WOMEN IN HUMAN EVOLUTION

Paleoanthropology, the study of human evolution, has constructed itself as a science at a high cost: by focusing largely on only one half of the species – males. *Women in Human Evolution* challenges the traditional invisibility of women in human prehistory, rejecting the conventional relegation of women to the realm of reproduction in order to ask what *else* our female ancestors were doing.

This collection raises key questions about both the existing archaeological evidence and the theoretical models which influence its interpretation. The contributions, drawn from a variety of disciplines, query whether scientific inquiry can be regarded as objective and value-free. They suggest re-interpretations of existing evidence to construct a model of human evolution which places women at its center. Shifting their focus on to the nature of the discipline itself, they ask what impact women paleoanthropologists have had on the field's theoretical assumptions and working practices, and what work remains to be done.

Women in Human Evolution boldly reconfigures women's traditional place in paleoanthropology – both as subjects of research and as researchers.

Contributors: Leslie Aiello, Yewoubdar Beyene, Rebecca Cann, Margaret W. Conkey, Dean Falk, Lori D. Hager, Linda Marie Fedigan, Camilla Power, Susan Sperling, Alison Wylie and Adrienne Zihlman.

Lori D. Hager is currently a Visiting Scholar at the Archaeological Research Facility, University of California, Berkeley.

WOMEN IN HUMAN EVOLUTION

Edited by
Lori D. Hager

London and New York

First published 1997
by Routledge
11 New Fetter Lane, London EC4P 4EE
Simultaneously published in the USA and Canada
by Routledge
29 West 35th Street, New York, NY 10001

Typeset in Garamond by
Ponting–Green Publishing Services, Chesham,
Buckinghamshire

Printed in Great Britain by
Biddles Ltd, Guildford and King's Lynn

British Library Cataloguing in Publication Data
A catalogue record for this book is available from the
British Library

Library of Congress Cataloging in Publication Data
Women in human evolution / edited by Lori D. Hager.
p.   cm.
Includes bibliographical references and index.
1. Human evolution.   2. Women–Evolution.
3. Feminist theory.
I. Hager, Lori, D., 1953–
GN281.W65   1997
573.2–dc20   96–29128
CIP

ISBN 0–415–10833–0 (hbk)
ISBN 0–415–10834–9 (pbk)

CONTENTS

ILLUSTRATIONS

CONTRIBUTORS

Leslie Aiello Department of Anthropology, University College London, Gower Street, London WC1E 6BT England.

Yewoubdar Beyene Medical Anthropology Program, University of California, San Francisco, CA 94143–0848.

Rebecca Cann Department of Genetics and Molecular Biology, University of Hawaii at Manoa, 1960 East-West Road, Honolulu, HI 96822.

Margaret W. Conkey Department of Anthropology, University of California, Berkeley, CA 94720.

Dean Falk Department of Anthropology, State University of New York at Albany, Albany, NY 12222.

Linda Marie Fedigan Department of Anthropology, University of Alberta, Edmonton, Alberta, Canada T6G 2H4.

Lori D. Hager Archaeological Research Facility, University of California, Berkeley, CA 94720.

Camilla Power Department of Anthropology, University College London, Gower Street, London WC1E 6BT England.

Susan Sperling Medical Anthropology Program, University of California, San Francisco, CA 94143–0848.

Alison Wylie Department of Philosophy, University of Western Ontario, London, Ontario N6A 3K7.

Adrienne Zihlman Board of Studies in Anthropology, University of California, Santa Cruz, CA 95064.

PREFACE

The motivation for putting this book together began when I was teaching a seminar on "Women in Human Origins Research" at Stanford University in 1990. This was a new class in an anthropology department with strong feminist ties. I expected anthropology students in the class, but I also hoped students outside the discipline would enroll. The class was cross-listed in human biology and feminist studies. The focus of the class was to be twofold: (1) examine the contribution of females in prehistory as agents of evolutionary change, and (2) examine the contribution of women as researchers in the field of paleoanthropology.

Although issues related to women and gender have been an important aspect of research within the larger field of anthropology for at least twenty years, paleoanthropology has traditionally been a discipline where women are under-represented and where studies on females in prehistory are rarely taken seriously. In sociocultural anthropology, for example, books and articles on gender and society have been circulating since the landmark volume *Women, Culture and Society*, edited by Michelle Rosaldo and Louise Lamphere in 1974. Books concerned with gender studies in sociocultural anthropology now abound. By anthropological standards, the 1984 article by Margaret Conkey and Janet Spector entitled "The Archaeology of Gender" was a relative latecomer, but has since been followed by two recent volumes on similar topics: *Engendering Archaeology*, edited by Joan Gero and Margaret Conkey, and *The Archaeology of Gender*, the publication of the Chacmool Conference of the same title held in Calgary in 1990, edited by Dale Walde and Noreen Willows. The success of these books and several other recently published books and articles which examine gender within the context of archaeological inquiry suggest that an "archaeology of gender" has merit. No comparable book which specifically incorporates issues of gender into the literature at large exists in human origins research. The seeds of this volume were thus sown.

I am particularly indebted to the guest speakers who came to that first seminar: Margaret Conkey, Elaine Chang, Phyllis Dolhinow, Ruth Doell, Diane Gifford-Gonzalez, Frieda Rickenbach, Susan Sperling, Alison Wylie, and Adrienne Zihlman. From them, the book began to take shape. To my good fortune, four of these women were able to contribute to this volume (Conkey, Sperling, Wylie, Zihlman). I was also greatly aided by the students of that class, and the ones in the next class taught two years later, who helped clarify the various paradigms which have structured human origins research by asking difficult, thought-provoking questions. This book is the direct result of the guest lectures, the students' responses, and the lively discussions in those classes as we attempted to elucidate the role of females as active participants in the prehistoric past and to examine the role of women as contributors to the science of human origins research.

All the contributors to this book are women. They are diverse in backgrounds, coming from the philosophy of science, primatology, genetics, medical anthropology, archaeology, and paleoanthropology. None of the men asked to contribute to this book were able to for a variety of reasons. So the book stands as a contribution by women about women. Some of these essays are personal accounts of women as researchers in the cadre of men. Some discuss the perspective of prehistoric females within an historical context. Some are presentations of new ideas and new areas of research. But all are concerned with females as fundamental to the evolution of the species in areas beyond procreation.

Even though this book is written only by women, it does not, however, represent one voice. The reader will be keenly aware of differences of opinions among the authors. As the editor, I made a conscious decision to let the authors express their opinions even though I knew they were at variance with other contributors. Just as there is not one "male voice," I do not believe there is, or should be, one "female voice." On many issues, we do not always agree.

The goal of these essays is to consider females in prehistory and women in paleoanthropology, just as I set out to do in that first seminar. I begin the book with an introductory chapter with these two topics as my primary concern. Since many critiques of science have been broadly based in feminist scholarship, the next two essays discuss feminist approaches to science, one a view from outside the discipline (Wylie), and the other a view from primatology (Fedigan). The reconstruction of the past has taken many forms, based on many lines of evidence. The fourth essay is a personal account of the reception of the controversial "Eve" hypothesis of modern human origins from a researcher who was intimately involved in the construction of the hypothesis (Cann). By examining the historical context of the portrayal of females in prehistory, the next essay is a less than optimistic view of women in paleoanthropology in the 1990s by a woman who has challenged the androcentric paradigms of the discipline for more than twenty years (Zihlman). The next essay is concerned with how sex and gender differences are used to depict females in the past, with particular reference to the evolution of the brain (Falk). Because females in prehistory have been defined more by their reproductive capabilities than any other attribute, the next two essays explore issues related to reproduction in nonhuman primates and humans. The goal of these essays is to explore commonly held beliefs about the female reproductive cycle (e.g, estrus, menstruation) and consider the relationship between biology and culture in what it means to be a woman in evolutionary perspective (Sperling and Beyene; Power and Aiello). The final paper explores issues of gender and the construction of ideologies in our attempt to visualize the past through the example of Upper Paleolithic "art" (Conkey).

The end result of these essays is a consideration of females in prehistory from alternative perspectives where females are active participants in the evolutionary process. The writings in this book hopefully reflect a new direction in paleoanthropology where females are centrally located, both in prehistory and as researchers.

Just as this book was about to go to press, I learned of the death of the matriarch of paleoanthropology, Mary D. Leakey. Like so many others in the discipline, men and women alike, I was truly inspired by her devotion to human origins research. Mary Leakey will be missed by scientists throughout the world but her legacy will live on for many years to come.

Finally, I would like to thank my family for their belief in this book from its inception and their abiding patience through all the stages of its publication.

Lori D. Hager
Berkeley, CA

REFERENCES

Conkey, M. W. and Spector, J. D. (1984) "Archaeology and the Study of Gender," in M.B. Schiffer (ed.) *Advances in Archaeological Method and Theory*, vol. 7, New York: Academic Press, pp. 1–38.

Gero, J. and Conkey, M. W. (eds) (1991) *Engendering Archaeology: Women and Prehistory*, Oxford: Basil Blackwell.

Rosaldo, M. and Lamphere, L. (eds) (1974) *Women, Culture and Society*, Stanford: Stanford University Press.

Walde, D. and Willows, N. (eds) (1991) *The Archaeology of Gender*, Calgary: Archaeological Association, University of Calgary.

ABBREVIATIONS

Acta Anat.	Acta Anatomica
Amer. Anthrop.	American Anthropologist
Amer. Antiquity	American Antiquity
Amer. J. Anat.	American Journal of Anatomy
Amer. J. Phys. Anthrop.	American Journal of Physical Anthropology
Amer. J. Psychiatry	American Journal of Psychiatry
Amer. Scientist	American Scientist
Anat. Rec.	Anatomical Record
Animal Behav.	Animal Behavior
Ann. N.Y. Acad. Sci.	Annals of the New York Academy of Science
Ann. Rev. Anthrop.	Annual Review of Anthropology
Arch. Neurol.	Archives of Neurology
Arch. Pathol. Lab. Med.	Archives of Pathology and Laboratory Medicine
Behav. Brain Res.	Behavioural Brain Research
Behav. and Brain Sci.	Behavioral and Brain Sciences
Behav. Neurosci.	Behavior Neuroscience
Brain Res.	Brain Research
Chronobiology Int.	Chronobiology International
Cold Spr. Harb. Symp. Quart. Biol.	Cold Spring Harbor Symposia on Quantitative Biology
Comp. Physiol.	Comparative Physiology
Curr. Anthrop.	Current Anthropology
Fem. Studies	Feminist Studies
Folia Primatol.	Folia Primatologica
Hum. Evol.	Human Evolution
Int. J. Primatol.	International Journal of Primatology
J. Anthrop. Res.	Journal of Anthropological Research
J. Archaeol. Sci.	Journal of Archaeological Sciences
J. Biosoc. Sci.	Journal of Biosocial Science
J. Hirnforsch.	Journal fur Hirnforschung
J. Hum. Evol.	Journal of Human Evolution
J. Mammal.	Journal of Mammalogy

J. Natl. Cancer Inst.	*Journal of the National Cancer Institute*
J. Neurophysiol.	*Journal of Neurophysiology*
J. Neurosci.	*Journal of Neuroscience*
J. Zool.	*Journal of Zoology*
NSF	National Science Foundation
Palaeontol. Africana	*Palaeontology Africana*
Phil. Trans. R. Soc. London	*Philosophical Transactions of the Royal Society of London*
Proc. Natl. Acad. Sci.	*Proceedings of the National Academy of Sciences*
Psych. Sci.	*Psychological Sciences*
S. Afr. J. Sci.	*South African Journal of Science*
Scient. Amer./Sci. Amer.	*Scientific American*
Signs	*Signs: Journal of Women in Culture and Society*
Soc. Neurosci.	*Society of Neurosciences*
Trans. NY Acad. Sci.	*Transactions of the New York Academy of Sciences*
Visual Anthrop. Rev.	*Visual Anthropology Review*
Yrbk. of Phys. Anthrop.	*Yearbook of Physical Anthropology*

1

SEX AND GENDER IN PALEOANTHROPOLOGY

Lori D. Hager

Paleoanthropology – the study of human origins – is and always has been a highly visible field of anthropological research. The search for our ancestors is in the forefront of scientific investigations. It is also the focus of considerable popular interest. Many people are curious about the past and are fascinated by the evolutionary path leading to modern humans. Evidence of this past is disseminated to a hungry audience in the scientific literature and in the pages of the *New York Times*, *National Geographic*, *Scientific American*, and other popular publications. As a result, many fossils and "fossil-hunters" have gained considerable notoriety outside the discipline at large. Names like "Leakey," "Johanson" and "Lucy" are recognizable to a wide variety of people who have never seen a human fossil nor stepped a foot outside of an urban, industrialized context.

The ultimate goal of human origins research is to reconstruct past life ways as fully as possible. In doing so, paleoanthropologists attempt to account for the very nature of what it is to be a modern human – Who were our ancestors? Why do we look the way we do? Why do we behave the way we do? Why are our brains so large relative to our body size? When did language begin? Are men and women inherently different due to our particular evolutionary past? What social systems did our ancestors practice? By examining events in the past, paleoanthropologists, and the lay public who eagerly follow their work, hope to link the past to the present to better understand who we are.

However, in spite of the avowed goal to understand who *we* are, the study of human origins has tended to minimize or ignore the role of females in prehistory, or worse, to cast females in the gender stereotypes of the time and place out of which the researcher came. For example, it has traditionally been held that hominid females are responsible for producing and caring for their offspring – but not much else. On the other hand, males have frequently been credited as active agents of evolutionary change – and reproduction is only one of a long list of their achievements.

Both as objects of study and as researchers, women have occupied a low profile in the study of human origins. The history of women as researchers

1

in paleoanthropology is a short one because very few women have been engaged in this field. This is especially evident where field work is concerned.

Fame has, however, come to three females in paleoanthropology. Mary Leakey, renowned archaeologist and the discoverer of several important hominids and stone tools, is well known for her contributions to the discipline. But she is an anomaly in paleoanthropology. The measure of success Mary Leakey has achieved in the study of human origins has generally been reserved for men.

In addition, two ancestral hominids have gained a certain amount of recognition, in part because of their "femaleness." "Lucy," a 3.2 million-year-old fossil hominid from Ethiopia, was declared a female since the day "she" was discovered. Interpretations about life 3–4 million years ago have been highly dependent upon the reconstruction of "Lucy" as the diminutive female of a highly sexually dimorphic species.

Another female who has gained a certain amount of fame in paleoanthropology is "Eve," a hypothetical female who lived in Africa 150–200,000 years ago and is thought to be the progenitor (along with her female kin) of all anatomically modern humans. The "Eve" hypothesis is a matrilineal account of the origins of modern humans that traces mtDNA from mother to daughter over thousands of generations. Rebecca Cann, one of the principal architects of the "Eve" hypothesis (Cann *et al.* 1987; Wilson and Cann 1992), offers compelling evidence that the "femaleness" of "Eve" has been an important factor in the negative reception of this model (Cann, this volume).

How does the reconstruction of these females' lives affect us today? It is readily apparent that questions about the origin and meaning of sex roles and gender differences are commonplace in today's society. Popular books purporting to explain why men and women are different have been hugely successful (e.g., *Men Are From Mars, Women Are From Venus* by John Gray (1992)). Explanations of sex roles and gender differences that have an evolutionary basis are particularly noteworthy because they supposedly link past behaviors with present ones. The "missing link" is not only the fossil which takes us from ape to human, but also the link between how we behaved in the past and how we behave today. But are past behaviors actually "knowable?"

Fossil hominids represent the remains of real individuals who once lived on the African or Asian or European landscape; hominids who were infants, teenagers and adults; hominids who once breathed, found food and water each day, eluded predators (sometimes), reproduced, raised offspring and eventually died. With some confidence, we can reconstruct what these hominids may have looked like, how long ago they lived, approximately how old they were at the time of death, and even what foods they potentially ate. However, behaviors do not fossilize and the reconstruction of past behaviors is therefore a more difficult task of interpretation.

2

Based on the principles of the scientific method, "scientific" interpretations are expected to be more than "just stories." They are intended to be the most logical, plausible and objective explanations of the observable facts. And because paleoanthropology conducts its research within the realm of "science," it is often assumed that it is objective and bias-free, and that what paleoanthropologists tell us about past behaviors are the "facts" of evolution. Because of this, interpretive narratives, such as those concerning males and females in the past, take on the cloak of fact. To be sure, the "facts" of the evolutionary process for the human lineage do exist, such as the fossils themselves which are indisputable evidence that humans did evolve over millions of years of prehistory. However, the inferential basis on which the structural and functional interpretations of fossils is based is more secure (but still highly controversial) than those contributing to our knowledge of past behavior. It is not that the process of constructing such knowledge is any different, it is simply that the inferences we draw from the evidence are different when we, on the one hand, interpret a fossil bone as a human ancestor, and on the other, interpret a particular morphology as evidence of behavior.

Generally speaking, paleoanthropologists interpret the past by constructing models of human origins based on one or more lines of evidence including comparative anatomical and behavioral studies of nonhuman primates; the chronological and paleoenvironmental context of hominid fossils; the archaeological record; and aspects of modern humans, with special emphasis on genetics and ethnographic analogy. Over the last one hundred years, several models have been constructed which focus on the roles of males and females (see Fedigan 1986 for an excellent review of these models within an historical context; also Falk, this volume; Zihlman, this volume). From Charles Darwin (1871), who portrayed men as "active and ardent" and women as "passive and reclusive," to the formulation of gender-explicit models such as "Man the Hunter," "Woman the Gatherer," and "Man the Provisioner," the behaviors and relative contributions of males and females in human evolution have been at the core of the discussion on past hominid life ways. That the models of human origins have changed since Darwin put humans into an evolutionary framework is due in large measure to an increase in the data base. But the models have also changed over the years because of changing world views, sociopolitical factors, historical circumstances and changing attitudes of the interpreters. In other words, interpretations, while logical and plausible, have a human aspect. This is why it is so important to reflect on the kind of knowledge being produced and the social and political context of the people producing it.

For example, many models of early hominid life are replete with assumptions about males and females which are based on western views of modern men and women. Unacknowledged stereotypes of modern male/female roles are too often used to interpret the past so that the past becomes a cultural

3

construct steeped in presentist views. Thus, when a link is made from our ancestors to us, behaviors such as sex and gender roles become credible and justifiable since they are then seen as "inherent" or "natural" to the species. These features become identifiable as part of "human nature," and because of this it is inferred that they cannot be easily modified or altered. Thus, evolutionary models function to reify what may be problematic images of modern men and women, even though a past constructed by reference to the present is problematic in itself. For these reasons, it becomes crucial to examine the inferential bases upon which knowledge of human origins is constructed.

As a means of discussing sex and gender in paleoanthropology, there are two principal questions I will be concerned with: (1) how have females been depicted in reconstructions of past life ways, and (2) how has the inclusion of women as researchers in human origins impacted these reconstructions, especially as they pertain to the portrayal of females? To address these questions, I begin with an overview of how females have been portrayed in prehistory, with special reference to the last 30 years. Second, because the reconstruction of past life ways described by anthropologists is disseminated to the public, I examine briefly how gender stereotypes purportedly based on evolutionary models are perpetuated in the public sphere. Third, I consider a specific example in the reconstruction of early hominid phylogeny and behavior, especially as it relates to females, where the determination of the "femaleness" of the fossil has been critical to the interpretations. For the fossil "Lucy," I discuss how sex was determined, and then outline the consequences of "Lucy" being female rather than male in these interpretations. Lastly, I consider women as paleoanthropologists. I focus on Mary Leakey's career in order to explore issues related to being a woman and a paleoanthropologist because she is one of the few women to be successful in this field. The goals of this chapter are to consider how inferences of females in our past have been dependent upon many factors, including "non-scientific" ones, and to show that the past is only as "knowable" as we want it to be.

HOMINID FEMALES IN PREHISTORY

The view of hominid females in prehistory has often been tied to preconceived ideas about what is "natural" to the species. In particular, the role of females in the prehistoric past has focused almost entirely on their reproductive abilities, or perhaps more appropriately stated, their reproductive "duties" to their species and their mates. Many theorists have viewed females as passive participants in evolutionary change, relegated to the bearing, nursing, and transporting of young – and little else. Males, on the other hand, have traditionally been seen as responsible for the many uniquely "human innovations" such as bipedalism, enlargement of the brain, the making of tools, cooperative communication, symbolic representation, and so on.

In the highly influential "Man the Hunter" model of the 1960s, Washburn and DeVore (1961) and Washburn and Lancaster (1968) suggested that the pursuit and acquisition of meat by males accounted for *all* morphological, technological, and social innovations which were the hallmark of "mankind." The trials and tribulations of the "hunt" precluded females from participating in such evolutionarily significant activities, so except in the capacity of bearing and raising children, females were seen as peripheral to our evolutionary history.

Given that the seeds of this model were actually sown in the 1950s (see Zihlman, this volume), it is no coincidence that the view of life in the past advocated by Washburn, DeVore, Lancaster and others at this time paralleled the one already in place in western cultures, especially post World War II America: the woman stayed at home having and raising the kids, and the man went out "hunting" for food ("bringing home the bacon"). "Science" was used to bolster the "preferred" image of women in a reproductive, home-maker role.

Particularly ironic with regard to these images of the fifties and sixties woman at home is the active participation of American women in the workforce during World War II. During the war years, and especially by 1942 when much of the male population was overseas fighting, American women were actively recruited to become welders, machinists, bomb-makers, electricians, and other traditionally held "male" jobs (Gluck 1987; Campbell 1984; Wise and Wise 1994; Hartman 1982). Magazine and newspaper advertisements told women how capable and competent they were, how they could be welders, machinists, electricians and the like, and how they were very much needed in the workplace (Honey 1984; Rupp 1978). Special government-sponsored housing and day care centers were built to encourage women to help out in the war effort. And many women loved it (Gluck 1987; Wise and Wise, 1994; Anderson 1981).

But as the war ended, and the returning GIs needed jobs, the need for women in the workforce declined and their competency was called into question (Campbell 1984; Chafe 1972). Instead of being encouraged to go to work, they were told they were no longer needed and no longer competent to hold jobs that males traditionally held. They were encouraged to return to their "true calling": as housewives and mothers. The "Man the Hunter" model gave *credibility* to these late forties, fifties, and sixties sex roles of women as mothers and homemakers. And, perhaps even more importantly, it pointed to the *inevitability* of these roles because they were "natural" or "inherent" to our species. It is not surprising that the "Man the Hunter" model was so thoroughly embraced at this time.

In part due to increasing numbers of women in primatology and paleo-anthropology in the sixties and seventies, some investigators began to consider women in prehistory less as passive reproductive agents than as central participants in human evolution. For example, Sally Slocum (Linton),

Adrienne Zihlman, and Nancy Tanner formulated the controversial "Woman the Gatherer" model (Slocum 1975; Tanner and Zihlman 1976; Zihlman and Tanner 1978; Zihlman 1978, 1981). This model counterpoised the starkly androcentric "Man the Hunter" model with an alternative view of prehistoric females. It suggested that these females were more than reproductive receptacles: prehistoric females in fact were major contributors to the diet, they formed the core social unit with their offspring, and they were inventors.

The advocates of the "Woman the Gatherer" model correctly argued that hunting must have come later in our evolutionary history than previously thought, because fossils of early humans predate the oldest stone tools. Therefore, hunting alone could not account for who we were at our beginnings. Alternatively, they suggested that collecting and gathering plant materials and small animals were the primary subsistence activities of our human ancestors. They argued, with convincing evidence from the ethnographic and nonhuman primate record, that this kind of foraging was done primarily by females who were anything but the sedentary "do-nothings" suggested in earlier models. Moreover, females were likely to have been the earliest inventors as they developed tools in relation to gathering and in relation to carrying infants who no longer had a grasping big toe due to morphological changes related to bipedalism. This new model invited scholars to see females as central to human evolution, as foragers, as inventors, and as active agents of change.

Looking back at the articulation of this model in the seventies, it is tempting to speculate on its relationship to the feminist movement of the time. From this perspective, the "Woman the Gatherer" model is the logical extension of a newly empowered group of contemporary women researchers. However, Adrienne Zihlman, one of the primary architects of the "Woman the Gatherer" model, argues that this new model was not developed as a "feminist" response to the "Man the Hunter" one. Zihlman (1987) quite explicitly states that the model was presented in response to the overwhelming data she and her colleague Nancy Tanner had compiled from the fossil, nonhuman primate, and ethnographic record. In other words, it was a "data-inspired" model rather than a "feminist-inspired" one. Zihlman does concede that the feminist movement provided the "social climate" for asking such questions as "where are the women?" and "what were the women doing?" but she insists that the "Woman the Gatherer" model was not formulated as a rebuttal to the "Man the Hunter" one. That the model put females at the center of the evolutionary process was due to the data set, not to any "feminist" notions on how to interpret the data.

Over the last twenty years, Zihlman has clearly had to combat those who are unwilling to see the merits of her model in large measure because it focused too heavily on females. For the most part, the "Woman the Gatherer" model was dismissed outright or ignored by many (mostly male) paleoanthropologists on the grounds that it was simply a feminist counterattack to the

"Man the Hunter" model, and that it therefore could not be a viable interpretation of the data (see Fedigan 1986). It was deemed too "gynecentric" and "female-biased" to be taken seriously. It somehow made no difference to these critics that the "Man the Hunter" model was exclusively androcentric and there were no adequate data to support it. Perhaps by distancing herself from any feminist roots, Zihlman, like many other female researchers, simply wanted to see her work examined in a fair manner without being criticized about underlying motives.

On the other hand, for many of us our experiences as women preclude us from accepting a model that renders females as meaningless and/or invisible. Does this mean these models are necessarily "feminist" in origin and should therefore be dismissed, or should we view alternative perspectives as just that: a new way of looking at the data? We all carry "baggage" – it does matter what our gender is, just as it matters who we studied with, where we studied, when we studied, what our religion is, our cultural heritage, and so on. As Ruth Hubbard has said, "There is no such thing as objective, value-free science" (1979: 47) (also see Harding 1986; Keller 1985; Wylie, this volume). If we recognize that "science" has a human aspect, and that everyone, male and female, is influenced by many factors, then and only then can we begin to understand the nature of those influences on our work.

The "Woman the Gatherer" model has never been a prevailing paradigm in human origins research. Other models were being proposed at roughly the same time; some of these enjoyed greater acceptance than others. Among the more favored alternatives to the "Man the Hunter" model was the "Food-sharing" hypothesis forwarded by Glynn Isaac (1978, 1980, 1981a, b, 1983a) and his students. This model suggested that there was a sexual division of labor early in our ancestry: the males hunted or scavenged large game, the females collected plant foodstuffs and small game. Each sex spent their day hunting or foraging, delaying consumption for the most part, thereby bringing a good portion of these foods back to a central base to exchange with each other. This made for a rather appealing egalitarian scenario involving an explicit sexual division of labor. It also emphasized a broad-based, flexible dietary subsistence pattern versus a hunting-only one as in the "Man the Hunter" model. As Isaac and his students attempted to find archaeological support for the "Food-sharing" model in the Early Pleistocene record of East Africa, Isaac came under sharp criticism by Binford regarding this hypothesis, especially as it related to site formation processes (e.g., Binford 1977, 1981; Isaac 1983b; see Blumenschine 1991b for an excellent review of the context of these criticisms and of the development of Isaac's "Food-sharing" hypothesis). As a result of the intense debates between Binford and Isaac over the next few years, Isaac refined the "Food-sharing hypothesis" and ultimately replaced it with the "Central Foraging Concept," while still maintaining a sexual division of labor (Isaac 1983b). Due largely to the tremendous insight, innovative thinking, and charismatic spirit that characterized the late Glynn

Isaac, many of his former students in Old World archaeology continue to have strong ties to underlying concepts of the "Food-sharing/Central Foraging" hypothesis (e.g., Blumenschine 1987, 1988, 1989, 1991a; Blumenschine and Selvaggio 1988; Bunn 1986, Bunn and Kroll 1986; Gifford-Gonzalez 1989; Marshall 1986; Sept 1986; Toth 1987).

In the eighties some investigators simply appropriated and inverted the basic concepts of these earlier models for their own purposes. For example, Owen Lovejoy (1981) posited a model, often dubbed "Man the Provisioner," in which gathering was indeed given status as the primary subsistence activity rather than hunting (without reference to Zihlman, Tanner or Slocum) (see Fedigan 1986; Falk, this volume). But in this new model, who was doing the gathering? Men were. According to Lovejoy, bipedalism evolved because it enabled the food-gathering male to increase the amount of food he could carry to *his* pair-bonded female and *their* offspring who remained back at camp. Females ensured the males would return to them (and them only) by "losing estrus," having enlarged breasts and buttocks as sexual cues, and being "continually sexually receptive." A "sex for food" bargain was thus made. In this scenario, females were dependent upon their males to provide for them and their offspring, and the role of females was once again reduced to a reproductive one. In Lovejoy's model, females became bipedal through a mechanism first outlined by Darwin (1871) in his sexual selection theory – through the equal transmission of characters, or on the "coat-tails" of the males.

Even though Lovejoy's model has been effectively challenged on many grounds (Hrdy 1981; Cann and Wilson 1982; Harley 1982; Isaac 1982; Wolfe *et al.* 1982; Wood, J. 1982; McHenry 1982; Zihlman 1985; Falk, this volume), it is nevertheless one of the models presented in introductory and upper-division textbooks, described in popular articles and books, and even featured in special television productions (e.g., *In Search of Human Origins*, 1994), often to the exclusion of "Man the Hunter," "Woman the Gatherer," and other models. Is this the preferred image of males and females in the past, in the present, or both?

PUBLIC KNOWLEDGE: GENDER, GIRAFFES AND GINGRICH

Based loosely on the evolutionary models developed by paleoanthropologists, notions of the evolutionary past are often used to explain present-day gender differences by a variety of people: politicians, celebrities, academics, and the popular media in general. Thus, the supposedly "known" evolutionary history of males and females has been used to account for modern male/female differences from map-reading to locating items on a desktop, to the ability to participate in combat duty. For instance, in a 1992 *Time* magazine article on "Why Men and Women are Different?" it is stated that men are able to read maps better than women because men can rotate "objects in three dimensional space . . . *due to ancient evolutionary pressures related to hunting which requires orienting oneself while pursuing prey*" (emphasis mine) (Gorman 1992: 45). This statement is based on the premise that males hunted in our evolutionary past and that females did not – premises that have been assumed but not demonstrated. Moreover, this example uses hunting as the primary defining quality of men (not humans) that is clearly reminiscent of the "Man the Hunter" model. Whether males are actually better at reading maps than females is in itself a debatable issue.

On the other hand, this same *Time* article states that women are better at remembering "items found on a desktop – perhaps reflecting *evolutionary pressures on generations of women who foraged for their food. Foragers must recall complex patterns formed of apparently unconnected items*" (emphasis mine) (Gorman 1992: 45). Ethnographic data suggest that foraging requires a complex knowledge of the landscape, where plants and trees are indeed "connected." Foraging for plant foods also requires a long-term acquisition of knowledge in order to judge the seasonal availability of food items and the toxicity of other vegetation. Who is to say that foraging does not also require "orienting oneself in three-dimensional space?" And who is to say that females foraged and males did not? Again, these are assumptions of life in the past – not known facts.

Politicians have also used notions of the past to account for gender differences, even invoking the past to promote one policy over another. For example, the current Speaker of the United States House of Representatives, Newt Gingrich, a powerful government figure, recently stated in a class on "Renewing American Civilization" at Reinhardt College that women are better on cruises and airplanes than men because men get restless "sitting in a chair all the time" due to the fact that they are "biologically driven to go out and hunt giraffes" (as cited in Abelson 1995; Buchwald 1995; Gingrich 1995). The idea that women have an evolutionary history that demanded activity and movement seems to have escaped Gingrich.

With regard to the "inherent" unsuitability of women for combat duty, Gingrich suggests that "females have biological problems staying in a ditch for 30 days because they get infections" (1995). What can he possibly mean by this? Is it related to Gingrich's misguided sense of menstruation and how "incapacitating" it must be for women? On the other hand, according to Gingrich, men are biologically suited for combat duty, because they "are basically little piglets; you drop them in the ditch and they roll around in it" (as cited in Abelson 1995; Buchwald 1995). There is clearly no support in the evolutionary record for any of these statements. However, this type of thinking, which explains present-day gender differences based on a supposedly "knowable" past, is all too common. Acceptance of statements based on stereotypes and/or preconceived notions about our past, especially as they relate to people today, must be cautionary at best in light of what we actually know.

SEX AND THE FOSSIL RECORD: "LUCY" VS. "SGT. PEPPER"

It should be intuitively obvious that if we are to discuss sex roles in prehistory, we should first have a fair understanding of the nature of any sex differences in the fossil record. What did our male and female ancestors look like? Did the way they look affect the way they behaved? While the terms "sex" and "gender" are often used interchangeably, when determining the "sex" of fossil specimens (or any skeletal material), the goal is to assess *biological sex* only. "Gender," as a cultural construct, is more appropriately concerned with what it *means* to be a man or a woman in a social context. However, in the reconstruction of models of human origins, some paleoanthropologists use sex determination to discuss sex as well as gender roles, even though it may be stretching the meaning of "gender" to consider it relevant to early hominid fossils. The fossil hominid known as "Lucy" is a good example of this.

The discovery of "Lucy" in Hadar, Ethiopia, by Johanson and his colleagues in 1974 instantly captured the imagination of the public. Nearly 40 per cent complete, and of great antiquity (one of the oldest known hominids at the time), "Lucy" quickly became the most famous woman in prehistory, and Johanson one of the most famous "fossil-hunters." But controversy soon surrounded this fossil, as paleoanthropologists debated taxonomic issues (Day *et al.* 1980; Tobias 1980; Leakey and Walker 1980; Olson 1981, 1985; Falk and Conroy 1983; Senut and Tardieu 1985; Zihlman 1985; White *et al.* 1981; Kimbel and White 1988; McHenry 1982, 1986c; McHenry and Corruccini 1980; Johanson and White 1980), locomotor adaptations (Stern and Susman 1983; Susman *et al.* 1985; Tuttle 1981; Jungers 1982; Senut 1981; Senut and Tardieu 1985; Tardieu 1983; Schmid 1983; Marzke 1983; Lovejoy *et al.* 1982), and behavioral interpretations (Lovejoy 1981; Zihlman 1985). Did "Lucy" and the Hadar fossils found in later field seasons and at other sites (e.g., Laetoli, Tanzania) belong in one species or two? Were they highly sexually dimorphic? Was "Lucy" fully bipedal or did she and others of her species spend a great deal of time in the trees? Were the females more arboreal than the males? Did this species, named *A. afarensis* in 1978 (Johanson *et al.* 1978; Johanson and White 1979), live in kin-related bands? What was their social structure? How did they behave?

Fundamental to answering many of these questions was the determination that "Lucy" was a female. That is, the "femaleness" of this specimen was crucial to the interpretations being made at the taxonomic, phylogenetic and behavioral levels. In order to correctly interpret the fossil record, it is essential that paleoanthropologists are able to recognize *variation due to sex differences* as opposed to *variation due to taxonomic differences*. In other words, we need to be able to account for all levels of variation before we can assign a fossil to a taxonomic category and before we can understand its evolutionary history.

Determining if fossil specimens are male or female is an essential means of assessing variation, but it is not always easy. In order to establish as "fact" that an individual is male or female would require examination of the genitalia – soft tissue that does not generally preserve, or a sample of ancient DNA which has not been found to date. Thus sex determination of skeletal material is an interpretation based on skeletal morphology with reference to known-sex populations. Since the pelvis is the most reliable indicator of sex in modern humans, a trained osteologist can accurately determine sex with a high probability of success (95–99 per cent), based on well-documented sex differences in the size and shape of the modern human pelvis (see Hager 1989, 1996; Krogman and Isçan 1986; Bass 1971). When pelvic elements are available for fossil hominids, modern pelvic dimorphisms have been the standard by which to determine sex (see Hager 1989 for a review of sex determinations for fossil hominids). The underlying assumption is that because modern humans are sexually dimorphic in their pelves, hominid fossils will show similar dimorphisms.

"Lucy" has been female since its first description in the mid-1970s (Johanson and Taieb 1976; but cf. Häuseler and Schmid 1996), or even more precisely, since the day it was found and given the name "Lucy." This fossil was named on the night of its discovery after the Beatles song "Lucy in the Sky with Diamonds" which was playing on a tape-recorder in camp (Johanson and Edey 1981: 18). In other words, Johanson and his colleagues immediately thought this fossil was female, calling it "Lucy" rather than "Sgt. Pepper," a designation which strongly suggests that the criteria for determining sex were readily visible to the finders on the *very day* this famous fossil was found.

This is an important point that has often been overlooked: Johanson and his colleagues immediately believed this fossil was female, not based on her small size as is now stated (Johanson *et al.* 1978; Johanson and White 1979; White *et al.* 1981; Johanson *et al.* 1982a, b; Kimbel and White 1988; McHenry 1986a, b; Tague and Lovejoy 1986), because the larger *afarensis* specimens such as those from Hadar locality 333 came later (Johanson *et al.* 1982a, b). Rather, "Lucy" was sexed as female because the morphology of the skeleton, and the hipbone in particular, was suggestive of the modern human female condition. That is, they had pelvic elements and they immediately determined the fossil's sex according to modern standards of pelvic dimorphisms. The question that needs to be asked, however, is whether the criteria they used are appropriate when sexing early hominids.

In 1981 Johanson and Edey wrote a popularized account of the Hadar Expedition. In this, they discuss how they determined that "Lucy" was female:

From her pelvis. We had one complete pelvic bone and her sacrum. Since the pelvic opening in hominids has to be proportionately larger in females than in males to allow for the birth of large-brained infants, you can tell a female.

(p. 18)

However, later in the book they state:

Lucy, in short, demonstrates the first of two steps that must be taken in the evolution of apes into humans. Her pelvis has evolved sufficiently for her to become a biped. But she has not yet taken the second step: further evolution of the pelvis to permit the birth of large-headed infants.

(p. 348)

Which is it then? Is "Lucy" female because the pelvis has been under selection pressures for an increase in size to accommodate the birth of those "large-brained" infants? Or should we even expect the australopithecines, these early small-brained and small-bodied hominids, to have the same level of pelvic dimorphisms as modern humans?

I have argued elsewhere (1989, 1991, 1996) that modern standards of pelvic dimorphism cannot be used to sex fossil hominids, especially not the australopithecines. The evolution of sex differences in the hominid pelvis was a complex process that did not begin as soon as we became bipedal. Analysis of fossil pelves over the last 3 million years suggests that sex differences in the hominid pelvis first became apparent approximately 2 million years ago (myr), a time that coincides with the increase in brain size in hominids. Sex differences in the pelvis continued to develop from about 2 myr to the present such that it is only with anatomically modern humans that we see the full development of modern pelvic dimorphisms. Thus I would argue that the criteria originally employed to assign "Lucy" as female, i.e., the hipbone, cannot be used for sex determination in early hominids.

In the absence of pelvic elements, overall body size also plays a role in determining the sex of fossil material. When fossil specimens show differences in size, such as in body size, but not in shape, and are otherwise morphologically similar, it is inferred that the specimens belong to the same species but are sexually dimorphic at varying degrees of magnitude. In this case, the underlying assumption is that males are larger than females, as in many extant primates, and that differences in size are typical of living primates who are sexually dimorphic.

With the *afarensis* material we have fossils which are roughly contemporaneous and obviously hominid, but some are quite large and others are small (Johanson and White 1979; White *et al.* 1981; Johanson *et al.* 1982a, b; McHenry 1986a, b). How do we account for the significant size differences in these fossils? One way is to consider the variation in size as a result of sexual dimorphism. Even though there are clearly large and small morphs represented in the sample, many investigators consider all the specimens to be members of one highly dimorphic species: the large ones are males and the small ones females. That is, these fossils, large and small, are considered to be a single species, *Australopithecus afarensis*. Thus the interpretation of the size variation is that it is the result of intraspecific variability. Of the Hadar fossils, "Lucy" represents one of the smallest specimens found, and because this fossil was sexed as "female" based on the hipbone, it has been assumed that all other small specimens are female also.

On the other hand, what if these fossils are morphologically different – that is, what if they exhibit not just size differences but also shape differences? The variation under these circumstances would be the result of *interspecific variability* or between-species differences. Some paleoanthropologists argue that the material categorically known as "*afarensis*," in addition to having different sizes, is also morphologically distinct (Senut 1981; Senut and Tardieu 1985; Tardieu 1983; Olson 1981, 1985; Zihlman 1985; Falk 1990) and, on this basis, they argue that these fossils belong in two separate species or even two different genera, *Australopithecus* and *Homo*. This viewpoint is currently in the minority.

It is interesting to note that for the first few years after the discovery of "Lucy," both Johanson and his French colleague Maurice Taieb argued that the smaller "Lucy" represented a different taxon than the larger ones. They argued that "Lucy" and the other small individuals were australopithecines, while the larger specimens were possibly early forms of *Homo* (Johanson and Taieb 1976). In other words, they originally believed size was *not* related to sex, but to taxonomy. A few years later Johanson *et al.* (1978) and Johanson and White (1979) advanced their own views of *A. afarensis* as a single species that was highly sexually dimorphic. They have stayed with this interpretation ever since.

More recent postcranial finds of early hominids from Hadar announced by Kimbel *et al.* (1994) are of the large robust variety, as is the new humerus from Maka from the Middle Awash region of Ethiopia announced by White *et al.* (1993). Not surprisingly, these new finds have been sexed as male. It has even been said that the controversy concerning *afarensis* as one or two species is now over (Gee 1993; Aiello 1994). How was sex determined for these hominids? Kimbel *et al.* (1994: 450) determine sex from the humerus (A.L. 137–50) based on its large size and its similarity to the humerus from Maka and from Hadar locality 333 (A.L. 333–107). White *et al.* (1993) sex the Maka humerus as male based on a comparison with A.L. 288–1 ("Lucy"). In this comparison, these authors believe the differences in the humeri "parallels human sex-related morphological differences" (White *et al.* 1993: 262), and because they believe "Lucy" is a female, then the Maka humerus is therefore male.

13

As with the pelvis, we need to first ask if the use of modern human standards of sex differences is relevant to these early australopithecines. Secondly, the humerus of modern humans is not an especially good predictor of sex, particularly in the absence of the proximal humerus (Bass 1971; Krogman and Isçan 1986; Dittick and Suchey 1986) as in the case of the Maka humerus. Even with these new finds, we are still left with the large discrepancies in the size of these early hominids – does this reflect high levels of sexual dimorphism? Or are these hominids too different in size and/or morphology to be in the same taxon?

It is obvious then that the determination of sex is critical to the taxonomic and phylogenetic assessments of this species (and other hominid species) whether based on pelvic morphology or body size. If "Lucy" is not a female, the advocates of the two-species hypothesis would certainly be on stronger ground to argue their case. On the other hand, if this fossil is indeed a small female, then those who argue for the single-species hypothesis can reasonably suggest the larger ones are the males and that sexual dimorphism among our earliest hominid ancestors was high. Thus knowing the sex of fossil specimens is the primary means by which we can determine the nature, extent and evolution of sexual dimorphism in the hominid line.

Evaluating the level of sexual dimorphism in hominids can be important in reconstructing past life ways because it has been argued that the amount of sexual dimorphism displayed by a species is directly linked to a particular kind of mating/social system (Leutenegger 1977, 1978, 1982; Leutenegger and Kelley 1977; Leutenegger and Chevrud 1982; Martin 1980; see Frayer and Wolpoff 1985 for a review of sexual dimorphism). In nonhuman primates, for example, highly sexually dimorphic species *tend* to live in multi-male, multi-female groups, or single-male, multi-female groups (Leutenegger 1977, 1978; Leutenegger and Kelley 1977). By contrast, in nonhuman primates where males and females show little to no sexual dimorphism, as with gibbons, there is a *tendency* for these primates to live in monogamous pairs with their dependent offspring (ibid.). Of course, there are exceptions and variations to this within the primate order as well as in other mammalian orders (e.g., see Rowell and Chism 1986; Wilner and Martin 1985; Rodman and Mitani 1986). Nonetheless, whether the link between sexual dimorphism and mating/social system is real or not, the level of sexual dimorphism present in hominid fossils is often used as a yardstick by which to measure the social organization of the early hominids.

If *A. afarensis* was one highly sexually dimorphic species, what kind of social structure might we infer from nonhuman primates? Was the social life more like baboons or gorillas who are highly sexually dimorphic in body size or more like chimpanzees who are only moderately dimorphic in body size? If canine size is not that dimorphic in *afarensis* even though body size is, does this imply less competition between the males and therefore a different social structure than either chimpanzees or gorillas? If *afarensis* is really two species not one, what can we then infer about social structure in these hominids? Accurate sex assessments of the fossil material, and thus the interpretation of the level of sexual dimorphism, are important in the formulation of models attempting to answer these questions and, by doing so, explain early hominid social structure and behavior (e.g. Lovejoy 1981, 1993; Johanson *et al.* 1994).

In sum, when evidence of early human origins is found, it invites re-construction of the past life ways. It is tempting to put flesh on the bones. But what form best describes those hominids? In a recent reconstruction at the newly renovated American Museum of Natural History exhibit on human biology and evolution, we see "Lucy" and her "mate" walking across the plains of Tanzania, implying that these hominids are responsible for the footprints at Laetoli (even though "Lucy" was found thousands of miles away in Ethiopia!). We see "Lucy" with a larger male walking beside her, his arm around her shoulders, protecting and comforting her. Visual representa-tions such as this are highly suggestive ways of disseminating evolutionary models to the lay public by presenting a visual text for these models (Moser 1992, 1993; Gifford-Gonzalez 1993, 1995; Conkey, this volume; Zihlman, this volume). Is this really the way it was? Examining sexual dimorphism in the hominid fossil record and how sex is determined is essential for understanding not only taxonomic issues, but also for elucidating our past life ways and helping to clarify the roles of males and females in that past. "Lucy" is pivotal to this reconstruction, and knowing whether this fossil was a female or not is ultimately of great consequence to understanding ourselves.

WOMEN AS PALEOANTHROPOLOGISTS

Paleoanthropology has traditionally been a male domain, with but a few women in its ranks. Even today, there are only a handful of women who are active in field work, the most valued aspect of the discipline. As in related disciplines (e.g., Gero 1985, 1993; Gero and Conkey 1991; Hanen and Kelley 1992), issues of gender tend not only to compromise women's participation in field work, but also in the formulation of ideas, recognition of their work, and their impact on the field in general. Shipman (1995) provides a particularly disturbing account of her career as a woman in paleoanthropology; an account which is no doubt shared by many women in science (Rossiter 1982; Sheperd 1993).

Overall, women graduate students in paleoanthropology have not been encouraged to participate in field work until quite recently, and perhaps just as importantly, women graduate students have not been encouraged to work directly with the human fossils, the second most valued aspect of the discipline. Rather, many women tend to work on collateral studies, often in laboratories and museums, which provide indirect evidence of our evolutionary history (e.g., paleoenvironmental studies). Even though the considerable importance of these studies for understanding the context of human evolution is widely recognized across disciplines, these collateral studies unfortunately are not given the credit due to them relative to those who do field work and those who work with the fossils. Thus many women (and men also) end up playing "back-up" roles to the more "famous" fossil-hunters.

There have been, however, great strides in recent years to include more women in the study of human origins. Women are graduating in paleo-anthropology from top universities in increasing numbers. Many of these women are not necessarily "feminists" by any means, nor are they focusing on issues of women in prehistory, but they are bright, competent, innovative, and ambitious. Yet, in spite of the increasing number of women getting into the field, fewer women than men are involved in the analysis of human fossils, nor have women been given equal opportunities for field work where the coveted fossils can be found. Whether or not the increasing numbers of recent women graduates will ultimately reach parity with men in these two areas is still open to question, but whatever happens, the level of female participation will no doubt have an effect on the future of the discipline.

Notwithstanding the generally low numbers of women in paleoanthropology in its first one hundred years, one woman has been tremendously successful: Mary Douglas Leakey. She has lived and worked in East Africa since the thirties, leading a somewhat unconventional life as she excavated some of the most important prehistoric sites in the world, and raised a family along the way. Wife of the well-known paleoanthropologist Louis Leakey, and mother of the equally famous Richard, a good part of her fame comes from her association with these men. Yet the paleoanthropological community has been aware of her valuable individual contribution to human origins research for many years.

Born in 1913, Mary Nicol Douglas had a rather unorthodox childhood, as she toured France, Switzerland and Italy with her mother and artist father. Early on she became fascinated by archaeology when she visited numerous Paleolithic sites with her father, especially in the Les Eyzies and Périgord regions of France. After her father's death, the 13-year-old Mary and her mother returned to England to live near her grandmother and aunts. Attempts were made to formally educate Mary, but she was an unwilling student and quickly learned what to do in order to ensure expulsion from more than one school. However, when Mary was 17 years old, her fascination with archaeology was rekindled and she began attending lectures in archaeology and geology at University College, London. But it was field work that Mary longed for, and soon she was accepted by Dorothy Liddell, a well-known archaeologist, to join excavations at an early Neolithic site in Devon.

Mary Leakey spent several summer seasons in the early thirties excavating in Devon under Dorothy Liddell's direction. Mary was also an accomplished artist and Liddell soon had her drawing the stone tools from these excavations for publication. It was these drawings that caught the attention of Dr

Gertrude Caton-Thompson, a prominent archaeologist who had directed excavations at the famous Fayum site in Egypt. Mary describes Caton-Thompson as

> the epitome of that remarkable breed of English ladies who for archaeology's sake would go out alone in the harsh desert environments and by determination, skill, expertise and endurance achieve discoveries of major and permanent importance.
>
> (Leakey, M.D. 1984: 39)

Mary could well have been speaking of herself. The influence of Liddell and Caton-Thompson on Mary's archaeological career is undoubted. But, indirectly, Mary's life was also changed dramatically because of the Fayum drawings she did for Caton-Thompson. Another archaeologist was looking for an illustrator for an upcoming book and Caton-Thompson recommended Mary. This other archaeologist was Louis Leakey.

Thus, by 1935 the young Mary Douglas was at the center of a great scandal when she went to Africa to join an archaeological expedition led by the ambitious, brash and highly spirited Louis Leakey, who happened to be married to someone else at the time. Upon their return to England later that year, Louis and Mary openly lived together, marrying after Louis was divorced from his first wife. Despite being shunned by the Cambridge community, Mary and Louis continued their work in archaeology, seemingly undaunted by the less than warm reception to their affair. Not long after their marriage in 1936, they returned to work in East Africa and remained there.

Mary Leakey's career centered on field work, not academic-oriented archaeology; she holds honorary doctoral degrees. Both Louis and Mary promoted a "hands-on" acquisition of knowledge, a legacy that has been avidly embraced by their sons and, more recently, their grandchildren. Field work is highly prized in archaeology and paleoanthropology – there is no doubt that her brilliance in the field has been an important factor in Mary Leakey's gaining credibility within the scientific community.

Mary Leakey is also the mother of three children (a fourth one died in infancy). In her autobiography (1984) she says little about her pregnancies or about the trials of raising young children in Kenya. It seems clear that she did not let pregnancy or child-rearing interfere with her work. Work simply became a family matter with the children accompanying their parents to various sites in East Africa. In fact, the children were encouraged to go off and find their own fossils – and sometimes they did!

Mary and Louis worked as a team for many years, conducting archaeological reconnaissance and excavation at several sites, but most importantly at Olduvai Gorge in Tanzania. In July 1959 Mary Leakey set out from their camp at Olduvai to scour the sediments for fossils and tools, just as she had for the past twenty-five years. That day she made a discovery of such magnitude that not only her life, but the lives of her husband and children, would never be the same again. Indeed, the discipline of paleoanthropology "came of age" that day. The discovery of *Zinjanthropus boisei*, the first hominid to be found at Olduvai and the oldest well-dated hominid at that time, plunged Mary and Louis into public life in a manner unprecedented for archaeologists or paleoanthropologists of that time. Through the pages of *National Geographic*, whose society generously funded the work at Olduvai for many years after this discovery, "Leakey" became a household name, as did "Nutcracker man," "Olduvai Gorge" and Africa as the "cradle of humankind." Yet while the discovery of "Zinj" catapulted the Leakeys into a life of fame and recognition, in the end it was the catalyst that led to the breakdown of this remarkable husband-and-wife team. Soon after "Zinj" was found, Louis embarked on numerous lecture and fund-raising tours that took him away from his family for long periods of time. Mary eventually moved from Nairobi to Olduvai to conduct large-scale excavations in search of more hominid fossils and stone tools. The once close-knit family was scattered, and they were never able to fully reconcile.

After more than thirty years of working together, Louis and Mary separated in 1968, four years before Louis died. After his death, Mary continued to do research, and in fact made some of the most spectacular discoveries of her career at the site of Laetoli in the seventies. But these discoveries put her in the middle of the controversy surrounding the inclusion of the Laetoli material within the *A. afarensis* species (Johanson *et al.* 1978; Leakey, M.D. 1978, 1979; Leakey, M.D. and Hay 1979; Day *et al.* 1980; Leakey, R.E.F. and Walker 1980) at a time when she was in ill health and at a difficult point in her personal life.

Mary Douglas Leakey remains a world authority on African prehistory and human origins. Her contributions to archaeology are many: she has examined and described the stone tools of Africa in great detail, she has made numerous fossil discoveries of tremendous significance, she has conducted extensive excavations at world-renowned sites, and she has located, described, and redrawn rock paintings throughout Africa.

Although she has made a significant contribution to paleoanthropology, Mary Leakey's life offers a multitude of contradictions common to women in science, especially women of her generation (Rossiter 1982). For example, she was both dependent upon and independent from Louis. They were a team in which Louis, clearly the dominating personality, received most of the credit for their finds. Mary meanwhile continued to do her work in a straightforward, nearly obsessive manner regardless of her lack of public recognition. She has always been a "maverick" of sorts, and certainly is considered to be a "strong" woman, yet she is shy and modest. Public lecturing and fund-raising were always Louis's duties, but after his death it became necessary for Mary to take on these responsibilities. She did this reluctantly, but has since grown to enjoy public lecturing (Leakey, M.D. 1984) and in a sense has become less shy.

Within the scientific community, Mary Leakey is the most famous female paleoanthropologist, specifically because of her accomplishments. In 1993, numerous colleagues from around the world gathered in Arusha, Tanzania, for a conference in her honor. The outpouring of praise and immense respect for Mary Leakey from her colleagues – people who know her contributions in intimate detail – was extraordinary. In the public sphere, however, Mary Leakey still seems to be better known as the wife and mother of famous paleoanthropologists than for her own achievements in that field. This alone speaks volumes for the place of women in the discipline. For example, much of the lay public does not know that she alone was responsible for the methodical, often tedious, excavations at Olduvai Gorge that yielded some of the most significant finds in paleoanthropology. Many are surprised to know she is an archaeologist at all.

Husband-and-wife teams are a common theme in the sciences – marriage has certainly been one means by which women have been able to enter the sciences in the first place (Rossiter 1982; Schiebinger 1989; Irwin-Williams 1990). Had she not been married to Louis, would Mary Leakey have become so famous? The answer to this question is anything but clear. Louis, besides being a native Kenyan, had already launched several archaeological expeditions to East Africa by the time Mary joined him in 1935. Without a doubt, Louis provided Mary with an opportunity to make notable finds, but she provided the archaeological methods and techniques to carry out much of the work. East Africa was wide-open territory for any sort of archaeological investigation at that time. In fact, Mary Leakey excavated a number of sites of different ages, not only early human ones. The Leakeys were in a frontier situation, so that with fortitude, ambition, drive, and perseverance they were able to make discoveries that were unprecedented. For many years, Mary was part of a team and she certainly benefited from Louis's flamboyant, audacious, energetic style, which promoted their finds to the scientific community and to the lay public alike. For her part, Mary was more concerned with the field work and generally shied away from making interpretations about the materials she uncovered. In this sense, it is difficult to imagine what Mary Leakey's career might have been had she not married Louis. By doing so, she reaped the benefits of exploring a part of the world with little archaeological precedent and of having a partner as confident and vocal as Louis. But it is equally important to remember that Mary is well known for being methodical, highly skilled, and driven. Her colleagues consider her to be an archaeologist of the highest caliber. Louis, whether he acknowledged it publicly or not, benefited greatly from the partnership too.

As a woman in what was a predominantly male domain, has Mary Leakey been a "voice" for women in paleoanthropology? The answer is no. Often the only female paleoanthropologist mentioned in textbooks, popular articles and media broadcasts, Mary Leakey is nonetheless quick to disengage herself from feminism or feminist ideas. With regard to this, she has said:

Women's Lib is something for which I carry no banner, though quite often people expect me to do so. What I have done in my life I have done because I wanted to do it and because it interested me. I just happen to be a woman, and I don't believe it has made much difference.

(Leakey, M.D. 1984: 193)

No matter how Mary Leakey perceives the role of her sex in her success, many women in science have experienced gender bias as a significant impediment to their careers (Rossiter 1982; Schiebinger 1989). Not many women in paleoanthropology have accomplished what Mary Leakey has. Yet in her work, she has never focused on women in particular and her writings clearly reflect this. Her renderings of the past do not portray women much differently than do the writings of her male contemporaries. She does not in fact believe that being a female has had any impact on her view of the past, any more than being a woman has meant much of anything to her career (Leakey, M.D. 1984). This seems typical of her generation of women scientists (Rossiter 1982; Holloway 1994).

Mary Leakey has nonetheless been an inspirational role model for many women. That she in turn was influenced early in her career by women seems certain. She comes from a generation of British-trained archaeologists where women not only were actively involved and accepted, but also where women conducted archaeological excavations in leadership roles (e.g., Dorothy Garrod, Dorothy Liddell, Gertrude Caton-Thompson) (Irwin-Williams 1990). That they did not focus on women's issues does not mean they have not made an impact in their discipline. Much of Mary Leakey's strength and resilience may in some measure derive from her female role models in archaeology, and in part from having spent much of her formative years in the company of her mother and maternal aunts. But it is equally clear that her father also greatly influenced her and that his interest in archaeology was certainly a major factor in her becoming an archaeologist in the first place.

CONCLUSIONS

In this chapter I have discussed how assumptions about life in the past inform our perceptions of modern sex and gender roles, and conversely, how our lives color interpretations of the past. Females have routinely been portrayed as bystanders in the evolutionary process; reproductive issues have often been used to restrict women to certain roles. Models where women are central to human evolution are few and those that exist are routinely dismissed, ignored, or worse, have their ideas appropriated by men who little value women's contribution to prehistory. We are but one species, composed more or less equally of men and women, and yet the view of males and females in prehistory continues to be polarized. For modern men and women, the polarization is equally acute as we debate gender differences and their meanings. Within the public sphere, ideas founded in some measure on evolutionary models have been used to forward gender stereotypes in a largely unsubstantiated fashion, often contributing to this opposition between genders.

In paleoanthropology, the presence of male/female differences and their origins are actively debated. An accurate interpretation of the fossil record relies heavily on the correct interpretation of variation – whether it is due to differences between the sexes or between species. Variation due to sexual dimorphism was invoked in the case of *A. afarensis* based, in large part, on the inferred "femaleness" of "Lucy." From this basic inference, other interpretations of taxonomic, phylogenetic, and behavioral significance followed. Thus the "femaleness" of this particular fossil became critical to the interpretations being made, and our view of females early in prehistory was essentially shaped on the very day that "Lucy" was found.

As has become evident in many other scientific disciplines, the very participation of women as researchers in the field brings new perspectives into the discipline. The participation of women in field work and in analyses which directly examine the fossil hominids can only serve to broaden the view of life in the past. In the future, new and alternative views of men and women in prehistory may be proposed as more women play active roles in paleoanthropological research and as more paleoanthropologists, men and women, become open to the idea that women are capable of more than bearing, nursing and transporting young.

Mary Leakey is one example of what one woman has accomplished as a scientist, a wife and a mother. Her fame comes partly from her relationships with famous men, but also from her many achievements as an archaeologist. Like her female mentors, Mary Leakey challenged long-standing beliefs concerning what women were capable of doing in frontier situations without necessarily being conscious of having done so. She has not been directly concerned about the interpretation of women's roles in prehistory, but she has encouraged other women to become paleoanthropologists, and thus has indirectly influenced perceptions of females in the past.

If our goal is to reconstruct past life ways, and, in doing so, explore what it is to be human – male or female – we must be aware of biases when they appear, and recognize "scientific" interpretation as having a human, "non-scientific" aspect. This awareness by no means radically undermines the value of scientific research; rather it should encourage attention to one's social and political context when constructing models of the past, especially because they are interpretations made in the present, on the basis of present understanding. It is all too easy to take gender models implicit in our contemporary world and project them uncritically onto the past. As paleoanthropologists, when we encounter these models and the evidence for them, cognizance of historical and present-day views of gender must be one of our principal goals.

ACKNOWLEDGEMENTS

This chapter is an expanded version of a paper presented at "The Women, Gender and Science Question" conference held at the University of Minnesota, May 12–14, 1995. This contribution was significantly informed by attendance at this conference. I have also benefited from discussions with a number of colleagues over the last several years on issues of sex and gender in paleoanthropology and related disciplines, including many who are contributors to this volume.

BIBLIOGRAPHY

Abelson, A. (1995) "High on the Hog," *Barron's* 75(4): 5–6, January 23.
Aiello, L. C. (1994) "Variable but Singular," *Nature* 368: 399–400.
Anderson, K. (1981) *Wartime Women: Sex Roles, Family Relations and the Status of Women during World War II*, Westport, Conn.: Greenwood Press.
Bass, W. M. (1971) *Human Osteology: A Laboratory and Field Manual of the Human Skeleton*, Columbia, Missouri: Missouri Archaeological Society.
Binford, L. R. (1977) "Olorgesailie Deserves More Than an Ordinary Book Review," *J. Anthrop. Res.* 33: 493–502.
—— (1981) *Bones: Ancient Men and Modern Myths,* New York: Academic Press.
Blumenschine, R. J. (1987) "Characteristics of an Early Hominid Scavenging Niche," *Curr. Anthrop.* 28: 383–407.
—— (1988) "An Experimental Model of the Timing of Hominid and Carnivore Influence on Archaeological Bone Assemblages," *J. Archaeol. Sci.* 15: 483–502.
—— (1989) "Man the Scavenger," *Archaeology* 42 (4): 26–33 [editor's title: originally titled "Fleshing-out ancestral life-styles," see *Archaeology* 42(6): 10].
—— (1991a) "Hominid Carnivory and Foraging Strategies, and the Socio-Economic Function of Early Archaeological Sites," *Phil. Trans. R. Soc. Lond.* Series B 334: 493–502.
—— (1991b) "Breakfast at Olorgesailie: the Natural History Approach to Early Stone Age Archaeology," *J. Hum. Evol.* 21: 307–327.
—— and Selvaggio, M. M. (1988) "Percussion Marks on Bone Surfaces as a New Diagnostic of Hominid Behaviour," *Nature* 333: 763–765.
Buchwald, A. (1995) "Piglets in Foxholes," *The Washington Post*, February 2.
Bunn, H. T. (1986) "Patterns of Skeletal Representation and Hominid Subsistence Activities at Olduvai Gorge, Tanzania and Koobi Fora, Kenya," *J. Hum. Evol.* 15: 673–690.
—— and Kroll, E. M. (1986) "Systematic Butchery by Plio-Pleistocene Hominids at Olduvai Gorge, Tanzania," *Curr. Anthrop.* 27: 431–452.
Campbell, D' A. (1984) *Women at War with America: Private Lives in a Patriotic Era*, Cambridge, Mass.: Harvard University Press.
Cann, R. L., Stoneking, M. and Wilson, A. C. (1987) "Mitochondrial DNA and Human Evolution," *Nature* 325: 32–36.
Cann, R. L. and Wilson, A. C. (1982) "Models of Human Evolution," *Science* 211: 303–304.
Chafe, W. (1972) *The American Woman: Her Changing Social, Economic and Political Roles, 1920–1970*, New York: Oxford University Press.
Cole, S. (1975) *Leakey's Luck: The Life of Louis Seymour Bazett Leakey, 1902–1972*, New York: Harcourt, Brace Jovanovich.

Conkey, M. W. and Spector, J. D. (1984) "Archaeology and the Study of Gender," in M. B. Schiffer (ed.) *Advances in Archaeological Method and Theory*, vol. 7, New York: Academic Press, pp. 1–38.

Darwin, C. (1871) *The Descent of Man and Selection in Relation to Sex*, London: Murray.

Day, M. H., Leakey, M. D. and Olson, T. R. (1980) "On the Status of *Australopithecus afarensis*," *Science* 207: 1102–1103.

Dittick, J. and Suchey, J.M. (1986) "Sex Determination of Prehistoric Central California Skeletal Remains Using Discriminate Analysis of the Femur and Humerus," *Amer. J. Phys. Anthrop.* 70: 3–9.

Falk, D. (1990) "Brain Evolution in *Homo*: the 'Radiator' Theory," *Behavioral and Brain Sciences* 13: 333–381.

—— and Conroy, G. C. (1983) "The Cranial Venous Sinus System in *Australopithecus afarensis*," *Nature* 306: 779–781.

Fedigan, L. M. (1986) "The Changing Role of Women in Models of Human Evolution," *Ann. Rev. Anthrop.* 15: 25–66.

Frayer, D. W. and Wolpoff, M. H. (1985) "Sexual Dimorphism," *Ann. Rev. Anthrop.* 14: 429–473.

Gee, H. (1993) "Why We Still Love Lucy," *Nature* 366: 207.

Gero, J. (1985) "Sociopolitics of Archaeology and the Woman-at-Home Ideology," *Amer. Antiquity* 50: 342–350.

—— (1993) "The Social World of Prehistoric Facts: Gender and Power in Prehistoric Research," in H. DuCros and L. Smith (eds) *Women in Archaeology: A Feminist Critique*, Occasional Papers in Prehistory, No. 23, Canberra: The Australian National University.

—— and Conkey, M. W. (eds) (1991) *Engendering Archaeology: Women and Prehistory*, Oxford: Basil Blackwell.

Gifford-Gonzalez, D. (1989) "Shipman's Shaky Foundations," *Amer. Anthrop.* 91: 180–186.

—— (1993) "You Can Hide, But You Can't Run: Representations of Women's Work in Illustrations of Paleolithic Life," *Visual Anthrop. Rev.* 9: 23–41.

—— (1995) "The Drudge-on-the-Hide," *Archaeology* 48(2): 84.

Gingrich, N. (1995) Quote in *Newsweek*, January 30, p. 17.

Gluck, S. B. (1987) *Rosie the Riveter Revisited: Women, the War, and Social Change*, Boston: Twayne Publishers.

Gorman, C. (1992) "Why Are Men and Women Different?" *Time*, January 20.

Gray, J. (1992) *Men Are From Mars, Women Are From Venus*, New York: Harper Collins.

Hager, L. D. (1989) "The Evolution of Sex Differences in the Hominid Bony Pelvis," Ph.D. dissertation, University of California, Berkeley.

—— (1991) "The Evidence for Sex Differences in the Hominid Fossil Record," in D. Walde and N. Willows (eds) *The Archaeology of Gender*, Calgary: Archaeological Association, University of Calgary, pp. 46–49.

—— (1996) "Sex Differences in the Sciatic Notch in Great Apes and Modern Humans," *Am. J. Phys. Anthrop.* 99: 287–300.

Hanen, M. and Kelley, J. (1992) "Gender and Archaeological Knowledge," in L. Embree (ed.) *Metaarchaeology: Reflections by Archaeologists and Philosophers*, Boston: Dordrecht, pp. 195–225.

Harding, S. (1986) *The Science Question in Feminism*, Ithaca: Cornell University Press.

Harley, D. (1982) "Models of Human Evolution," *Science* 211: 296.

Hartman, S. (1982) *The Home Front and Beyond: American Women in the 1940s*, Boston: Twayne.

Häuseler, M. and Schmid, P. (1996) "Comparison of the Pelves of STS 14 and AL 288–1: Implications for Birth and Sexual Dimorphism in Australopithecines," *J. Hum. Evol.* 29: 363–383.

Holloway, M. (1994) "Mary Leakey," *Scient. Amer.* 271: 37–40.

Honey, M. (1984) *Creating Rosie the Riveter: Class, Gender and Propaganda during World War II*, Amherst, Mass.: University of Massachusetts Press.

Hrdy, S. B. (1981) "Lucy's Husband: What Did He Stand For?" *The Science Watch*, July-August.

Hubbard, R. (1979) "Have Only Men Evolved?" in R. Hubbard, M. Henifin and B. Fried (eds) *Biological Woman: The Convenient Myth*, Cambridge, Mass.: Schenkman.

—— (1990) *The Politics of Women's Biology*, New Brunswick, New Jersey: Rutgers University Press.

Irwin-Williams, C. (1990) "Women in the Field: The Role of Women in Archaeology before 1960," in G. Kass-Simon and P. Farnes (eds) *Women of Science*, Bloomington: Indiana University Press.

Isaac, G. Ll. (1978) "The Food-Sharing Behavior of Protohuman Hominids," *Sci. Amer.* 238: 90–108.

—— (1980) "Casting the Net Wide: a Review of Archaeological Evidence for Early Hominid Land Use and Ecological Relations," in L. K. Konigsson (ed.) *Current Arguments on Early Man*, Oxford: Pergamon Press, pp. 226–251.

—— (1981a) "Archaeological Tests of Alternative Models of Early Hominid Behaviour: Excavations and Experiments," *Phil. Trans. R. Soc. Lond.* Series B 292: 177–188.

—— (1981b) "Stone Age Visiting Cards: Approaches to the Study of Early Land-Use Patterns," in I. Hodder, G. Ll. Isaac and N. Hammond (eds) *Patterns of the Past: Studies in the Honour of David Clarke*, Cambridge: Cambridge University Press, pp. 131–155.

—— (1982) "Models of Human Evolution," *Science* 211: 295.

—— (1983a) "Aspects of Human Evolution," in D. S. Bendall (ed.) *Evolution from Molecules to Men*, Cambridge: Cambridge University Press, pp. 509–543.

—— (1983b) "Bones in Contention: Competing Explanations for the Juxtaposition of Early Pleistocene Artifacts and Faunal Remains," in J. Clutton-Brock and C. Grigson (eds) *Animals and Archaeology, Volume 1: Hunters and Their Prey*, Oxford: British Archaeological Reports International Series 163, pp. 3–19.

Johanson, D.C. and Edey, M. (1981) *Lucy: the Beginnings of Humankind*, New York: Simon and Schuster.

Johanson, D.C., Johanson, L. and Edgar, B. (1994) *Ancestors: In Search of Human Origins*, New York: Villard Books [also NOVA special, April 1994].

Johanson, D.C., Lovejoy, C.O., Kimbel, W. H., White, T. D., Ward, R. C., Asfaw, B. and Coppens, Y. (1982a) "Morphology of the Pliocene Partial Hominid Skeleton (A.L. 288–1) from the Hadar Formation, Ethiopia," *Amer. J. Phys. Anthrop.* 57: 403–451.

Johanson, D. C. and Taieb, M. (1976) "Plio-Pleistocene Hominid Discoveries in Hadar, Ethiopia," *Nature* 260: 293–297.

Johanson, D.C., Taieb, M. and Coppens, Y. (1982b) "Pliocene Hominids from the Hadar Formation, Ethiopia (1973–1977): Stratigraphic, Chronologic, and Paleoenvironmenal Contexts, with Notes on Hominid Morphology and Systematics," *Amer. J. Phys. Anthrop.* 57: 373–402.

Johanson, D.C. and White, T. D. (1979) "A Systematic Assessment of Early African Hominids," *Science* 203: 321–330.

—— (1980) "Reply: On the Status of *Australopithecus afarensis*," *Nature* 207: 321–330.

—— and Coppens, Y. (1978) "A New Species of the Genus *Australopithecus* (Primates: Hominidae) from the Pliocene of Eastern Africa," *Kirtlandia* 28: 1.

Jungers, W. L. (1982) "Lucy's Limbs: Skeletal Allometry and Locomotion in *Australopithecus afarensis*," *Nature* 297: 676–678.

Keller, E. F. (1983) *A Feeling for the Organism: The Life and Work of Barbara McClintock*, New York: Freeman.

—— (1985) *Reflections on Gender and Science*, New Haven, CT: Yale University Press.

Kimbel, W. H., Johanson, D. C. and Rak, Y. (1994) "The First Skull and other New Discoveries of *Australopithecus afarensis* at Hadar, Ethiopia," *Nature* 368: 449–451.

Kimbel, W. H. and White, T. D. (1988) "Variation, Sexual Dimorphism and the Taxonomy of *Australopithecus*," in F. Grine (ed.) *The Evolutionary History of the Robust Australopithecines*, New York: Aldine, pp. 175–192.

Krogman, W. M. and Işcan, M. Y. (1986) *The Human Skeleton in Forensic Medicine*, (2nd edition), Springfield, Ill.: C. C. Thomas.

Leakey, M. D. (1978) "Pliocene Footprints at Laetoli, Northern Tanzania," *Antiquity* 52: 133.

—— (1979) "3.6 Million Year Old Footprints in the Ashes of Time," *National Geographic* 155: 446–457.

—— (1984) *Disclosing the Past: An Autobiography*, New York: Doubleday.

—— and R. L. Hay (1979) "Pliocene Footprints in the Laetolil Beds at Laetoli, Northern Tanzania," *Nature* 278: 317–466.

Leakey, R. E. F. and Walker, A. C. (1980) "On the Status of *Australopithecus afarensis*," *Nature* 207: 1103.

Lee, R. B. and DeVore, I. (eds) (1968) *Man the Hunter*, Chicago: Aldine.

Leutenegger, W. (1977) "Sociobiological Correlates of Sexual Dimorphism in Body Weight in South African Australopiths," *S. Afr. J. Sci.* 73: 143–144.

—— (1978) "Scaling of Sexual Dimorphism in Body Size and Breeding System in Primates," *Nature* 272: 610–611.

—— (1982) "Scaling of Sexual Dimorphism in Body Weight and Canine Size in Primates," *Folia Primatol.* 37: 163–176.

—— and Chevrud, J. (1982) "Correlates of Sexual Dimorphism in Primates: Ecological and Size Variables," *Int. J. Primatol.* 3: 387–402.

—— and Kelley, J. T. (1977) "Relationship of Sexual Dimorphism in Canine Size and Body Size to Social, Behavioral, and Ecological Correlates in Anthropoid Primates," *Primates* 18: 117–136.

Lovejoy, C. O. (1981) "The Origin of Man," *Science* 211: 341–350.

—— (1993) "Modeling Human Origins: Are We Sexy Because We're Smart, or Smart Because We're Sexy?" in D. T. Rasmussen (ed.) *The Origin and Evolution of Humans and Humanness*, Boston: Jones and Barlett Publisher, pp. 1–28.

—— , Johanson, D. C. and Coppens, Y. (1982) "Hominid Lower Limb Bones Recovered from the Hadar Formation: 1974–1977 Collections," *Amer. J. Phys. Anthrop.* 57: 679–700.

McHenry, H. M. (1982) "The Pattern of Human Evolution: Studies on Bipedalism, Mastication and Encephalization," *Ann. Rev. Anthrop.* 11: 151–173.

—— (1986a) "Size Dimorphism in the Postcranium of Early *Australopithecus*," *Amer. J. Phys. Anthrop.* 70: 238.

—— (1986b) "Size Variation in the Postcranium of *Australopithecus afarensis* and Extant Species of Hominoidea," *Hum. Evol.* 1: 149–155.

—— (1986c) "The First Bipeds: A Comparison of the *A. afarensis* and *A. africanus*

Postcranium and Implications for the Evolution of Bipedalism," *J. Hum. Evol.* 5: 177–191.

—— and Corruccini, R. S. (1980) "On the status of *Australopithecus afarensis*," *Nature* 207: 1103–1104.

McIntyre, J. (1989) "Mary Douglas Nicol Leakey," in U. Gacs (ed.) *Women Anthropologists*, Urbana: University of Illinois Press, pp. 222–230.

Marshall, F. (1986) "Implications of Bone Modification in a Neolithic Faunal Assemblage for the Study of Early Hominid Butchery and Subsistence Practices," *J. Hum. Evol.* 15: 661–672.

Martin, R.D. (1980) "Sexual Dimorphism and the Evolution of Higher Primates," *Nature* 287: 273–275.

Marzke, M. W. (1983) "Joint Function and Grips of the *Australopithecus afarensis* Hand, with Special Reference to the Region of the Capitate," *J. Hum. Evol.* 12: 197–211.

Morell, V. (1996) *Ancestral Passions: The Leakey Family and the Quest for Humankind's Beginning*, New York: Simon and Schuster.

Moser, S. (1992) "The Visual Language of Archaeology: A Case Study of the Neanderthals," *Antiquity* 66: 831–844.

—— (1993) "Gender Stereotyping in Pictorial Reconstructions of Humans Origins," in H. DuCros and L. Smith (eds) *Women in Archaeology: A Feminist Critique*, Occasional Papers in Prehistory, No. 23, Canberra: The Australian National University.

Olson, T. R. (1981) "Basicranial Morphology of the Extant Hominoids and Pliocene Hominids: The New Material from the Hadar Formation, Ethiopia, and its Significance in Early Human Evolution and Taxonomy," in C. B. Stringer (ed.) *Aspects of Human Evolution*, London: Taylor and Francis, pp. 99–128.

—— (1985) "Cranial Morphology and Systematics of the Hadar Formation Hominids and 'Australopithecus' africanus," in E. Delson (ed.) *Ancestors: The Hard Evidence*, New York: Alan R. Liss, pp. 102–119.

Pickford, M. (1986) "On the Origins of Body Size Dimorphism in Primates," *Hum. Evol.* 1: 77–90.

Rodman, P. S. and Mitani, J. C. (1986) "Orangutans: Sexual Dimorphism in a Solitary Species," in B. B. Smuts, D. L. Cheney, R. M. Seyfarth, R. W. Wrangham, and T. T. Struhsaker (eds.) *Primate Societies*, Chicago: University of Chicago Press, pp. 146–154.

Rossiter, M. W. (1982) *Women Scientists in America: Struggles and Strategies to 1940*. Baltimore: Johns Hopkins University Press.

Rowell, T. E. and Chism, J. (1986) "Sexual Dimorphism and Mating Systems: Jumping to Conclusions," *Hum. Evol.* 1(3): 215–219.

Rupp, L. J. (1978) *Mobilising Women for War: German and American Propaganda, 1939–1945*, Princeton: Princeton University Press.

Schiebinger, L. (1989) *The Mind Has No Sex?: Women in the Origins of Modern Science*, Cambridge, Mass.: Harvard University Press.

Schmid, P. (1983) "Eine Rekonstruktion des Skelettes von A.l. 288–1 (Hadar) und deren Konsequenzen," *Folia Primatol.* 40283–306.

Senut, B. (1981) "L'humerus et ses Articulations chez les Hominides Plio-Pleistocenes," *Cahiers de Paléoanthrop.*, Paris: CNRS.

—— and Tardieu, C. (1985) "Functional Aspects of Plio-Pleistocene Hominid Limb Bones: Implications for Taxonomy and Phylogeny," in E. Delson (ed.) *Ancestors: the Hard Evidence*, New York: Alan R. Liss, pp. 193–201.

Sept, J. M. (1986) "Plant Foods and Early Hominids at site FxJj 50, Koobi Fora, Kenya," *J. Hum. Evol.* 15: 751–770.

Sheperd, L. J. (1993) *Lifting the Veil: The Feminine Face of Science*, Cambridge, Mass.; Cambridge University Press.

Shipman, P. (1995) "One Woman's Life in Science," *Amer. Scientist* 83: 300–302.

Slocum, S. (1975) "Woman the Gatherer: Male Bias in Anthropology," in R. R. Reiter (ed.) *Toward an Anthropology of Women*, New York: Monthly Review Press, pp. 36–50.

Stern, J. and Susman, R. (1983) "The Locomotor Anatomy of *Australopithecus afarensis*," *Amer. J. Phys. Anthrop.* 60: 279–317.

Susman, R., Stern, J. and Jungers, W. J. (1985) "Locomotor Adaptation in the Hadar Hominids," in E. Delson (ed.) *Ancestors: the Hard Evidence*, New York: Alan R. Liss, pp. 184–192.

Tague, R. and Lovejoy, C. O. (1986) "The Obstetric Pelvis of A.L.288-1 (Lucy)," *J. Hum. Evol.* 15: 237–255.

Tanner, N. and Zihlman, A. (1976) "Women in Evolution. Part I. Innovation and Selection in Human Origins," *Signs: Journal of Women in Culture and Society*, 1(3): 585–608.

Tardieu, C. (1983) "L'articulation Genou: Analyse Morpho-fonctionelle chez les Primates et les Hominides Fossiles," *Cahiers de Paléoanthrop.*, Paris: CNRS.

Tobias, P. V. (1980) "'*Australopithecus afarensis*' and *A. africanus*: A Critique and an Alternative Hypothesis," *Palaeontol. Africana* 23: 1–17.

Toth, N. (1987) "Behavioral Inferences from Early Stone Artifact Assemblages: An Experimental Model," *J. Hum. Evol.* 16: 763–787.

Tuana, N. (1989) *Feminism and Science*, Bloomington: Indiana University Press.

Tuttle, R. H. (1981) "Evolution of Hominid Bipedalism and Prehensile Capabilities," *Phil. Trans. R. Soc. Lond.*, Series B: 292: 89–94.

Washburn, S. L. and DeVore, I. (1961) "Social Behavior of Baboons and Early Hominids," in S. L. Washburn (ed.) *Social Life of Early Man*, Chicago: Aldine, pp. 91–105.

Washburn, S.L. and Lancaster, C. S. (1968) "The Evolution of Hunting," in R. Lee and I. DeVore (eds) *Man the Hunter*, Chicago: Aldine, pp. 293–303.

White, T. D., Johanson, D. C., and Kimbel, W. H. (1981) "*Australopithecus afarensis*: its Phyletic Position Reconsidered," *So. Afr. J. Sci.* 77: 445–470.

White, T.D., Suwa, G., Hart, W. K., Walter, R. C., WoldeGabriel, G., Heinzelin, J., Clark, J. D., Asfaw, B. and Vrba, E. (1993) "New Discoveries of *Australopithecus* at Maka, Ethiopia," *Nature* 366: 261–265.

Wilner, L. A. and Martin, R. D. (1985) "Some Basic Principles of Mammalian Sexual Dimorphism," in J. Ghesquiere, R. D. Martin and F. Newcombe (eds) *Human Sexual Dimorphism*, London: Taylor and Francis, pp. 1–42.

Wilson, A. C. and Cann, R. L. (1992) "The Recent African Genesis of Humans," *Scient. Amer.* 266(4): 68–73.

Wise, N. B. and Wise, C. (1994) *A Mouthful of Rivets*, San Francisco: Jossey-Bass Publishers.

Wolfe, L. D., Gray, J. P., Robinson, J. G., Lieberman, L. S. and Peters, E. H. (1982) "Models of Human Evolution," *Science* 211: 302.

Wood, B. A. (1985) "Sexual Dimorphism in the Hominid Fossil Record," in J. Ghesquiere, R. D. Martin and F. Newcombe (eds) *Human Sexual Dimorphism*, London: Taylor and Francis, pp.105–123.

Wood, J. (1982) "Models of Human Evolution," *Science* 211: 297–298.

Zihlman, A. L. (1978) "Women in Evolution. Part II. Subsistence and Social Organization among Early Hominids," *Signs: Journal of Women in Culture and Society* 4(1): 4–20.

—— (1981) "Women as Shapers of the Human Adaptation," in F. Dahlberg (ed.) *Woman the Gatherer*, New Haven: Yale University Press, pp. 75–120.

—— (1985) *"Australopithecus afarensis*: Two Sexes or Two Species?" in P. V. Tobias (ed.) *Hominid Evolution: Past, Present, and Future*, New York: Alan R. Liss, pp. 213–220.

—— (1987) "American Association of Physical Anthropologists Annual Luncheon Address, April 1985: Sex, Sexes and Sexism in Human Origins," *Yrbk. of Phys. Anthrop.* 30: 11–19.

—— and Tanner, N. (1978) "Gathering and the Hominid Adaptation," in L. Tiger and H. Fowler (eds) *Female Hierarchies*, Chicago: Beresford Book Service, pp. 163–194.

2

GOOD SCIENCE, BAD SCIENCE, OR SCIENCE AS USUAL?

Feminist critiques of science

Alison Wylie

INTRODUCTION

I am often asked what feminism can possibly have to do with science. Feminism is, after all, an explicitly partisan, political standpoint; what bearing could it have on science, an enterprise whose hallmark is a commitment to value-neutrality and objectivity? Is feminism not a set of personal, political convictions best set aside (bracketed) when you engage in research as a scientist? I will argue that feminism has both critical and constructive relevance for a wide range of sciences, and that feminism has much to gain from the sciences, including at least some of those that even the most querulous of my interlocutors would dignify as "real" science.[1] I will concentrate here on the critical import of feminism for science, but will identify constructive implications as I go.

But first, some ground work. Let me begin with some brief comments about what it is I take feminism to be, and why feminists have been interested in science – why they have undertaken to comment on, scrutinize, and actively engage in science. In the body of this chapter I want to disentangle several quite distinct kinds of feminist critiques of science. I will conclude with some suggestions about what feminism and science have to offer one another that could be, indeed that is, already proving to be very substantially enriching for both a range of scientific disciplines and for feminism.

WHAT IS FEMINISM?

On a cross-country drive in December 1994 I spent one evening in a roadside motel watching, with horrified fascination, a late-night edition of "Firing Line," in which a wildly incongruous assemblage of public figures debated the proposition "Is feminism as a movement dead?" Betty Friedan spoke first; she made a plug for her new book, evidently supporting the "not dead" position by ostentation: if she, a founding mother of the contemporary women's movement, was still publishing and active clearly feminism could not be dead. She was teamed up with, among others, Camille Paglia, who used the debate as an occasion to promote her bad girl image; she believed feminism was still alive, if not well, despite its unfortunate affiliation with a variety of women and men who identify as feminist. And on the "feminism is dead" side were arrayed William F. Buckley Jr., the feminist historian Elizabeth Fox-Genovese, and Arianna Huffington, prominent right-wing advocate from California. Buckley began by reading a passage from a feminist tract that firmly located pornography on a continuum of sexual harassment and violence against women; it was of the genre, "pornography is the theory; rape is the practice." He wanted to know what this could possibly mean. On one thing he was quite clear. However incoherent this passage might be, on Buckley's view it represented, in its most virulent form, precisely the sort of threat to principles of free speech (and to an implied subsidiary right to consume whatever appeals to you) that he finds most abhorrent in contemporary political movements like feminism. I was unclear how this was supposed to establish that feminism is dead. It seemed more an exercise in wishful thinking on Buckley's part: if feminism is not dead it should be.

Fox-Genovese was, by contrast, full of regret that feminism had not realized its promise, that it had passed away before its time. On one hand, she objected that contemporary feminism had been derailed by its elitism and its failure to address the real bread-and-butter issues of concern to most (non-elite) women in the world: childcare, poverty, education, health care. But on the other hand, making common cause with at least some of those on the other side of the "firing line," she insisted that if feminists had just followed Betty Friedan's sensible lead (e.g., as set out in Friedan 1963), second-wave feminism would still be a viable political movement. Fox-Genovese made no mention of the vast range of feminist literature and activism that repudiates Friedan's liberal feminism as a chief exemplar of precisely the narrowness of vision she was calling into question, a narrowness that has alienated many from the popular women's movement in North America because it privileges, as normative, the frustrations and ambitions of class- and race-privileged women who found themselves, in the 1960s, unfulfilled by Friedan's "feminine mystique" (see, e.g., hooks' 1984 discussion of Friedan). The women Friedan spoke to and for were justifiably outraged at the squandering of their human talent but, as a great many feminists have objected since 1963 (when *The Feminine Mystique* appeared), they were also systematically uninformed about the needs and interests and agendas of the vast majority of women who, for example, never have had the option of staying home in suburbia, much less of demanding a more fulfilling "career" as an alternative to the stifling domestic roles open to them in "Father Knows Best" America.

The rear was brought up by Huffington who opened her remarks with the observation that she and Buckley had been on opposing teams years ago in a debate at the Oxford Union; she was grateful to be aligned with him now and was eager to endorse his main points. In her view the defining flaw of contemporary feminism is that its main proponents are, at bottom, naive little girls who expect big government, a substitute for Dad, to make things all right; in this she seemed to be targeting, from another direction, the formal equality liberal feminists (of roughly the 1960s and 1970s) that Fox-Genovese also took to be definitive of contemporary feminism.

It was one of those late night shows you cannot bear to watch, and cannot bear to turn off. Certainly it was one of the most frustrating discussions of contemporary feminism I have ever witnessed although, in many respects, it was all too familiar. Sweeping claims were made about what "feminism" has done, or failed to do, for women or for society as a whole, with almost no consideration of specific positions or programs of activism, or political gains or failures that might be attributed to (or blamed on) feminists in the more than thirty years since Friedan's *Feminine Mystique* was published. Some of the sharpest exchanges came between those who might otherwise have found themselves on the same "team." There was some pleading that Fox-Genovese should change sides since she is a feminist after all, and I suspect Friedan would have been pleased to pass Paglia off to Buckley. But wherever they found themselves positioned on the question of whether feminism is dead (yet), clearly everyone was engaging something – some set of ideas, political stances, policies, programs, laws, influences, collective actions – that was impinging on their lives in a significant way, whether welcome or abhorrent, disappointing or still bright with promise. I found myself thinking of Mark Twain: "the reports of my death are greatly exaggerated" (1897).

While this seemed hopeful, at the same time I found the general disarray of the debate – the sense of it being a mad tea-party replete with non sequiturs and gross incoherences – deeply disconcerting. For the most part it was an exercise in futility. There was virtually no contact, no exchange between parties to the debate; indeed, there was no real debate. Advocates and critics of feminism (on both sides of the official debate) were talking past one another, jousting with the most grotesque and reductive stereotypes of "feminism" and of "feminists." The one sane voice, in my estimation, was Helen Weinstein, a third party to the "not dead" side of the debate (a lawyer and Long Island representative to the New York State Assembly). She began her position statement with the objection that this sort of point-winning confrontation was really not very productive. She was sternly reprimanded by the moderator; evidently comments on the "Firing Line" debate format are not allowed. She took a different tack. She drew attention to the implausibility of various of the stereotypes that were defining the terms of the debate. She cited examples of feminist activism on child support and daycare issues and, as I remember, of feminist anti-poverty activism and involvement in the wages for housework movement to counter the claim that feminists are all anti-family radicals who have never taken seriously the interests and needs of the normative "ordinary" woman (for Huffington, it seemed, women committed to their roles as mothers and wives; for Fox-Genovese, non-elite women more generally). She noted the contradiction involved in condemning feminists for being too extreme in their anti-establishment politics, on one hand, and objecting, on the other (as Huffington had done), that they are perpetual dependants on the good offices of patriarchal institutions, lacking initiative and naively invested in a "liberal" faith in formal remedies and big government. She drew attention to the vibrant, deep-rooted traditions of feminist and womanist activism that have long flourished outside the narrow circle of privileged women addressed by Friedan in the early 1960s – for example, in the Black and Hispanic and Native communities in North America, and in Latin American, Eastern European, Middle Eastern, Asian/South Asian, and African contexts – countering the erasure perpetuated by claims that contemporary feminism is exclusively a movement of white, middle-class women, that it begins and ends with Friedan's brand of "American" liberal feminism. She could, as well, have challenged Buckley's selective and reductive reading of the anti-pornography literature by drawing attention to the enormous diversity of positions feminists have taken on pornography and to the vast array of initiatives they have taken in combating violence: violence against women, violence against children and, indeed, violence in general (when you consider the close ties between the women's movement and the peace movement). In short, Weinstein pointed out just how diverse a range of positions and actions and policies is encompassed by the term "feminism."

What was very largely missing from this debate – what Weinstein challenged all parties to the debate to consider – was an appreciation that feminism is quite different from many of the movements we dignify as "political" in North America. Both its strengths and its weaknesses lie in its grassroots diversity, its diffuseness, its multi-fronted, situational, and local/personal brand of political activism. The fact is, the women's movement is nothing more or less than women in movement, and women of all kinds have been "in movement" as women for a very long time, on many different fronts and in many different contexts, arguing and acting against gender-based inequities from positions that lie across the whole length and breadth of the social and political spectrum. Contemporary feminism, the "second wave women's movement," does not fit the monolithic stereotypes that the parties to the "Firing Line" type of debate eagerly declare dead or hopefully promote as alive. No wonder there was so little meaningful exchange across this particular "Firing Line."

Given this diversity – a vision of feminism as a grassroots movement, vigorously alive in many different local niches and configurations – it would seem that feminism must escape the confines of any clear-cut definition. I am reminded of Rebecca West's famous statement: "I myself have never been able to find out precisely what feminism is: I only know that people call me a feminist whenever I express sentiments that differentiate me from a doormat . . .".[2] I am inclined to this view, especially in face of definitions of feminism that involve a specification of what one must be or believe to be a feminist;

the essentialism immanent in many such definitions seem to me inimical to the enterprise (although, unfortunately, it is by no means foreign to feminism). Nonetheless, I think it is possible to distinguish three general types of claim or commitment that are characteristic of a broad range of feminisms.

First, feminists typically hold that gender categories, gender relations, gendered social structures are a crucial, even a fundamental, dimension along which our lives are organized. This does not necessarily mean that feminists consider gender to be the sole or most important of structuring principles, or that it is autonomous of other factors, although there certainly are feminists who have embraced positions of this sort. It does mean that feminists are inclined to be suspicious of positions that categorically reduce gender to other factors, naturalizing it or rendering it epiphenomenal. Typically, too, feminists believe that sex/gender systems are to some degree amenable to change or, at least, to revaluation.

Second, feminists hold that those categorized as women under existing sex/gender conventions tend to be, in varying ways and to different degrees, systematically disadvantaged as women, compared to men who otherwise share their status or social location. That is to say, gender categories and relations are typically hierarchically structured. In many areas they do not simply define different but equal or complementary roles and identities, rather they delimit for individuals quite different ranges of opportunities, privileges, resources, and rewards depending on their gender.

Third, feminists believe that these gender-based inequalities are unjust or otherwise unacceptable (morally or politically), and they are committed to changing these inequities.

It is important to note two things about this core of defining commitments. First, they contain two very different kinds of claim: empirical claims about the way the social, political world actually is (various components of the first two tenets); and a normative or explicitly evaluative commitment about the acceptability of this world, so understood (the third tenet). Philosophers are fond of saying that you cannot get an "ought" (a normative conclusion) from an "is" (empirical premises) and, in fact, it is perfectly possible to accept some version of the first two claims while yet rejecting the third. The famous sociobiologist E. O. Wilson does just this.[3] In *On Human Nature* (1978) he argues that, where humans are concerned, the enormous volume of evidence he had compiled of ways in which our biological inheritance shapes our behavior establishes that "at birth the twig is already bent a little" (1978: 132). But he acknowledges that these relatively "modest genetic differences [that] exist between the sexes" at birth (1978: 129) – the "slight biological component" he discerns in sexually dimorphic patterns of behavior (1978: 132) – must be substantially amplified (e.g., by "later psychological development by cultural sanctions and training": 1978: 129) to arrive at the strongly marked differences we associate with existing gender roles and identities. The biological tilt he documents cannot be said to uniquely or strictly determine the complex array of sex/gender differentiated behaviors we associate with masculine vs. feminine roles, sensibilities, psychology, patterns of interaction, and so on (see chapter 6, "Sex," in Wilson 1978; reprinted in Jaggar and Rothenberg 1984: 99–104).[4] Nevertheless, Wilson concludes that even if sex/gender systems are not an exclusively biological legacy – even if they are contingent and plastic enough that they could be changed "through an exercise of will" (1978: 196) – they are by now so entrenched in the fabric of our society that it would be enormously costly (both in energy and individual freedom) to change them. Thus he agrees with much that has been central to feminist argument: that sex/gender systems are fundamental, structural features of virtually all contemporary societies; that they are often in-equitable; and that they are not an unalterable given. But he insists that these considerations do not necessarily justify challenging or changing gender inequities. At just the point where feminists argue, as a matter of moral, political commitment, that we must redress gender inequities, Wilson argues for conservative caution; one option that must be weighed by any society contemplating such change is that the greater good may be better served by allowing the status quo to persist, even if this means sacrificing the interests (and capabilities) of those who are disadvantaged by existing conditions.

A second feature of the central tenets I have identified is that they leave enormous room for divergence among feminists on a number of fronts. Feminists disagree on empirical questions about just what sort of structuring principle gender is. They diverge on the question of whether biological sex differences are in any sense separable from gender constructs and whether, if so, biology makes a difference (perhaps a positive difference) in women's sensibilities and capabilities that feminists must reckon with in formulating programs for change. Even those who agree that sex/gender systems are entirely social, historical constructs frequently disagree about how malleable sex/gender systems are. And feminists disagree, crucially, on how gender systems relate to other dimensions of social organization, especially class and race, sexual identity, ethnicity, nationality, and disability. In recent years the central focus of debate among feminists has been questions such as whether it is ever meaningful to analyze the effects of sex/gender systems inde-pendently of these other structuring principles and dynamics, and whether there is anything at all common to women's experience as women across all these other dimensions of difference (see, for example, contributions to Mohanty, Russo, and Torres 1991; Bannerji 1993; Hirsch and Keller 1990).

Feminists also disagree in their empirical assessment of how consistently or seriously, and in what areas, existing gender structures disadvantage women, and in their understanding of how and why gender structures have emerged – what generated and what sustains them, and therefore how amenable to change they may be. Some take the position that "sex/gender" structures have "organized social life throughout most of history and in every culture today"; that they are "an organic social variable . . . not merely an effect of other more primary causes, that limits and creates opportunities within which are constructed the social practices of daily life, the characteristics of social institutions, and of all our patterns of thought" (Harding 1983: 312). Some argue that it remains an open question, to be settled by close examination of particular historical and social contexts, just how important a role is played by "sex/gender" structures, compared with other structuring principles. And many insist that there is no such thing as "gender" that is separable from the specific forms that gender relations or ideologies or identities take in particular social locations defined, for example, by race and by class, by sexual orientation, and by a wide range of other key factors and affiliations.

Given these differences in empirical understanding, it is not surprising that feminists also hold widely divergent moral and political views about the sorts of change we should be trying to make: what kinds of feminist ideals we should be striving to realize, what aspects of existing gender inequity are unacceptable and should be the primary target for political action, and what strategies are appropriate for making change. The result is a broad spectrum of feminist positions including the stereotypic liberal feminism that was centrally at issue in the "Firing Line" debate (with its focus on achieving equity before the law and within existing political and economic structures), as well as a range of socialist and "radical" feminisms (which call for more fundamental change in these encompassing structures), alongside various forms of "cultural" and spiritual feminism (some of which retain existing gender stereotypes and seek to valorize rather than transform the "feminine" principle they articulate). There are, as well, a great many other distinctive traditions of feminist activism and theory which incorporate elements of these political stances but rarely fit neatly into any of them: "womanism," Black and Hispanic feminism (see, e.g., Collins 1990 on "Black feminist thought"), lesbian feminism, various forms of feminist separatism, and issue-specific feminist alliances (e.g., the shelter movement, women against violence against women and the anti-pornography movement, wages for housework, pay and employment equity activism, reproductive rights groups, and so on), as well as a constantly evolving panoply of deliberately hybrid positions. So, contrary to much popular wisdom and the caricatures that dominated the "Firing Line" debate, "feminism" is not a monolithic entity that could plausibly be judged "dead" or "alive" as a singular whole. Neither is it an entirely arbitrary collection of individual "points of view." It is a family of positions that depend on quite specific empirical claims and normative commitments, some of which have a bearing on the enterprises we identify as scientific.

SO WHY ARE (SOME) FEMINISTS CONCERNED ABOUT SCIENCE?

I believe there are really two sorts of reasons why feminists have concerned themselves with science. One is that if we are committed to making change in the world, as feminists, it matters a great deal that we understand with accuracy, subtlety, and explanatory precision, the nature and extent and sources of the inequitable sex/gender systems we hope to transform;[5] we need detailed and reliable knowledge of the conditions and forces we oppose. Scientific modes of inquiry are among the most powerful tools we have for doing this; indeed, one of the chief motivations for much science – its Enlightenment legacy – is precisely the commitment to ground action, including political action, in a sound empirical understanding of the human, social, biological, and natural conditions that impinge on our lives. So feminists have a prima facie interest in the sciences and in scientific methods as, in principle, a crucial source of just the kind of understanding we need to proceed effectively in the pursuit of our goals of creating a gender-equitable world.

At the same time, however, feminists have long been suspicious of science as a bastion of male privilege, as male-dominated, as infused with masculinist values and interests, and as an important source and ground of men's gender privilege and control over women's lives. Consider Virginia Woolf on the subject: "science it would seem is not sexless; he is a man, a father and infected too" (as cited in Harding 1986: 135). Despite their reputation for an all-consuming curiosity about the world and for unflinching objectivity in pursuing this curiosity, scientists often betray, at best, a pervasive disinterest in the questions of concern to women and to feminists. At worst, several decades of close analysis and critique reveal that the most relevant sciences for feminist purposes – the social and life and medical sciences – often reproduce and legitimize precisely the ideology of gender inequity that feminists find they have reason to question. So the second reason feminists have taken an interest in the sciences is because these disciplines of inquiry are, in various ways, part of the problem. They are one important locus and source of the inequalities that feminists mean to challenge at the same time as they are a resource for addressing this problem.

Let me now consider, first, some of the ways in which feminists have found the institutions of science to be inequitable and then turn to some of the implications that these inequities may have for the practice and content of science, and for the kinds of knowledge they have provided us for navigating the social and natural worlds.

EQUITY ISSUES IN SCIENCE

In a recent popular discussion, Michael Schrage begins an assessment of the current status of women in the natural sciences and engineering with the observation that "historically, culturally, and economically, science and technology are overwhelmingly male enterprises . . . there's the occasional Madame Curie and Ada, Countess of Lovelace, but they're atypical to the point of anomaly" (Schrage 1990). In fact, although this is true of the broad sweep of science as it has developed in Euro-American contexts in the last 300 years, women did play an important role in the founding of science, and a great many talented women have since contributed to the development of a whole range of sciences – from astronomy, physics, and chemistry through to anatomy, biology and, later, the social sciences – despite the substantial institutional barriers they have had to overcome. There is a growing historical literature which shows that the overwhelmingly masculine profile of science as it has developed was by no means a given; it was a deliberately enforced and closely protected institutional construct.

Londa Schiebinger, a key contributor to this literature, argues that, in the seventeenth and eighteenth centuries, the emerging New Science "st[ood] at a fork in the road" with respect to the inclusion of women (Schiebinger 1989: 100). Women had been active both in the craft traditions and in the learned circles of aristocrats out of which emerged early modern science. The best known of these women are noblewomen, not surprisingly, and they included such prominent figures as Queen Christina of Sweden (who commissioned Descartes to draw up regulations for a scientific academy she sought to establish in the mid-seventeenth century); Laura Bassi, a professor of physics at the University of Bologna in the mid-eighteenth century who was known for her innovative early experimentation with electricity (Italy was an exception in allowing women to teach in universities); Margaret Cavendish, Duchess of Newcastle, who was active in science circles that included many members of the Royal Society in London, and who visited the Society in the late seventeenth century but was never admitted to it; the physicist Madame du Châtelet (Emilie du Châtelet; a prominent mathematician and Newtonian physicist in eighteenth-century French science circles), and her seventeenth-century predecessor Madeleine de Scudery, both of whom were denied membership of the French Academie Royale but were admitted to Italian academies (see Schiebinger 1989, among others, for a much-expanded catalogue of women who contributed substantially to the development of science).

By contrast with these craft and aristocratic traditions, however, most of the European/English universities in which the sciences were to become established drew on monastic traditions that systematically excluded women. Schiebinger argues that, in the seventeenth and eighteenth centuries, when science was still a "new enterprise forging new ideals and institutions," its proponents could either have affirmed the presence and contributions of elite women and craft specialists, or followed the conventions of the universities and excluded them. For the most part those building the formal academies and other institutional bases that came to define science as we know it chose the latter path. Despite the presence of learned women, women who had had "access to the tools of science" and had put them to good use, women and, more generally, all things "feminine" were purged from the emerging traditions of modern science (Schiebinger 1989: 9, chapter 8).

With few exceptions the major academies of science maintained strict policies of not admitting women. In fact, Marie Curie was denied membership of the prestigious Académie des Sciences after winning her first Nobel Prize, and was admitted reluctantly only after becoming the first person ever to win two Nobel Prizes (Ramey 1992); no other woman was elected to the Académie until 1979, "more than three hundred years after it first opened its doors" (Schiebinger 1989: 2). The US National Academy of Sciences did not admit its first woman until 1925, and even now just 4 per cent of its members are women (this is a calculation based on data reported in a review article in the *Washington Post*: Ramey 1992). A similar story can be told not only about other prestigious science academies, but about virtually all of the institutions that have trained and employed scientists since they formed their first formal associations and these policies of exclusion were adopted.

The view that science is a largely male enterprise, both literally and ideologically, is by no means unique to feminists. As Schiebinger has argued in historical terms, and Evelyn Fox Keller with reference to contemporary science (most influentially in Keller 1985), the conception of science as a masculine domain has been an essential feature of its self-definition, and the literal exclusion of women from scientific institutions is by no means anomalous or inadvertent given this self-definition. There are numerous examples of founding figures and pre-eminent practitioners who have been quite explicit about this. Bacon is famous for advocating, in the early seventeenth century (at the dawn of the New Science), a thoroughly masculine (and British) natural philosophy – an "active, virile, generative" science, distinguished by its commitment to the experimental method from the "passive, speculative, and effeminate [natural] philosoph[ies]" of antiquity and of the continent (Schiebinger 1989: 137). He made liberal use of rape metaphors to characterize this new scientific methodology: "you have but to follow and as it were hound nature in her wanderings, and you will be able when you like to lead and drive her afterward to the same place again" (an argument for the experimental replication of results); "neither ought a man to make scruple of entering and penetrating into these holes and corners, when the inquisition is his whole object" (an argument for regarding nature not as sacred or inviolate but as something to be explored and exploited to its fullest potential) (as quoted in Merchant 1980: 168). More recently Richard Feynman, a Nobel Prize laureate, is cited by Harding, among others, as having described the theory that brought him recognition as a mistress he had originally loved with youthful abandon, who had grown old and unattractive, but proved nonetheless to be a solid workhorse of a wife who had borne him a number of "very good children" (Harding 1986: 120).

While these metaphors may be dismissable as extrinsic to the actual content and practice of science, they are often aligned with quite literal claims to the effect that women are inherently incapable of doing science, or that it is inappropriate for them to try. Their intellects are too weak, or if exercised, will drain energy from their ovaries, rendering them infertile, and their presence is disruptive for those who are equipped to do science: "female company so enervates and relaxes the mind, and gives it such a turn for trifling, levity, and dissipation, as renders it altogether unfit for that application which is necessary in order to become eminent in any of the sciences" (Alexander 1779, as quoted by Schiebinger 1989: 152–153). Clearly here the subject position of the scientist is not only gendered male, as it is in the case of Bacon's and Feynman's statements, but the capacity of the scientist to exercise his faculties to the fullest is understood to depend on eliminating "feminine" distractions and weaknesses. Moreover, closing the circle, the life and social and psychological sciences have often, themselves, been used to rationalize the exclusion of women from scientific and other preeminently masculine domains by "demonstrating" that they (along with criminals, members of the "lower" classes, and members of a shifting catalogue of despised "other" cultures, ethnicities, and races) are inherently less intelligent than the race- and class-privileged men who have predominantly done science.

Despite devastating critiques brought against the conceptual foundations of these sorts of racialist and sexist research programs over many years, due to such prominent figures as Steven J. Gould (e.g. Gould 1983), they are now enjoying a resurgence of popularity (see, e.g., Herrnstein and Murray 1994, and the commentaries assembled by Jacoby and Glauberman 1995). And one of their effects is to reinforce widely held "pre-judgements" to the effect that science is no place for a woman, a conviction that has proven to have considerable powers of self-realization since the time it was entrenched in the sciences in the seventeenth and eighteenth centuries. Taking stock of where we now stand, it is clear that since the beginnings of organized science in the Euro-American tradition, women have figured predominantly as technicians and assistants, they have had walk-on roles which were usually gender-stereotypic (see Rossiter 1982, especially chapter 3, "'Women's Work' in Science"). Those who did excel and make significant original contributions are, indeed, remarkable exceptions and typically they were quickly forgotten, their accomplishments often, it is turning out, attributed to husbands, fathers, colleagues.[6]

Certainly some things have changed, and are changing, for the better. With the substantial, if uneven, inroads that women (largely middle-class, white women) have made in a whole range of disciplines and professions since their first admission to universities and colleges in the 1860s, women have improved their position in the sciences – especially in the last couple of decades. In the 1920s, figures reported in the publication *American Men of Science* (Cattell 1906; see Rossiter 1982: 326 note 59, and 358 note 3) indicate that under 5 per cent of all scientists working in the US were women (including engineering and technology, physics, mathematics, the life sciences). By the 1940s, according to Margaret Rossiter, there were "thousands of . . . women working in a variety of fields and institutions, whereas sixty or seventy years earlier there were about ten at a few early women's colleges" (Rossiter 1982: xviii; see also discussion by Harding 1986: 60). This was an achievement realized by "the best efforts of a host of talented women, who, seeing how both science and women's roles were changing around them, took steps to carve out a legitimate place for themselves in the new order" (Rossiter 1982: xviii). And despite being vulnerable to reversal as this "new order" was itself reshaped – there was a sharp downturn in women's training and employment in the sciences in the 1950s – women have continued to build on these gains, doubling and quadrupling their representation in college and graduate programs in science, and among employed scientists and engineers.[7]

Today women account for easily twice as many employed engineers and scientists in the US as in the 1940s, but this is still just 16 per cent of the employed science and engineering workforce at a time when women constitute 45 per cent of the employed workforce in the US (Alper 1993: 409). And their numbers remain comparatively low in the "training pipeline" for scientists, compared to other professional and graduate training programs. Women are still awarded less than a quarter of the advanced degrees granted in the sciences on the most generous construal. Between 36 per cent and 50 per cent of PhDs go to women in various of the social/human sciences (this figure is inflated by psychology in which 50 per cent of new PhDs are awarded to women if you include clinical and applied psychology) while the typical percentage of women among new PhDs in the natural sciences is as low as 8 per cent for engineering, and well under 20 per cent for mathematics, computer science, physics, and environmental science (Alper 1993: 409). This is in an era in which over 50 per cent of the undergraduate student body in the US and Canada has been women since the mid-1980s (taking all fields of study together); in which women have proven to have a higher completion rate for undergraduate degrees than their male counterparts, and now take roughly half of all Master's degrees and over a third of PhDs (all fields); and in which between 30 per cent and 40 per cent of completing students in law and medicine are women. Only biology and chemistry approach this level of representation for women PhDs among the natural sciences and engineering (35 per cent and 24 per cent respectively; Alper 1993: 409). As Schrage observes, in the article I referred to earlier, the persistently low number of women in many sciences serves to "reinforce [a long-established] historical pattern . . . women probably have greater influence over the future of baseball than they do over emerging technologies" (1990: D1) – a sobering thought, given the current state of baseball.

Just as disturbing is an increasing body of evidence that these statistics cannot altogether be attributed to women's lack of natural "aptitude" for science and mathematics or, indeed, to a lack of preparatory training in science. As Rossiter observes, "th[e] great growth [in the participation of women in the sciences seen in the first half of the century] . . . occurred at the price of accepting a pattern of segregated employment and under-recognition which, try as they might, most women could not escape" (Rossiter 1982: xviii, see also discussion by Harding 1986: 60). Women who do succeed in getting trained in the sciences find themselves disproportionately unemployed and underemployed. A recent Canadian report describes a situation that seems endemic to the sciences: "although jobs for all highly trained scientists [have been] in short supply [since the mid-1970s], women particularly have had a difficult time finding permanent jobs . . . the percentage of women with PhDs [in science and engineering] form a pool that seems to be at least twice as great as the percentage of women hired as professors" (Dagg 1985: 74; see Flam 1991 for a comparable discussion of the status of women in astronomy and physics in the US). Even more worrisome, women are disproportionately deflected from the training programs that feed the job market for scientists in the academy, in industry, and in the public sector, not only at the level of preliminary training, but at various points where they already have the qualifications to go on in science but choose other fields. As declared by the title of a contribution to the 1993 *Science* special feature on "Women in Science," "The Pipeline is Leaking Women All the Way Along" (Alper 1993; this special feature is entitled, as a whole, "Gender and the Culture of Science").

This 1993 *Science* article on "pipeline" issues echoes the title and central theme of a Presidential Address that was presented to the AAAS (American Association for the Advancement of Science) by Sheila Widnall in 1988. Her title was "Voices from the Pipeline" and her point of departure was a review of statistics that were then a matter of serious concern to the various agencies and policy-makers in the US who monitor demographic trends in science and technology. Evidently the number of qualified students with BSc and engineering degrees who were choosing to go on to doctoral work in the sciences had dropped dramatically (from 12 per cent to 6 per cent since the mid-1960s) and showed no signs of reversing themselves; a further 26 per cent decrease was projected by the turn of the century. What Widnall juxtaposed with these statistics are the results of a number of studies which suggest that this loss of qualified candidates from the training pipeline is especially high for women, and for foreign and "minority" students. Focusing on women Widnall identified two major points at which women drop out of "the pipeline": at entry to college and mid-way through graduate school, between masters and doctoral programs.

Taking 2,000 girls and 2,000 boys beginning public school as a comparison group, she reports that 220 girls, compared to 280 boys, get the necessary high-school training in mathematics and science to go on to college science programs. Given Widnall's figures, this means that fully 44 per cent of those qualified for science programs in college are girls (14 per cent of the cohort of boys who begin school together, compared to 11 per cent of girls, complete high school with the qualifications to go on in the sciences). But, most striking, of these science-qualified high-school students, three times as many young men as women choose science programs in college. Widnall reports that only 44 women, compared to 140 men of the original cohort (that is, less than 20 per cent of the qualified women, compared to half of the men), continue their training in science at a college level. She observes that women more than hold their own through college; the figures she cites suggest that half of the women who start science programs in college finish with a BSc, compared to a third of the men. Moreover, roughly the same proportion of women as men who complete their BSc decide to go on to science programs in graduate school. The second sharp drop in the representation of women comes at the point when they are mid-way through their graduate studies (when they have completed an MSc) and must decide whether or not to continue on to a PhD in science or engineering. Just 1 woman compared to 5 men, of the original cohort of 2,000 girls and 2,000 boys, will emerge at the end of the pipeline with a doctoral degree in these fields. That is, as the 1993 *Science* article reports, just 20 per cent of new PhDs in science and engineering will be women: this is less than half the proportion of women among the high-school students who are qualified to go on in science programs (i.e., where Widnall's figures suggest 44 per cent of science-qualified high-school students are girls).

On Widnall's account, then, the persistently low number of women in the sciences and engineering cannot be attributed solely or even primarily to their failure, at early stages in their education, to get the necessary qualifications to do science at an advanced level. Rather, it seems that when women reach the point of entering college and PhD programs, a disproportionate number of those who have the training to go on in the sciences and engineering choose against these programs. To account for this pattern of "leakage" of women from the training pipeline, especially in graduate school, Widnall turns to various student surveys (specifically ones done at MIT and Stanford in the mid-1980s) and argues on the basis of their findings that one crucial factor must be what she calls the "environmental" conditions women encounter in science – what the 1993 *Science* feature on "Women in Science" refers to as the "culture of science."

A graduate career is, Widnall says, a process of "continuous testing and trial of one's academic and personal characteristics" that shapes and reshapes your career aspirations as you proceed. As an "apprenticeship in research," much depends on the "quality of interaction with the advisor" and on the role students have an opportunity to play as members of a research team. While "white male students benefit from the self-reinforcing confidence that they belong" which they acquire in part through "self-identification with [largely] white male faculty" for others – women, minority and foreign students – "acceptance is not a presumption, the environment is not so reinforcing" (Widnall 1988: 1744). Widnall finds this reflected in a whole series of measures of self-esteem, confidence, comparisons between "objective" test results and subjective estimates of one's own capabilities and performance relative to that of peers. Instructors evidently expect less from their women students; women students find that their instructors spend less time with them than with their male peers; they report strikingly low rates of assignment to roles of responsibility on research teams (20 per cent of men, compared to 6 per cent of women); and roughly half of the women report various forms of sexual harassment. Not surprisingly, these women come to doubt their capabilities (they routinely report much lower self-assessments of how well they have done or will do than male students who achieve the same results on objective tests and other measures of their performance as students). And as their confidence is eroded, they lower their career aspirations – entering a downward spiral that is reflected in disproportionately high attrition rates among women in graduate programs.

Setting these contemporary experiences and their consequences in historical perspective, I believe that what Widnall reports is the deep-rooted legacy of precisely the masculinist vision of science that, on Schiebinger's account, a great many founders of modern science were intent on establishing; the attributes of personal style and patterns of interaction, the social dynamics and the culture that are valorized in the sciences are pervasively gendered male.[8] As such, they are systematically undermining for individuals who are otherwise inescapably women. Insofar as we do not fit the male mould we are not easily seen as authoritative, as part of "the team," much less as hard-driving, self-starting, dynamic, independent leaders. And often we do not see ourselves in this picture, at least not without considerable conflict and great cost to our own (highly gendered) sense of self and integrity.

Clearly, then, although much has changed, the exclusion (or loss) of women from science is not yet an historical artifact. Widnall's argument for taking seriously the need to turn this situation around – in particular, her argument that we must create a more hospitable environment for women and a great many others who are marginalized in the sciences – is not primarily inspired by a concern with the injustices done to those who are denied the opportunity to "be the best they can" and to make a contribution in the fields they have chosen. Rather, her central concern is that the US as a whole, and the research establishment in particular, cannot afford any more to squander the trained "human resources" represented by those (most especially women) who are so persistently "leaking" from the training pipeline. In this Widnall echoes the concern voiced by Madeleine du Châtelet more than two hundred years ago, when she objected that it was a terrible shame to waste the talents and potential contributions of women to the emerging sciences. In 1735 du Châtelet insisted that "women deserve the same education as men," adding that if she were king, she would "reform an abuse which cuts off . . . half the human race . . . [and ensure that] women participate [fully] in the rights of humankind, and above all in those of the intellect" (as quoted by Schiebinger, 1989: 65).

43

I would add to Widnall's assessment the argument that this pattern of exclusion of women exacts a cost not only from women and from the larger communities of which we are a part, but also from the sciences themselves. Our sciences are not all they could be, measured against their own ideals of empirical rigour and explanatory power, when they deflect the insights and contributions of those potential science practitioners who could be drawn from well over "half the human race," if you consider not only the exclusion of women but of all those who constitute the so-called "minority" groups that Widnall's finds excluded as well.

IMPLICATIONS FOR SCIENCE: CONTENT CRITIQUES

The most controversial form of critique that feminists have levelled against the sciences is that it would be astonishing if the domination of science by men and by a highly masculinized culture did not have an impact on the doing of science – and, ultimately, on the content and results of science. The most straightforward of these critiques focuses on the questions asked and the uses made of scientific inquiry. Key examples often come from the medical sciences where, for example, feminists have objected that research tends to focus on the ailments of men rather than those of women, for example, on heart disease rather than osteoporosis and breast cancer.[9] But as important as these critiques are in practical terms, they leave untouched the conviction that the content and practice of science is value and interest neutral. The objection here is that reliable, empirically substantiated knowledge is being produced, but in areas that are of special interest to, or that stand to benefit, the members of one gender-defined group rather than another.

More challenging are critiques which purport to show that science is not only inequitable in who it recruits and rewards as practitioners and in who it serves, but that the understanding of the world it produces reflects, in its content, the social status, identities, and interests – in short, the standpoint – of its practitioners.[10] For many this is a radically counter-intuitive claim. In considering what such a claim might mean, it is important to recognize that it can be formulated in more and less radical terms, and that it has quite different import for the various disciplines we identify as scientific.

For one thing, the ways in which the content and practice of a science is gender-biased (either intentionally or inadvertently) are bound to be very different for sciences whose subject-matter is inherently or projectively gendered than for those that deal with seemingly non-gendered subjects. While some feminists have argued that the whole orientation of mathematics and theoretical physics is ideologically masculine (e.g., in their preoccupation with abstraction and control), it is not altogether clear how specific practices or results in these fields might reflect gender bias. To quote Schrage's popular discussion, however, this should not be taken to foreclose the question of whether the study of non-gendered subjects sustains gender bias:

> [The natural sciences and engineering raise] a fascinating question: Does gender matter in scientific research? Do women, because of their temperaments and backgrounds, bring ... different sensibilit[ies] to scientific research than their male counterparts? Talk with people at Johns Hopkins, Stanford, and MIT's Whitehead Institute, and it's immediately clear that the influx of women in molecular biology has influenced the nature of research ... [but] unless there are fundamental changes in society and the engineering infrastructure ... we may never know just what sort of a sensibility women can bring to the various disciplines of engineering.
>
> (Schrage 1990: D1)

Certainly a number of sociologists of science argue that class and national bias are evident not just in notorious instances of propagandistic science (the favourite examples are Nazi and Soviet science), but in much of the natural science and mathematics that was acclaimed as the best of its kind in its day. It may be that these seemingly pure exemplars of scientific objectivity reflect the gendered interests of their makers in ways we cannot fully comprehend, being located as we are within a culture permeated both by the authority of science and by sex/gender constructs that are thoroughly naturalized.

By contrast, it is by now well established that the gendered standpoint of practitioners has had a profound impact on the content of the social sciences and many of the life sciences. But even here critiques of androcentrism – of gender bias – take a number of different forms depending on where this bias is located, how it is understood to arise, how pervasive it is, and how deeply rooted it proves to be. Here are some examples that illustrate this diversity.

First, feminists have identified pervasive domain definition bias in a number of social and life sciences; frequently research in these fields simply leaves women and gender out of account. One famous example is Lévi-Strauss's description of one morning's experience, entered in his field journal in the 1930s: "the entire village left the next day in about thirty canoes, leaving us alone in the abandoned houses with the women and children" (1936, as cited by Eichler and Lapointe 1985: 11). Another is the long tradition of anthropological research among "hunter–gatherers" that has characterized these societies almost exclusively in terms of the hunting activities of the men (e.g., as critiqued by Slocum 1975; see also contributions to Lee and DeVore 1968, and overviews by Dahlberg 1981, and Fedigan and Fedigan 1989). A third is Kohlberg's famous and influential study of moral development in children which is fundamentally flawed, Gilligan has argued, by its dependence on samples comprised entirely of little boys (see Gilligan 1982; Kohlberg 1958, 1969).

A second, closely related form of bias, indeed one that is often a consequence of domain definition bias, is that of treating masculine attributes and activities as typical of, or normative for, humankind and society as a whole – the tendency to "count the part as whole." Alternatively, when gender is acknowledged as an important variable, a third tendency is to treat gender differences as a given, as absolute, and to characterize gender roles and identities in terms of stereotypes derived, uncritically, from our own society. For example, as Gilligan develops her critique of Kohlberg's account (Gilligan 1982), she was initially responding to the puzzle of why, on his model of moral development, female children should systematically test several stages behind males in the middle years of their development; here male experience was treated as normative for the population as a whole (the second form of bias). She argues that if you listen to the emerging moral "voice" of girls you will recognize in it a quite different pattern of development than is manifested by most of the boys of Kohlberg's samples (e.g., as discussed in Kohlberg 1958, 1969). Rather than seeing little girls as deficient or immature when they do not fit male-defined norms, she argues that we should recognize divergent paths to moral maturity. Boys later develop the capacity to think empathetically in terms of responsibilities and mutual connection that girls are developing in the middle stages of maturation, and girls later learn to manipulate principles and concepts of rights in the ways that become second nature for boys immersed in rule-governed schoolyard games in their middle years of development.

In a similar vein, detailed ethnographic studies of women's roles and activities in "hunter–gatherer" societies reveal that, among temperate, desert-dwelling, and subtropical groups, the small game and plant resources provided by women gatherers may account for as much as 70 per cent of the group's total dietary intake (see contributions to Lee and DeVore 1968); in many cases it is fundamentally misleading to characterize these groups in normatively male terms as "hunting" societies. In addition, women gatherers often proved to be highly mobile (not tied to a home base), to control their own fertility to an extent not previously acknowledged, and to take the lead in determining community movement and strategies for survival – by sharp contrast with the stereotypes of women's "natural" roles that were projected onto them when they did figure in traditional accounts of "hunter–gatherer" societies. These findings have profound implications not only for what we understand of contemporary "gatherer–hunter" or "foraging" societies (as they were renamed), but for models of human evolution that depend, in part, on ethnographic models of the subsistence patterns and social organization of such groups; they were the inspiration for corrective "woman the gatherer" models of human evolution. In a parallel development, androcentric theories of human evolution have also been undermined by the findings of largely female (although not always feminist) primatologists who have transformed our understanding of our nearest relatives: e.g., chimpanzees (Goodall), gorillas (Fossey), orangutans (Galdikas), and baboons

(Fedigan). This quite recent tradition of research has demonstrated that, *contra* many deeply entrenched assumptions about what counts as "natural" in the domain of sex/gender relations, wild primate populations exemplify much greater diversity in social organization than previously recognized, that mother–infant bonds are often central in structuring primate social relations, and that the females of many species are not just the passive recipients of the attentions of dominant males but are "endowed with sexual strategies of their own" (Morrell 1993: 429).

Cases like these have both depended on, and generated, a great deal of what has since come to be known as "remedial research." In the initial "add women and stir" phase of feminist research, as many now describe it, a great many women and men influenced by feminist critiques undertook to recover, in their various fields, what had been left out of account by research that had manifestly ignored women, that had treated male experience and activities as normative, or had characterized women in gender-stereotypic terms; this was an enterprise of recovering "women worthies, women victims, and women's contributions" (see Harding 1986, chapter 2). Very quickly, however, it became evident that the sorts of errors remedial researchers were bent on redressing had much deeper roots than they initially recognized and could not be corrected by simply augmenting existing accounts with details about women's lives and experiences. Broadening these various fields of inquiry to consider women all too often simply moved the reproduction of gender bias to a new level; the results were sexist or androcentric theories about women, or about a domain newly recognized to include gendered (specifically female) subjects.

Feminist researchers took up this deeper challenge as part of their program of critical inquiry. Soon after the advent of feminist programs of research in anthropology and primatology, history and psychology, the analysis of gender bias took a reflective turn, focusing on ways in which the underlying presuppositions of inquiry may embody ethnocentric, presentist assumptions not just about women, but about gender categories and social relations more generally. These include, for example, a growing body of critiques of Gilligan's continued dependence on a stage-schema model to characterize moral development; the presupposition of set stages and a dynamic of internally driven maturation begins to seem problematic when you expand the range of factors that make a difference in the moral "voice" of children beyond that of gender (see, e.g., Auerbach *et al.* 1985). They also include several powerful autocritiques published by feminist researchers within a decade of their initial critiques of androcentrism in their fields. One is M.Z. Rosaldo (but see also Ringelheim 1985, and Nicholson 1983), who argued that her earlier work as a feminist was flawed by a failure to recognize the ethnocentrism of an implicit assumption that the non-industrialized societies she studied are structured by the same principles of sharp separation and opposition between gendered domains as is familiar from Euro-American contexts: the public domain of men, the private domain of women (Rosaldo 1980). Given this assumption she had held that the errors of androcentric accounts could be corrected by refocusing attention on the private, domestic domain of women. In fact, she came to argue, these dichotomous gender categories are highly specific to Anglo-American society, indeed, they are of quite recent origin (they date to the emergence of a middle class in the late nineteenth century) and cannot be projected onto cultures of other times and places. To do so is to retain precisely the androcentric and ethnocentric assumptions about gender roles that, as feminists, we should be prepared to question.

The turn to searching internal critique exemplified by Rosaldo is also evident in Fedigan's arguments that we should resist the tendency to replace "man the hunter" models of early hominid evolution with "female the gatherer" models; both betray the limitations of current taken-for-granteds about the fundamental and oppositional nature of gender difference and neither are adequate to the complexity of extant data (Fedigan 1986; see also Fedigan 1982; Sperling 1991). It is a mistake, Fedigan insists, to simply invert and revalue the categories central to our current sex/gender system; all indications are that our ancient ancestors lived in social groups, utilizing subsistence strategies, that are unlike any we know through historical, ethnographic, or primatological research. The compulsion to find elements of our own gender relations in the social lives of contemporary non-human primates, and to project these back onto our earliest (proto-human) ancestors, ignores the fact that evolutionary processes have as long a history for non-human as for human primates. In all cases it is as likely as not that paleontological populations were quite different in their behavior and social dynamics from any of the forms we now know among their descendants. Finally, there have been numerous feminist critics within the social sciences who have called into question simplistic assumptions to the effect that women in contemporary societies are everywhere disadvantaged, in the same ways and to the same degrees, by the sex/gender conventions that structure their lives. An early example in sociology/anthropology comes from those who had studied women in so-called "peasant" societies. Here the public subordination of women to men proved to be counter-balanced by the decisive control that women exercise over many aspects of family and community decision-making, so long as the domestic sphere in which they operate continued to be the primary locus of economic activity for such communities (see, e.g., Rogers 1975; Sanday 1974). To characterize these women as disenfranchised victims of an inequitable sex/gender system is to impose on them profoundly ethnocentric and, indeed, androcentric notions about what counts as power (for a more detailed discussion of this example see Wylie 1992).

In all of these cases, what began as an enterprise of adding a missing piece to a complex puzzle led to a reconfiguration of the puzzle as a whole. The central insight to emerge is that studies of literally or projectively gendered subject-matters are pervasively shaped by presuppositions which reflect our standpoint in a society structured by a range of deeply entrenched pre-suppositions about the nature and roles and capacities of those gendered female vs. male. These not only result in ignoring or stereotyping women but also determine, more generally, the range of variables we consider salient, the dimensions of the subject domain we document, the array of explanatory hypotheses we consider plausible enough to be worth testing, and even what we can recognize as "evidence" relevant for evaluating these hypotheses.

In the process, as the net of feminist critique is cast wider and turns up fresh examples of gender bias at increasingly fundamental levels, the question arises of just how deeply scientific practice is impugned. Certainly the cases I have cited make it clear that many sciences are pervasively gender-biased in ways that have escaped attention until quite recently. But is this just a matter of human error – a failure to apply the tools of science carefully or widely enough – or are the tools themselves part of the problem, either in generating some of the biases that feminists document or, more modestly, in allowing bias to be reproduced, failing to be as thoroughly and automatically self-cleansing as we might have hoped? Is the problem we face one of correcting surprisingly widespread instances of "bad science," or must we reconsider the scope and powers of "science as usual," good science, even our best science (see Harding 1986: 19, 102–105)? A feminist biologist, Anne Fausto-Sterling, frames this question in particularly stark terms, after having de-scribed case after case in which it has been found that sex-difference researchers in psychology and physiology ignored negative results, failed to use appropriate control groups and generalized from inappropriately small samples, misapplied techniques of statistical analysis, manipulated variables to produce tautological results, and sometimes even falsified their data (Fausto-Sterling 1985: 7–9). Fausto-Sterling expresses considerable puzzle-ment over the "paradox" that much of this exceedingly bad research was done by "intelligent, serious men and women . . . trained at the best institutions in the country. By all conventional measures, they are good scientists" who frequently built prestigious careers on results that are now proving to be seriously flawed, in terms they would have to respect (1985: 9). In the end she rejects the option of "denouncing the entire scientific enterprise as intellectually corrupt" (*ibid.*), not least, it would seem, because she wants to claim that the research by which feminists have called entrenched wisdom into question is *better* science, science enriched by the fresh "angle of vision" brought to bear by feminist researchers who notice "things about research methods and interpretations that many others have missed" (1985: 11).

I am sympathetic to Fausto-Sterling's position but would add that the cases I have cited – and many of those that she describes in *Myths of Gender* – seem to require a quite thorough-going reassessment of what we can reasonably expect of the tools of inquiry that have been honed by the sciences. These cases bring into view not just piecemeal error, but systematic error made possible by a misplaced confidence in the powers of scientific method to neutralize, to counter or wash out, the effects of the standpoint-specific interests that we inevitably bring to the endeavour of science. That range of "effects" born of the beliefs and practices that define sex/gender difference in contemporary society are just one example of the interests that impinge on science. Often these conventions are so completely transparent, especially to those who fit male norms and are privileged by existing sex/gender systems, that predominantly male science practitioners simply did not see the need to test framework assumptions about gender structures and were not alert to ways in which their research design and results might be biased by gendered presuppositions. It is perhaps not surprising that women who have become conscious of ways in which they are disadvantaged by contemporary sex/gender systems would be more sensitive to ways in which presuppositions about these systems structure our understanding, and would demand higher standards in these cases. Given this "angle of vision," they bring a critical perspective to bear that allows the quite literal discovery of errors and possibilities that had been overlooked. Not only do they use the existing tools of scientific inquiry more effectively in these cases, they often see more clearly the limitations of these tools and are creative in thinking around corners, exploring new ways of using them, and in some cases developing new tools.

The lesson I draw from the work of feminist practitioners and critics of science is that standpoint matters, in both a positive and negative sense. On the principle, "garbage in: garbage out," a great many of the framework assumptions that have informed scientific practice in the past must be subjected to critical scrutiny, especially in fields that study inherently or projectively gendered subject domains. We must become more accountable for the standpoint-specific assumptions we bring to inquiry, especially those that are so deeply entrenched we are barely aware that we hold them.

CONCLUSIONS

I close with three brief observations that I hope raise questions for discussion. First, the sort of bias in content I have identified suggests that inequities in who does science do have a bearing on how good science is. The argument is this: if bias is most likely to arise and persist where science is practiced by a fairly homogeneous group – a group whose values and interests are largely shared and unquestioned – then it would seem that a commitment to objectivity requires that we increase the diversity of those recruited to practice science (see Longino 1990: 214). It is not just that the institutions of science should be more tolerant or accommodating of the diverse standpoints and perspectives of women, as just one among a whole range of groups who have traditionally been excluded from science, but that those who have been excluded in the past may well bring to the sciences quite unique, even transforming, insights and approaches. Our sciences stand to be better – more rigorous, more creative, more inclusive – if a greater diversity of people is involved in their practice.

Second, where feminism is a political perspective based on empirical presuppositions about the way the world actually is – about the role of gender as a structuring principle and the relative status of women vs. men – it is crucial that feminists not reject science as a mode of inquiry, however masculinist and inhospitable it has become as an institution. If we are to be effective in changing the inequities that women still face, we need to make full use of the tools of science, and in the process transform them and the institutions that now control them.

Finally, a reflection that arises from conversation with Leo Block: I believe we should all enthusiastically endorse sunset clauses. My hope is that a genuinely feminist transformation of science and of society will realize a degree of human inclusiveness – intellectually, socially, economically – that will render feminism unnecessary both as a political movement and as a locus of intellectual, scientific engagement. The "Firing Line" debate brought home to me just how far we are from such a happy juncture. My own response to the framing proposition (that "feminism as a movement is dead") is that we have barely begun the task of dismantling the sex/gender systems that continue to limit the human potential, not just of women, but of men located in widely divergent contexts, including such traditionally masculine enter-prises as science. *Pace* E. O. Wilson, this is a challenge that I believe we cannot afford not to meet.

ACKNOWLEDGEMENTS

This essay was written for presentation as a public lecture to the staff, students, alumni, and friends of the University of Denver, at the end of my tenure as the 1994–95 Leo Block Professor. I thank everyone involved in the Women's Studies Program at the University of Denver, especially Anne Rankin Mahoney (Director of Women's Studies), and the administrative staff of the Special Programs Office, for all they have done to make this the most rewarding and enjoyable of visiting appointments. In particular, I thank Leo Block for his support of this chair and of the impressive initiatives being taken in education and scholarship at the University of Denver. I completed this paper for publication while a Fellow at the Center for Advanced Study in the Behavioral Sciences; I thank the Andrew J. Mellon Foundation and the University of Western Ontario for the financial support that made this fellowship year possible.

NOTES

1 Except when discussing the early modern founding of science (which pertains primarily to astronomy, physics and mathematics) or "science and engineering"

(a category used for statistical purposes which includes the natural and life sciences, as well as computing and some branches of psychology–cognitive science), I will use the term science to refer broadly to the whole range of disciplines committed to systematic empirical investigation of the human, social, and natural worlds that we now refer to as scientific.

2 Rebecca West (Cicily Isabel Fairfield) is widely cited as having made this statement in 1913, but I have been unable to find any more specific reference to it.

3 Wilson makes a case for taking this option seriously when he considers the responses open to a society that faces demands for change, e.g., given a growing and global "struggle for women's rights" (1978: 132).

4 Wilson calls for a "value-free assessment of the relative contributions of heredity and environment to the differentiation of behavioral roles between the sexes" (1978: 128–129), and urges that this can "help us to define the options and to assess the price of each" (1978: 132). Nonetheless he concludes that "the evidences of biological constraint alone cannot prescribe an ideal course of action" (1978: 132).

5 By way of a digression I am struck that just as "woman is not born, she is made" (de Beauvoir 1952), so too feminists are very largely not born but made. Often our feminism is inspired by evidence that shatters faith in the objectivity and fairness – specifically, the gender neutrality – of our educational and employment systems, and our social, economic, legal, and political institutions. At least, those who are privileged in other respects may have the luxury of growing up with the belief that if we work hard, get the right sorts of training, cultivate our talents, make ourselves useful and otherwise contribute to society, we can expect, in these lands of opportunity, to achieve various sorts of success. We may believe, more specifically, that the crucial rights and freedoms underpinning these ideals were won for women by our mothers and grandmothers and that it is now up to us to make the most of the hard-fought freedoms and opportunities they have secured for us. In such cases the catalyst for exploring feminist analyses is often a growing realization that, no matter how talented or hard-working we are as individuals, being a woman can make a substantial difference to the opportunities that come our way, and to the rewards we can expect in everything from the subtle reinforcement of full integration into our communities and working groups, through to the acknowledgement and compensation we realize for our achievements and contributions. This is not an easy recognition. Often it comes in agonizing response to a critical threshold of evidence that renders inescapable some version of the two empirical claims I have identified as central tenets of feminism: that gender makes a difference and that in many areas this difference is not just an idiosyncratic, personal/circumstantial problem, but a difference that systematically disadvantages those categorized as women, albeit in widely varying ways.

6 For example, Madeleine du Châtelet's key work in Newtonian physics was claimed by her tutor as his own (see Schiebinger 1989: 63), and by all accounts, Watson's and Crick's dismissive treatment of the contributions made by Rosalind Franklin to their discovery of the double helix – the work that earned Watson and Crick the Nobel Prize – is still by no means anomalous (Ramey 1992).

7 A more detailed discussion of these analyses of the status of women in the sciences, and in colleges and universities more generally, is included in Wylie (1995).

8 The sorts of issues Widnall raises, concerning inhospitable teaching and working environments in the sciences, are addressed more generally in the growing literature on the "chilly climate" that women confront not only in the sciences, but in academia as a whole (see, e.g., Sandler 1986; Aisenberg and Harrington 1988; Chilly Collective 1995).

9 In fact, recent news coverage suggests that medical researchers have not always been very effective in discerning sex/gender differences even in diseases that have been extensively studied, as in the case of heart disease.

10 I will focus here on critiques that consider the gendered standpoint of practitioners, but a wide range of counterpart critiques consider, as well, the class, race, national identity, and other aspects of standpoint.

BIBLIOGRAPHY

Aisenberg, Nadya and Mona Harrington (1988) *Women of Academe: Outsiders in the Sacred Grove*, Amherst, Mass.: University of Massachusetts Press.

Alper, Joe (1993) "The Pipeline is Leaking Women All Along the Way," *Science*, special issue on "Women in Science '93," 260: 409–411.

Auerbach, Judy, Linda Blum, Vicki Smith and Christine Williams (1985) "On Gilligan's *In a Different Voice*," *Feminist Studies* 11(1): 149–163.

Bannerji, Himani (ed.) (1993) *Returning the Gaze*: *Essays on Racism, Feminism, and Politics*, Toronto: SisterVision-Black Women and Women of Colour Press.

de Beauvoir, Simone (1952) *The Second Sex* (H. M. Parshley, trans.), New York: Bantam Books (originally published in French, 1949).

Cattell, James McKeen (1906) *A Bibliographical Dictionary of American Men of Science*, Garrison NY: Science Press (as discussed by Rossiter 1982).

Chilly Collective (1995) *Breaking Anonymity*: *The Chilly Climate for Women Faculty*, Waterloo, Ontario: Wilfrid Laurier University Press.

Collins, Patricia Hill (1990) *Black Feminist Thought*, New York: Routledge (originally Unwin Hyman).

Dagg, Anne Innis (1985) "The Status of Canadian Women PhD Scientists," *Atlantis* 11: 74.

Dahlberg, Frances (1981) "Introduction," in F. Dahlberg (ed.) *Woman the Gatherer*, New Haven: Yale University Press, pp. 1–33.

Eichler, Magrit and Jeanne Lapointe (1985) *On the Treatment of the Sexes in Research*, Social Sciences and Humanities Research Council of Canada, Ottawa.

Fausto-Sterling, Anne (1985) *Myths of Gender: Biological Theories About Women and Men*, New York: Basic Books.

Fedigan, Linda Marie (1982) *Primate Paradigms*: *Sex Roles and Social Bonds*, Chicago: University of Chicago Press.

—— (1986) "The Changing Role of Women in Models of Human Evolution," *Annual Review of Anthropology* 15: 25–66.

—— and Laurence Fedigan (1989) "Gender and the Study of Primates," in S. Morgan (ed.) *Gender and Anthropology*: *Critical Reviews for Teaching and Research*, Washington, DC: American Anthropological Association.

Flam, Faye (1991) "Still a 'Chilly Climate' for Women?," *Science* 252: 1604–1606.

Friedan, Betty (1983) *The Feminine Mystique*, New York: Laurel (originally 1963).

Gilligan, Carol (1982) *In a Different Voice*: *Psychological Theory and Women's Development*, Cambridge, Mass.: Harvard University Press.

Gould, Steven Jay (1983) *The Mismeasure of Man*, New York: W. W. Norton and Co.

Harding, Sandra (1983) "Why Has the Sex/Gender System Become Visible Only Now?" in Sandra Harding and Merrill B. Hintikka (eds) *Discovering Reality*: *Feminist Perspectives on Epistemology, Metaphysics, Methodology and Philosophy of Science*, Dordrecht: Reidel, pp. 311–324.

—— (1986) *The Science Question in Feminism*, Ithaca: Cornell University Press.

Herrnstein, Richard J. and Charles Murray (1994) *The Bell Curve*, New York: Simon and Schuster.

Hirsch, Marianne and Evelyn Fox Keller (eds) (1990) *Conflicts in Feminism*, New York: Routledge.

hooks, bell (1984) *From Margin to Center*, Boston: South End Press.

Jacoby, Russell and Naomi Glauberman (eds) (1995) *The Bell Curve Debate*, New York: Times Books.

Jaggar, Alison M. and Paula S. Rothenberg (eds) (1984) *Feminist Frameworks*, New York: McGraw Hill, second edition.

Keller, Evelyn Fox (1985) *Reflections on Gender and Science*, New Haven, CT: Yale University Press.

Kohlberg, Lawrence (1958) "The Development of Modes of Thinking and Choices in Years 10 to 16," PhD dissertation, University of Chicago.

—— (1969) "Stage and Sequence: The Cognitive-Development Approach to Socialization," in D. A. Goslin (ed.) *Handbook of Socialization Theory and Research*, Chicago: Rand McNally.

Lee, Richard B. and Irven DeVore (eds) (1968) *Man the Hunter*, Chicago: Aldine.

Lévi-Strauss, Claude (1936) "Contributions a l'étude de la organisation sociale des Indiens Bororo," *Journal de la Société Américanistes de Paris* 28: 267–304.

Longino, Helen (1990) *Science as Social Knowledge: Values and Objectivity in Scientific Inquiry*, Princeton NJ: Princeton University Press.

Merchant, Caroline (1980) *The Death of Nature: Women, Ecology, and the Scientific Revolution*, San Francisco: Harper and Row.

Mohanty, Chandra Talpade, Anne Russo and Lourdes Torres (eds) (1991) *Third World Women and the Politics of Feminism*, Bloomington: Indiana University Press.

Morell, Virginia (1993) "Seeing Nature Through the Lens of Gender," *Science* 260: 428–429.

Nicholson, Linda (1983) "Feminist Theory: The Private and the Public," in C. Gould (ed.) *Beyond Domination*, Totowa, NJ: Rowman and Allanheld, pp. 221–232.

Ramey, Estelle (1992) "A Look at Gender in Science," review of *The Outer Circle: Women in the Scientific Community*, Harriet Zuckerman, Jonathan R. Cole, and John T. Bruer (eds), *Washington Post*, April 21.

Ringelheim, Joan (1985) "Women and the Holocaust: A Reconsideration of Research," *Signs* 10(4): 741–761.

Rogers, Susan Carol (1975) "Female Forms of Power and the Myth of Male Dominance: Models of Female/Male Interaction in Peasant Society," *American Ethnologist* 2: 727–757.

Rosaldo, Michelle Z. (1980) "The Use and Abuse of Anthropology: Reflections on Feminism and Cross-Cultural Understanding," *Signs* 5: 389–417.

Rossiter, Margaret W. (1982) *Women Scientists in America: Struggles and Strategies to 1940*, Baltimore: Johns Hopkins.

Sanday, Peggy Reeves (1974) "Female Status in the Public Domain," in Michelle Z. Rosaldo and Louise Lamphere (eds) *Women, Culture and Society*, Stanford: Stanford University Press, pp. 189–206.

Sandler, Bernice R. (1986) *The Campus Climate Revisited: Chilly for Women Faculty, Administrators, and Graduate Students*, Project on the Status and Education of Women, Washington, DC: Association of American Colleges.

Schiebinger, Londa (1989) *The Mind Has No Sex?: Women in the Origins of Modern Science*, Cambridge, Mass.: Harvard University Press.

Schrage, Michael (1990) "Does it Matter if Women Aren't Into Physics? Well, Yes," *LA Times* July 5: D1.

Science (1993) special issue on "Women in Science '93," 260: 384–432.

Slocum, Sally (1975) "Woman the Gatherer: Male Bias in Anthropology," in Rayna

Reiter (ed.) *Toward an Anthropology of Women*, New York: Monthly Review Press, pp. 36–50. (Originally published under the name Sally Linton, in Sue-Ellen Jacobs (ed.) *Women in Perspective: A Guide for Cross-Cultural Studies*, Urbana: University of Illinois Press, pp. 9–21.)

Sperling, Susan (1991) "Baboons with Briefcases: Feminism, Functionalism, and Sociobiology in the Evolution of Primate Gender," *Signs* 17: 1–27.

Twain, Mark (1897) "Cable from London to the Associated Press," as cited in John Bartlett (ed.) *Familiar Quotations*, New York: Little Brown and Company, p. 625.

Widnall, Sheila (1988) "Voices from the Pipeline," *Science* 241: 1740–1745.

Wilson, E.O (1978) *On Human Nature*, Cambridge, Mass.: Harvard University Press.

Wylie, Alison (1992) "Feminist Theories of Social Power: Some Implications for a Processual Archaeology," *Norwegian Archaeology*, 25: 51–68.

—— (1995) "The Contexts of Activism on Climate Issues," in The Chilly Collective (eds) *Breaking Anonymity: The Chilly Climate for Women Faculty*, Waterloo, Ontario: Wilfrid Laurier University Press, pp. 29–60.

3

IS PRIMATOLOGY A
FEMINIST SCIENCE?

Linda Marie Fedigan

Primatology appears to have come of age. Historical analyses of our field are now being written. But exactly what sort of discipline has primatology grown up to be? Not for the first time, I found myself pondering this question recently as I spent a day reading some forty of the many reviews of Donna Haraway's 1989 book, *Primate Visions*. Most primatologists are aware of Haraway's nearly 500-page analysis of the history of ideas and practices in the science of primatology; some will have read the book, and many more will have read the reviews of the book that appeared in biological and anthropological journals. Thus, they will be aware that *Primate Visions* was almost universally panned by primatologists (e.g., Cachel 1990; Cartmill 1991; Dunbar 1990, cf., Stanford 1991; Jolly and Jolly 1990; Rodman 1990; Reynolds 1991; Small 1990). However, they may not know that the same book was greeted with much fanfare and the highest praise in a range of journals, from history to science to feminist periodicals (e.g., Fausto-Sterling 1990; Harding 1990; Hubbard 1989; Marcus 1990; Masters 1990; Nyhart 1992; Rossiter 1990; Scheich 1991). For example, one of the latter reviewers stated that *Primate Visions* "changed her life" and was the "most important book to come along in twenty years" (Fausto-Sterling 1990). Although there were exceptions, one can generalize that practicing animal-watchers did not like the book ("infuriating" was an adjective that appeared repeatedly in their reviews), whereas those who study the process of science, especially those feminists who study science, found it brilliant and stunning. A perfect example of this dichotomized reaction is the joint review by Alison Jolly and her daughter Margaretta in the *New Scientist* (1990): the primatologist mother found the book incomprehensible and wrong-headed, whereas the feminist, postmodernist daughter thought it noble and provocative.

It is possible to suggest several reasons why primatologists, male and female, younger and older alike, reacted so negatively to the book. First of all, as noted by Callan (1990) and Cartmill (1991), the deconstructionist analysis practiced by Haraway can be seen as a hostile act that challenges the authority of the scientist. Her fundamental assertions that facts are relative, that science is a form of story-telling, that sociopolitical forces have a major impact on how science is done, are deeply disturbing to many scientists. Secondly, Haraway is an "outsider," who, like a journalist with an agenda, reported a version of the history of primatology with which many of the people who lived that history cannot concur (e.g., Dunbar 1990; Rodman 1990; Small 1990). Thirdly, *Primate Visions* frustrated many readers because it is written in a prose that is inaccessible to them, a writing style referred to by Alison Jolly as "armor-plated, post-modern, feminist jargon." Haraway herself did not intend her analysis to be hostile to primatologists (1989: 366), and she may well have been surprised by the extent and depth of negative response she received from its practitioners. Indeed, it could be argued that Haraway's depiction of the history of primatology is that of a science becoming increasingly enlightened over time, especially, she implied, as more women entered the discipline. A thorough analysis of Donna Haraway's *Primate Visions* and the reactions to it is beyond the scope of this chapter, but I would like to pursue here the point that feminist scholars liked and approved of this book, and, in fact, many of them look very favorably on the discipline of primatology. Primatologists should be aware that Haraway is only one of a group of "science studies" scholars who are out there watching and evaluating scientists; turning the tables by following *us* around with tape recorders and notebooks.

A review of the literature on gender and science shows that feminist scholars often single out primatology as a discipline in which women have made a greater than average impact (see Fedigan 1994; Strum and Fedigan, in press), and one in which women have had a marked influence for the betterment of their science. Although such scholars may disagree as to whether women have always, or only recently, played an important role in primatology, and they may dispute the precise nature of this role, it is clear that primatology is often singled out for praise by feminists. Indeed, it is sometimes interpreted as a feminist science itself. For example, Rosser (1986: 175) said: "Primatology is the field within the sciences where the research has been most transformed by the feminist perspective." And Bleier (1986: 10) concluded that:

> Primatology thus serves as an example of the correction that a feminist perspective can effect in a field of knowledge ... primatology is a lone example in the natural sciences of dramatic changes made under feminist viewpoints. This is related, in part, to the presence of a critical mass of women and feminists within the field ...

Similarly, Keller (1987a: 235) commented that:

> Over the past 15 years, women working in the field [of primatology] have undertaken an extensive re-examination of theoretical concepts, often using essentially the same methodological tools. These efforts have resulted in some radically different formulations.

What strikes me as curious about such accolades from feminist science scholars is the possibility that theirs is an unrequited love affair, because there are so few primatologists who acknowledge that they are feminists or admire, much less pursue, feminist goals. Obviously, one may counter that it is not common scientific practice to declare one's sociopolitical allegiances, and that we have no objective data on the proportion of primatologists who could be considered feminists. Further, it is possible that some primatologists wish to disassociate themselves from the implications and repercussions of being labeled feminists, while at the same time adhering to principles congruent with those of feminism. Has primatology quietly, and without announcement, become a genre of feminist science? Or is this a case of mistaken identity? Is it possible that primatologists are doing things of which feminists approve for reasons not directly related to feminism? In order to consider this question, it is necessary to first address a set of prior issues. What *do* feminists approve of in science – what is the feminist critique of science? What are the criteria for a feminist science? Is primatology a discipline influenced by the woman's point of view? Is primatology a discipline influenced by the feminist point of view, indeed, a feminist science? I do not claim to give a definitive answer to the last question, but I will lay out the issues, offer an opinion, and make suggestions for how we might develop a better sense of primatology's place in science.

FEMINIST CRITIQUES OF SCIENCE

It took some time for feminist scholars to turn their critical eye on the natural sciences, and even today there is not a unified challenge to the conceptual framework of science or one coherent strategy for alleviating what feminists see to be the problems with the scientific enterprise. According to Fee (1986), feminists in the early stages of the women's movement saw science and technology as located in the (public) male world and having little to do with the politics of personal relationships, sexuality, and reproduction that were the focus of their concerns. Beginning in the mid-1970s and early 1980s, however, the growing issues of reproductive engineering, and the relationship between science and the technologies affecting the lives of women around the world, led feminist scholars to turn their analytical skills to addressing the production and application of scientific knowledge. In particular, many of these writers developed critiques of specific theories in the biological sciences, ranging from models of human evolution to deterministic explanations of differences between the sexes to endocrinological constructions of ontogeny (e.g., Birke 1986; Bleier 1984; Fausto-Sterling 1985; Haraway 1978, 1981; Hubbard *et al.* 1982; Keller 1992; Leibowitz 1983; Longino and Doell 1983; Lowe and Hubbard 1983; Sayers 1982; Tanner 1981; Tuana 1989; Zihlman 1978, 1981). Usually these critiques sought to expose the androcentric language and concepts seen as inherent in the theories, and sometimes they offered an alternative explanation – one from the female point of view.

As well, feminist scholars in the 1980s and 1990s turned their attention to critiquing the entire scientific enterprise as it has been traditionally conceptualized and conducted in the Western world (e.g., Harding 1986; Keller 1985, 1992; Longino 1990; Merchant 1980; Tuana 1993). These analysts concluded that the history of science in the West is founded on assumptions of male domination and patriarchal power. Keller and others have argued that, at least since the Renaissance, the language and metaphors of science have been those of domination and sexuality. The mind is male and nature is female, men gain knowledge (power) by conquering and penetrating nature. Although these metaphors may no longer be so overt as in the writings of Francis Bacon, the fundamental dualities of mind/body, objectivity/subjectivity, active/passive, detachment/attachment, dominance/subordinance, subject/object, rationality/emotionality have become fundamental in Western thinking, and in all cases the former are associated with men, and with science. This association is believed by some to be the reason why women, even today, are less attracted to, and comfortable in, science. According to this argument, the men who brought about the scientific revolution created an enterprise in their own idealized image. Keller (1985 but cf. 1992), Chodorow (1978), Dinnerstein (1976), and Merchant (1980) have offered psychoanalytic theories to explain why men in Western societies wish to associate themselves with characteristics such as detachment, objectivity and rationality, and to accord them higher value than their opposites.

Women have reacted to this model of science in various ways. Most have simply steered clear of the enterprise. Others have attempted to enter science, but, according to Fee (1986), found it strategic to deny that gender attributes play any role in science. Often women scientists have found it necessary to be "nonfeminine" in order to be accorded authority. However, others have argued that women should not have to remake themselves in a masculine manner in order to be scientists; rather, science itself should change.

Harding (1986) has identified five different types of feminist critique of science. The first are equity studies which document the obstacles that women face in obtaining the educational and employment opportunities available to similarly talented men. The second are studies of the sexist uses and abuses of science and technology in various fields such as reproductive technologies. The third line of feminist critique questions the concept and possibility of scientific objectivity by demonstrating that all steps in the process are value-laden, from the original selection of phenomena to be studied to the final interpretation of results. A fourth type of critique uses techniques from psychoanalysis, literary criticism, and historical interpretation to find hidden symbolic and structural meanings in scientific claims and practices. And the fifth area of feminist criticism involves the development of feminist epistemologies (e.g., feminist empiricism, standpoint, and postmodernism) to lay the foundation for an alternative understanding of how knowledge and beliefs are grounded in social experience.

Keller characterized the feminist critique of science as occurring along a political spectrum. Slightly left of center is the liberal critique that almost all scientists are men because of unfair employment practices. Compared to other criticisms, this critique would be relatively easy to address and correct. Further to the left is the radical critique that the predominance of men in science has led to bias in the choice of problems with which scientists have concerned themselves. In several sciences, such as the health sciences (and, I would argue, primatology), this criticism has begun to be addressed. Slightly more radical is the claim of bias in the design and interpretation of experiments. Finally, the most radical critique is to question the very assumptions of objectivity and rationality that underlie the scientific enterprise itself. Keller has cautioned against a view of science as pure social product and outlined the dangers of an intellectual descent into total relativity. In her opinion, we should reformulate and maintain the objective effort but abandon the objectivist illusion. "In short, rather than abandon the quintessentially human effort to understand the world in rational terms, we need to refine that effort" (Keller 1987a: 238).

Harding (1986) has also noted that the ultimate objective of feminist critiques should be to bring an end to androcentrism, not to systematic inquiry, even though an end to androcentrism will require far-reaching transformations of that inquiry. Although the feminist critiques are obviously diverse, it seems to me that they share two fundamental commonalties: (1) the assertion that the inferior status of women in science is related to the inferior status of women in society at large, and one will not change without reform in the other; and (2) the attempt to document and bring an end to androcentric bias in science.

FEMINIST MODELS OF SCIENCE

Just as there are various feminist critiques and many types of feminists, so there are a number of different models for feminist science. Some theorists have observed that the sciences are so diverse, it is unreasonable to expect them all to be transformed by one feminist framework, and that the search for one "correct" feminist approach is misplaced and runs the dangers of introducing a new orthodoxy (e.g., Longino 1989, 1990; Stanley and Wise 1983). Others have argued that it is not possible to even begin to design a feminist science until we have a more feminist and egalitarian society (Birke 1986; Bleier 1986; Fee 1983), or that asking us to envision a feminist science today is like asking a medieval peasant to design a space capsule (Fee 1983).

Nonetheless, a number of scholars have outlined their vision of what science would look like in a future, more feminist society, or how science might be, and indeed is, practiced by feminists today (e.g., Birke 1986; Bleier

1986; Fee 1986; Harding 1986; Longino 1990; Rosser 1989; Wylie 1992). Rather than describe each of these models in turn, I will attempt to extract the features that many of the descriptions have in common. Although I recognize that this risks oversimplification and the implication of one limiting orthodoxy, when in fact many views prevail, it does allow us to distill the elements of feminist ideology that have been applied specifically to the transformation of the practices of science. And such a distillation of the literature on feminist science is necessary before we can assess its application to the field of primate studies.

There are at least six features commonly outlined in models of feminist science. The first may be referred to as reflexivity, or the acknowledgement of the contextual values that influence everyone, including the scientists among us. Such contextual values are believed to act as constraints on the reasoning and interpretations that affect our world view, and usually are seen to be related to race, class, gender, and nationality, among other factors. In a feminist science, it is often proposed that practitioners would seek to understand their fundamental assumptions and how these affect their science; they would see themselves as people whose background and experiences are involved in the process of doing science. Such an acknowledgement of biases and of the role that sociopolitical considerations play in the scientific enterprise would clearly require a rethinking of the traditional concept of scientific objectivity.

In particular, feminists have been concerned that scientists acknowledge the role that gender plays in how they perceive the world, and that scientists explicitly factor gender into their research. This leads to the second feature common to many models of feminist science: the goal of empowering women by developing a way of understanding the world from the woman's point of view. As noted by Wylie (1992), such research would assist scientists to critically reassess the theory that distorts or devalues the lives and experiences of women, and would allow us to evaluate and understand the gendered dimensions of life that conventional categories of analysis ignore.

A third common feature of feminist models involves a reconceptualization of nature. In many models of feminist science, nature would be conceptualized not as passive and subject to human control, domination and manipulation, but rather as active, complex, and holistic. Science would be committed to understanding and working in cooperation with nature; and the language of scientists would shift away from metaphors of hierarchy and domination to those of comprehension and "empowerment." Related to this is a fourth feature suggested in many models; the move away from dualisms and reductionism. Many feminist scientists have argued for the lessening of boundaries between the scientist as knower, and the object of knowledge, between objectivity and subjectivity, dispassion and empathy, and a move toward seeing the elements of nature on a continuum rather than in binary opposition.

Fifth, scientific knowledge would be seen and used as a liberating tool rather than one of domination and nationalism; it would be geared to humanitarian values, and to the solution of world problems. Many models of feminist science speak of an enterprise that would serve humanity rather than the military–industrial complex of western nations ("human need rather than corporate greed": Birke 1986: 143). And finally, in feminist models, the scientific community itself would change; it would become less elitist and more accessible, egalitarian, diverse in make-up and background, and humble in the face of the complexity of life.

Clearly these are utopian goals, and perhaps we can understand now why many feminists argue that a feminist science is not possible in our present world. A more pragmatic approach is taken by Harding (1989, 1991), who concludes that there *are* feminist sciences already in existence today, and that we can recognize them by observing what feminist scientists *do* in fields such as anthropology and psychology, where feminist efforts are already a force with which to reckon. According to Harding, feminist scientists are characterized by being strongly reflexive, by focusing on gender as a variable that infuses behavior, views and society, and by "thinking from women's lives," thereby providing some of the crucial resources needed to develop science for the many, rather than for the elitist few.

FEMALE, FEMININE, AND FEMINIST SCIENCE

One of the confusing issues for nonfeminists and feminists alike is precisely what it means to "think from women's lives." Some have taken this to mean that women might possess a unified cognitive framework that can be brought to bear on the practices of science, and that women may thus do science differently from their male counterparts. Those adhering to this view can be broken into two categories. A very small minority of feminists have argued that women have biologically based traits which are superior to those of men, and that these traits should be espoused in science (e.g., Elshtain 1981; MacMillan 1982). This might be characterized as the argument for a "female science" based on biological sex differences. More commonly, theorists have suggested that the behavior and beliefs of women are *socially* constructed, and that it is the differential history, status, and socialization of women which provide them with a perspective on life and on science that is different from that of their male colleagues. This can be characterized as the argument for a "feminine science" based on socialized gender differences. Scattered through the literature on gender and science (see references in Fee 1983, 1986; Harding 1986; Longino 1990; Rosser 1986, 1989) are suggestions that, as a result of their experiences and position in life, women are more likely than men to possess certain characteristics that enable them to better understand the complexities of natural processes, or at least to develop an alternative world view to the traditional dualistic, hierarchical, "masculine view" of science. A short list of proposed "feminine characteristics" are: a sense of connectedness to nature, an integrative, holistic, contextual world view, a disposition to attend to details, complexities and interactions, a sense of patience and empathy, and a high valuation of pragmatic, experiential knowledge. Fee (1986), for example, has argued that, whether consciously articulated or not, women carry the seeds of an alternative epistemology, and several notable works in psychology (e.g., Belenky *et al.* 1986; Gilligan 1982) have pursued this argumentation.

Some theorists have implied that a feminist science, that is a science based on a theoretical/political stance, would incorporate these presumed feminine characteristics, but there have been objections to this conflation of feminine traits and feminist goals on several grounds. For example, Longino (1990) noted that some women scientists object to such a characterization of feminist science simply as "soft" science, as a new guise for the old argument that women cannot do real, quantitative, hard science. A related objection to the thesis that women scientists will exhibit socialized "feminine traits" is the counterargument that both women and men scientists have been strongly socialized as scientists, and thus gender differences should be minimized. And some feminists (e.g., Harding 1986; Keller 1987b; Longino 1990) have argued that these very traits ascribed to women are socially constructed categories that originated in the historical subordination of women, and are merely the converse of the culturally dominant "masculine" traits. As such, they may be as much characteristics of "outsiders" of the scientific mainstream as characteristics of women. At the very least, it would surely be an oversimplification to suggest that these "feminine" traits reflect the temperaments and world view of all women.

Thus, it is important to distinguish the concept of a feminist science from that of a feminine science: feminism is a theoretical/political stance, and thus the characteristics of *feminists* doing science may well be distinctive from those of *women* doing science (see also Keller 1987b, 1992 on the distinction between gender ideology and women doing science). Feminist theorists, such as Harding, Keller and Longino, are not proposing that feminine biases should replace masculine biases in science, rather they are proposing that an acknowledgement of biases (i.e., contextual values) and a greater diversity of contextual values through the inclusion of people of different backgrounds will result in better science.

In practice, however, it is not always easy to separate the idea of a feminine from a feminist science, since many feminists do see those values thought to be more characteristic of women as essential to a feminist science. As Schiebinger (1987) has noted, traditional feminine values alone may not serve well as an epistemological base for new philosophies of science, but feminist critiques do promote feminine values as an essential part of the human experience, and envision a science that would integrate all aspects of the human experience.

WOMEN AND PRIMATOLOGY

Having summarized the feminist critique of science and distilled the common features of feminist models of science, we are now in a better position to address the questions about primatology raised at the beginning of this chapter. Is primatology a discipline influenced by the woman's point of view? There are several levels at which this question may be addressed. First, there is the presence of a "critical mass of women" in primatology referred to by Bleier (1986) in the statement quoted earlier. A common perception among many observers of science is that there are more women in primatology than in similar fields. My recent analysis of proportions of women and men in professional societies in 1991–2 established that there *is* a significantly higher proportion of women in primatology than in analogous biological sciences, such as ornithology, mammalogy, and benthology (Fedigan 1994). However, there are *not* significantly more women primatologists than there are women anthropologists, psychologists and animal behaviorists, the latter being the three parental disciplines that gave rise to primatology. In 1991, women made up 48 per cent of the membership of the American Society of Primatologists and 38 per cent of the International Primatological Society. By 1992, French (1993) reported that women made up 52 per cent of the American Society of Primatologists. There has been a significant increase in the proportion of women members of primatological societies over the past decade. Thus, the perception that there is a critical mass of women in primatology is likely valid in a comparison across the biological sciences, but not particularly striking from the perspective of the behavioral sciences, such as anthropology and psychology.

Secondly, does the presence of relatively more women, or near gender parity, in a given science influence that discipline? As noted earlier, it has sometimes been argued that women may practice science differently from men, that is, they may tend to choose different topics, frame different questions, prefer different theories and hypotheses, select different methods, and favor different interpretations of scientific findings than do their male counterparts. There has been as yet little research into what male and female primatologists actually do, so there is not much evidence to support or reject the argument of gender differences in scientific practice. The primary assumption is that women scientists focus more on female animals, and there has been some, mainly indirect, evidence that this is the case (e.g., Adams and Burnett 1991; Burk 1986; Haraway 1989; Small 1984; cf. Holmes and Hitchcock 1992). It has also been suggested that women are more likely to try to see the social and physical environment from the female animal's point of view (Haraway 1989; Hrdy 1984; Rowell 1984). I have argued elsewhere (Strum and Fedigan, in press) that over the past two decades the image of female primates has been fleshed out to include much more than just their roles as mothers and sexual partners of males, the two primary descriptors used in earlier studies of primate behavior. In the past twenty years there have been many studies of the significance of female bonding through matrilineal networks, as well as analyses of female sexual assertiveness, female long-term knowledge of the group's local environment, female social strategies, female cognitive skills, and female competition for reproductive success. That women have been more responsible than men for developing our present model of the female primate has been suggested, but not documented. A quantitative scientist might examine whether there is a significant relationship between the relative proportions of women in primatology over the past four decades and the proportions of published papers written "from the female animal's point of view." This has not yet been done.

Finally, there is the possibility that primatology has been influenced by a distinctive cognitive and emotional framework or worldview of women described earlier as the "feminine" approach to science. Although there have been many criticisms of this suggestion, others have argued that women scientists are more likely than men to be patient and empathetic, to take a holistic, contextual approach, to attend to complexities and details, to favor pragmatic, empirical evidence, and integrative interpretations. Is this true of women primatologists? I think that this would be almost impossible to establish on any global scale. However, I have argued elsewhere (Fedigan and Fedigan 1989) that the women who were primarily responsible for transforming our model of baboon behavior in the 1970s and 1980s exhibited all of the characteristics just cited, albeit as did several of the men.

FEMINISM AND PRIMATOLOGY

Has primatology been influenced by the sociopolitical movement known as the women's movement and the theoretical/political stance known as feminism? Some scholars (e.g., Haraway 1989; Hrdy 1986; Sperling 1991) have argued it cannot be a coincidence that a strong shift in the perception of female primates began to occur in the mid-1970s, during the same years as those in which the second wave of western feminism urged scientists to take account of the female point of view. Apart from noting this apparent synchrony of historical events, how might we document the impact of feminism on primatology? Few primatologists, other than Hrdy (1986) and Smuts (in Rosenthal, 1991) have identified themselves in print as feminists, which does not mean that others were not influenced by feminism. It would be possible to ask those primatologists who focused on females and the female point of view, what influenced them to do so. However, this method would also run the risks of any self-reporting study (e.g., revisionist history).

Another approach would be to build a circumstantial case by showing that primatology in the past twenty years has shifted toward the values and practices of feminist science. One of the "science studies" scholars (Rosser

1986) has already made such an argument about primatology, and I will briefly outline her logic here, as well as offering my own examples for clarity.

Rosser modified a scheme originally developed to track the changes in curricula in the liberal arts and applied it to the feminist transformation of research and teaching in the sciences. Her scheme consists of six stages in the feminist transformation of science. Stage 1 is characterized by the failure to even note absence of women (or females). I would say that this stage would encompass the first wave of field studies following World War II (approximately 1950–65), during which time the male dominance hierarchy was often assumed to represent the entire social system of primates (see Strum and Fedigan, in press). Stage 2 begins the search for the missing females. Still working within the on-going paradigms of the science, the research that was formerly carried out on the males of the species was now conducted on the females as well. My interpretation is that in primatology, this stage was characterized by the deliberate attempt to collect more data on females and the publication of books such as *Female Primates* (Small 1984) and *Social Behavior of Female Vertebrates* (Wasser 1983). Stage 3 is characterized by a growing awareness that females have been a disadvantaged, subordinate group, and a questioning about why this is the case. Examples of this stage in primatology might be Hrdy and Williams (1983) and Fedigan (1982), both of which critiqued the past biases against females in primatological theory and data collection.

Stage 4 in Rosser's scheme represents the transition from questioning within the traditional paradigm of the given science, to a breaking free to study females on their own terms, that is, to develop a female point of view which may be outside the prevailing paradigm. This stage includes a rise in feminist consciousness on the part of the researcher. Rosser takes her example of this stage from Hrdy's description (1981, 1986) of how she (Hrdy) realized that the theories she had learned in graduate school did not apply to the female langurs she was studying. Hrdy noted that her shifting perception of female langurs was linked to her dawning awareness of male–female power relationships in her own life, and her attempts to understand and articulate the general experience of female primates. Stage 5 is characterized by the use of the newly discovered female point of view to challenge the traditional theories and models of the science. Gender is used as a category of analysis to test the traditional paradigms. Again, Rosser uses Hrdy's research as an example, and interprets Hrdy's studies of female competition, sexual assertiveness, and infanticide as examples of testing the established paradigms of sociobiology in the science of primatology. Other examples of testing and challenging established sociobiological theories using gender as a category of analysis would be Small (1993) and Smuts (1992; see also Smuts and Smuts 1992). Stage 6 represents a transformed, "balanced" view in which both female and male perspectives and experiences are included and integrated.

Thus, based largely on her reading of Sarah Hrdy's research, Rosser finds that primatology is the field within the sciences which has been most transformed by the feminist perspective. While it is certainly true that Rosser's interpretation would be strengthened had she read more widely in primatology, can we nonetheless concur with her general conclusion that our discipline has moved through the stages as outlined? I would argue, and have done so elsewhere (Fedigan 1994), that primatology has shown itself to be very responsive to criticisms of androcentric language and interpretations, and quite willing to redress the past focus on male behavior with a present focus on both sexes and on the relationship between the sexes. As primatologists, we have certainly seen more and more efforts to collect information on female lives and behaviors, and to develop equivalent understandings of how female and male primates perceive, behave, and interact in their worlds. If this is a feminist transformation, then it has happened in primatology. Below I will consider alternative explanations for why primatology in the past twenty years has better developed its knowledge and understanding of female primates.

A more generalized, if still circumstantial, case might be built by examining trends in primatology, especially changing trends over the past twenty years, in light of the six common characteristics of feminist models of science described earlier. Although I cannot pretend to a quantitative analysis or even a profound qualitative analysis here, I will offer my opinions as to whether or not primatology exhibits any or all of these six characteristics, as a vehicle for further discussion.

The most commonly mentioned feature of feminist science is "reflexivity," which, as noted above, refers to an awareness and acknowledgement of the contextual values that constrain our perception of the world, especially our views of our scientific subject-matter. Nothing in the published work of primatologists indicates that they are particularly reflexive about the role of race, class, or national biases in their work. However, there is one fundamental tenet in primatology which is highly reflexive and that is the awareness of the dangers of anthropomorphism. Primatologists work with animals that look and often seem to behave in ways familiar to humans, and one of the principles that is drilled into new recruits is that we must avoid ascribing human motivations, values, and understandings to our animal subjects. As scientists, primatologists are constantly reminded that we are limited by our human world view, and that this affects our understanding of our subjects, even as we strive to understand the animals in their own right. Further, most primatologists in North America are trained in anthropology departments (French 1993), and will be familiar with the taboo against ethnocentrism, the latter being the often unconscious view that one's cultural patterns are the only acceptable form of behavior. Although primatologists, like other scientists, strive for objectivity in their research, they have been made well aware that scientists come to their subject-matter with certain preconceptions.

A second feature common to feminist models of science is the factoring of sex and gender differences into research and the development of the female point of view. I would say that primatology has definitely developed a strong female point of view over the past fifteen years, and it may well be this attention paid to female primates on the part of scientists that drew the attention of feminist scholars in the first place. Why have primatologists developed a strong female point of view? As noted above, it may be the result of feminist ideology. It may also be that the nature of the subject-matter lends itself to a female-centered "world view" in primatologists. Many primate societies are female-bonded; thus kin-related females are the permanent core of the social group, competing with conspecifics for resources, defending themselves against predators, and finding enough food to feed themselves and their suckling young. This was not immediately recognized by primatologists, but it has now forced itself on the consciousness of these scientists, and possibly facilitated a strong focus on females as well as attracting more women to the discipline.

A third feature in feminist models is a reconceptualization of nature as a complex phenomenon with which humans would best attempt to cooperate rather than dominate. Does primatology exhibit this trait? I would answer a cautious yes, and suggest that the primatologists' conceptualization of nature, like the primatologist's concept of female primates, is based largely on their subject-matter – the primates. Primates are complex, long-lived animals who exist in a multi-layered web of environmental and social interactions. In order to observe them in the wild, many months, even years, of patient observation are necessary. One develops a very different attitude in this type of study than that developed, for example, when studying thousands of short-lived creatures whose populations are easily manipulated. Without belittling the laboratory work and experimental field work that does take place in primatology, I would say that the goal of most field observation is to better understand the subject-matter, rather than to manipulate or control it. Furthermore, all primatologists are concerned about the increasingly endangered populations of primates in the wild, and the destruction of their habitats. This renders almost all primatologists environmentalists, the latter being a group that is certainly dedicated to working with and not against nature.

Has primatology exhibited the fourth feature common to many models of feminist science, that is, a move away from reductionism and dualisms? Again, I would answer a qualified yes. I would not argue that most primatologists have lessened the boundaries between themselves as scientists and their subjects, nor do they usually have the ability or desire to let the "subject" speak for her or his self, as is recently the case in the human behavioral sciences. However, a very important trend in the past twenty years of primatology is to increasingly portray our subjects as cognizant, sentient, socially intelligent creatures, who are not simply automatons responding to genetic or hormonal directives. A good example is the study of social dominance relations. At first it was assumed by many primatologists that the bigger, stronger, tougher individuals would be socially dominant over their conspecifics. Now we realize the enormous role played by individual intelligence, social traditions, and social strategies in determining power relationships among nonhuman primates. We have moved from an over-simplified concept of "brute" force to a more complex one of "social finesse" (e.g., Strum 1987). I would say that a move from reductionist understandings of primate behavior to more sophisticated ones is characteristic of many areas of primatological research in the past couple of decades.

Fifth, is primatology geared to humanitarian values and to the solution of world problems rather than to serving nationalistic interests? Clearly, unlike such fields as physics and engineering, primatology does not lend itself particularly well to serving nationalistic, military–industrial interests. However, as pointed out by Haraway (1989), primatological research has some-times been carried out by and for military interests. I do not know if this is any less true today than in the past. I do know, however, that primates are often used as models for human problems, both behavioral and biological, and in that respect primatology does serve humanitarian ends. The study of primates allows us to put humans into a larger, cross-specific comparative perspective, and one of the ultimate rewards of studying our primate relatives is a better understanding of what it means to be human.

Finally, there is the question of the primatological community; has it become more diverse, accessible and egalitarian over time, as postulated in feminist models of science? Certainly, more and more women are entering the discipline, but there is little evidence in North America and Europe that people of diverse races and classes are pouring into this science. However, there is an increasingly good representation of different nationalities at international primatological meetings, and there have been attempts on the part of many primatologists working in Third World countries to train local people to become scientists. Furthermore, the two major primatological societies (the International Primatological Society and the American Society of Primatologists) have recently made available scholarships specifically targeted for Third World students and scholars. But clearly more could be done to encourage accessibility and diversity of background in this science.

CONCLUSION

In sum, primatology does exhibit several of the features that have been described in feminist models of science. Also, more and more women have entered the discipline over the past decade, and recently there are nearly equal proportions of women and men primatologists. Over the past twenty years, primatology has produced a strong, well-developed focus on the female as well as the male primate. Has primatology become a genre of feminist science? According to the published criteria available on feminist science, I would say, yes. But whether by design or not is a different question. Some primatologists are no doubt feminists. Others may subscribe to values and practices approved of by feminists for reasons that they do not directly relate to feminism.

If the correlation between feminist science and trends in primatology that has been suggested in this chapter were substantiated, at least two alternative explanations should be considered. The first is that the objectives of a feminist science may be similar to those of other alternative approaches to the scientific enterprise. For example, Fee (1986), Haraway (1989) and Montgomery (1991) have noted the similarities between the feminist critique of science and other epistemologies of science, such as the African, Indian, Chinese, Japanese and Marxist perspectives on natural knowledge. There may not be that many different ways to do science. The women's movement in the 1970s can also be seen as part of a larger liberation movement growing out of the "counter-culture" of the 1960s in North American and Europe. A thorough analysis would consider the possible influences of many social forces, and not just feminism, on the development of the discipline of primatology in North America and Europe.

Secondly, some of the trends in primatology that have been identified in this chapter, such as the development of a female as well as male perspective, and the move from reductionism and dualisms to increasingly complex, sophisticated explanatory models, could arguably result from the processes intrinsic to the maturation of all scientific disciplines. It is possible that any new science would go through initial stages of being relatively mechanistic and making simplifying assumptions. As the science matures, it would be expected to graduate to sophisticated models that are more complex, dynamic, and multi-factorial. Thus, the goals of those who try to develop a better, more mature science of primatology may sometimes dovetail with the goals of those aspiring to a feminist science.

Nonetheless, a good circumstantial case can be made that primatology has been influenced, if not transformed, by feminist perspectives and objectives, and I have suggested ways that this influence might be more directly documented. At the very least, we should give credit to the feminist critique for drawing our attention to androcentric bias in science, and for challenging us to develop a more balanced view in which both female and male perspectives and experiences are taken fully into account.

However, the reception of the feminist critique by practicing scientists, including women scientists, has often been less than positive, and Hammonds reviews the reasons for this lack of enthusiasm (Longino and Hammonds 1990). She suggests that a primary reason for the negative response is the perception by scientists that the feminist critique of science is a political rather than a scholarly enterprise. She also argues that scientists and feminists cast the "women in science" problem differently: scientists ask "what is it about women's lives that keep them from doing science?", whereas feminists ask "what is it about science that keeps women from participating?" The former question locates the problem with women; the latter formulation situates the problem in science.

Do these general observations on the chasm between many practicing scientists and feminist critics of science help us to understand the negative reaction to Haraway's history of primatology on the part of its practitioners? Longino (in Longino and Hammonds 1990) states that scientists may misread Haraway as an anti-realist who licenses any claim so long as it is in opposition to the mainstream discourse, and who sees primatology as nothing more than self-serving stories. Longino argues on the contrary that Haraway sees the production of primate knowledge as rule-governed (although the rules may change over time), and Haraway acknowledges that scientific representations, produced according to the rules of inquiry in given fields, have made it possible to interact with our material surroundings in reliable ways. However, she believes that scientists cannot inform us about human values and justice. According to Longino, Haraway does not dispute the role of science as representer of natural processes, but she does contest primatology's claim to hold objective blueprints for the transition from nature to culture and for the original form of human society and justice. Thus, Haraway has tried to convince her readers that "primatology is politics" and "political," as noted by Hammonds, is precisely what most practicing scientists do not wish to be. One of primatology's self-avowed tasks is to help us understand the evolution of primate and human sociality, and even those primatologists who would agree with many of the goals of feminist science may not be able to accept Haraway's fundamental questioning of their authority in this endeavor.

ACKNOWLEDGEMENTS

My research is supported by an on-going grant from the Natural Sciences and Engineering Research Council of Canada (NSERCC, Operating Grant no. A7723). Long walks and lively conversations with Shirley Strum over the past several years stimulated me to address the issues in this chapter, and I thank Shirley for her probing, but always courteous, questions about my assumptions. I also thank Pam Asquith, Mary Pavelka, Sandra Zohar and Lori Hager for their critical reading of the manuscript, and Meg Conkey for sharing her list of reviews of Donna Haraway's *Primate Visions*.

BIBLIOGRAPHY

Adams, E. R. and Burnett, G.W. (1991) "Scientific Vocabulary Divergence among Female Primatologists Working in East Africa," *Social Studies of Science* 21: 547–60.
Belenky, M. E., Clinchy, B. M., Goldberger, N. R., and Tarule, J. M. (1986) *Women's Ways of Knowing. The Development of Self, Voice, and Mind*, New York: Basic Books, Inc.

Birke, L. (1986) *Women, Feminism and Biology. The Feminist Challenge*, New York: Metheun.

Bleier, R. (1984) *Science and Gender. A Critique of Biology and its Theories on Women*, New York: Pergamon Press.

—— (1986) "Introduction," in R. Bleier (ed.) *Feminist Approaches to Science*, New York: Pergamon Press.

Burk, T. (1986) "Sexual Selection, Feminism and the Behavior of Biologists: Changes in the Study of Animal Behavior, 1953–85," *Creighton University Faculty Journal* 5: 1–16.

Cachel, S. (1990) "Partisan Primatology," *American Journal of Primatology* 22: 139–142.

Callan, H. (1990) "Writing Primates," *Anthropology Today* 6: 13–15

Cartmill, M. (1991) "Review of *Primate Visions*," *International Journal of Primatology* 12: 67–75.

Chodorow, N. (1978) *The Reproduction of Mothering: Psychoanalysis and the Sociology of Gender*, Berkeley: University of California Press.

Dinnerstein, D. (1976) *The Mermaid and the Minotaur: Sexual Arrangements and the Human Malaise*, New York: Harper and Row.

Dunbar, R. (1990) "The Apes as We Want to See Them," *New York Times Book Review* January 10: 30.

Elshtain, J. B. (1981) *Public Man, Private Woman: Woman in Social and Political Thought*, Princeton, NJ: Princeton University Press.

Fausto-Sterling, A. (1985) *Myths of Gender*, New York: Basic Books.

—— (1990) "Essay Review: Primate Visions, a Model for Historians of Science?", *Journal of the History of Biology* 23: 329–333.

Fedigan, L.M. (1982) *Primate Paradigms. Sex Roles and Social Bonds*. Chicago: University of Chicago Press.

—— (1994) "Science and the Successful Female: Why There Are So Many Women Primatologists," *American Anthropologist* 96: 529–40.

—— and Fedigan, L. (1989) "Gender and the Study of Primates," in S. Morgan (ed.) *Gender and Anthropology. Critical Reviews for Teaching and Research*, Washington DC: American Anthropological Association, pp. 41–64.

Fee, E. (1983) "Women's Nature and Scientific Objectivity," in M. Lowe and R. Hubbard (eds) *Woman's Nature. Rationalizations of Inequality*, New York: Pergamon Press.

—— (1986) "Critiques of Modern Science: the Relationship of Feminism to other Radical Epistemologies," in R. Bleier (ed.) *Feminist Approaches to Science*, New York: Pergamon Press.

French, J. A. (1993) "A Demographic Analysis of the Membership of the American Society of Primatologists: 1992," *American Journal of Primatology* 29: 159–165.

Gilligan, C. (1982) *In a Different Voice. Psychological Theory and Women's Development*, Cambridge, Mass.: Harvard University Press.

Haraway, D. (1978) "Animal Sociology and a Natural Economy of the Body Politic," *Signs* 4: 21–60.

—— (1981) "In the Beginning was the Word: the Genesis of Biological Theory," *Signs* 6: 469–481.

—— (1989) *Primate Visions. Gender, Race and Nature in the World of Modern Science*, New York: Routledge, Chapman, and Hall.

Harding, S. (1986) *The Science Question in Feminism*, Ithaca: Cornell University Press.

—— (1989) "Is There a Feminist Method?", in N. Tuana (ed.) *Feminism and Science*, Bloomington: Indiana University Press.

—— (1990) "Review of *Primate Visions*," *National Women's Studies Association Journal* 2: 295–298.

—— (1991) *Whose Science? Whose Knowledge?* Ithaca: Cornell University Press.
Holmes, D. J. and Hitchcock, C. L. (1992) "Gender as a Predictor of Research Topic in Animal Behavior," Paper presented at the Annual National Meetings of the Animal Behavior Society, University of North Carolina at Washington.
Hubbard, R. (1989) "Planet of the Apes, Dismantling the Empire of Science," *The Village Voice*, October 3: 63.
——, Henefin, M. S. and Fried, B. (eds) (1982) *Biological Woman: The Convenient Myth*, Cambridge, Mass.: Schenkman Press.
Hrdy, S.B. (1981) *The Woman That Never Evolved*, Cambridge, Mass.: Harvard University Press.
—— (1984) "Introduction," in M. Small (ed.) *Female Primates. Studies by Women Primatologists*, New York: Alan R. Liss.
—— (1986) "Empathy, Polyandry, and the Myth of the Coy Female," in R. Bleier (ed.) *Feminist Approaches to Science*, New York: Pergamon Press.
—— and Williams, G. C. (1983) "Behavioral Biology and the Double Standard," in S. K. Wasser (ed.) *Social Behavior of Female Vertebrates*, New York: Academic Press.
Jolly, A. and Jolly, M. (1990) "A View from the Other End of the Telescope," *New Scientist* 21: 58.
Keller, E. F. (1985) *Reflections on Gender and Science*, New Haven, CT: Yale University Press.
—— (1987a) "Feminism and Science," in S. Harding and J. F. O'Barr (eds) *Sex and Scientific Inquiry*, Chicago: University of Chicago Press.
—— (1987b) "Women Scientists and Feminist Critics of Science," *Daedalus* 116: 77–91.
—— (1992) *Secrets of Life. Secrets of Death. Essays on Language, Gender and Science*, New York: Routledge.
Leibowitz, L. (1983) "Origins of the Sexual Division of Labor," in M. Lowe and R. Hubbard (eds) *Woman's Nature: Rationalizations of Inequality*, New York: Pergamon Press.
Longino, H. (1989) "Can There be a Feminist Science?", in N. Tuana (ed.) *Feminism and Science*, Bloomington: Indiana University Press.
—— (1990) *Science as Social Knowledge*, Princeton: Princeton University Press.
—— and Doell, R. (1983) "Body, Bias and Behavior: a Comparative Analysis of Reasoning in Two Areas of Biological Science," *Signs* 9: 206–227.
—— and Hammonds, E. (1990) "Conflicts and Tensions in the Feminist Study of Gender and Science," in M. Hursch and E. Fox Keller (eds) *Conflicts in Feminism*, New York: Routledge.
Lowe, M. and Hubbard, R. (eds) (1983) *Woman's Nature. Rationalizations of Inequality*, New York: Pergamon Press.
MacMillan, C. (1982) *Woman, Reason, and Nature*, Princeton, NJ: Princeton University Press.
Marcus, G. E. (1990) "The Discourse of Primatology," *Science* 248: 886–887.
Masters, J. (1990) "Natural Selection, Cultural Construction," *The Women's Review of Books* VII (January): 18–19.
Merchant, C. (1980) *The Death of Nature: Women, Ecology and the Scientific Revolution*, New York: Harper and Row.
Montgomery, S. (1991) *Walking with the Great Apes*, Boston: Houghton Mifflin Co.
Nyhart, L. K. (1992) "Review of *Primate Visions*," *Signs* 17: 481–484.
Reynolds, V. (1991) "Review of *Primate Visions*," *Man* 26: 167–168.
Rodman, P. S. (1990) "Flawed Vision: Deconstruction of Primatology and Primatologists," *Current Anthropology* 31: 484–486.
Rosenthal, E. (1991) "The Forgotten Female," *Discover* 12: 22–27.

Rosser, S. (1986) "The Relationship between Women's Studies and Women in Science," in R. Bleier (ed.) *Feminist Approaches to Science*, New York: Pergamon Press.

—— (1989) "Feminist Scholarship in the Sciences: Where are We Now and When can We Expect a Theoretical Breakthrough?", in N. Tuana (ed.) *Feminism and Science*, Bloomington: Indiana University Press.

Rossiter, M.W. (1990) "Review of *Primate Visions*," *The Journal of American History* 77: 712–713.

Rowell, T.E. (1984) "Introduction," in M. F. Small (ed.) *Female Primates. Studies by Women Primatologists*, New York: Alan R. Liss.

Sayers, J. (1982) *Biological Politics: Feminist and Anti-feminist Perspectives*, New York: Tavistock Publications.

Scheich, E. (1991) "Review of *Primate Visions*," *American Historical Review* 96: 829–830.

Schiebinger, L. (1987) "The History and Philosophy of Women in Science: a Review Essay," in S. Harding and J. O'Barr (eds) *Sex and Scientific Inquiry*, Chicago: University of Chicago Press.

Small, M.F. (ed.) (1984) *Female Primates. Studies by Women Primatologists*, New York: Alan R. Liss.

—— (1990) "Review of *Primate Visions*," *American Journal of Physical Anthropology* 82: 527–532.

—— (1993) *Female Choices. Sexual Behavior of Female Primates*, Ithaca: Cornell University Press.

Smuts, B.B. (1992) "Male Aggression against Women," *Human Nature* 3: 1–44.

—— and Smuts, R.W. (1992) "Male Aggression and Sexual Coercion of Females in Nonhuman Primates and other Mammals: Evidence and Theoretical Implications," in P. J. B. Slater, M. Milinski, J. S. Rosenblatt, and C. T. Snowdon (eds) *Advances in the Study of Behavior* (vol. 22), New York: Academic Press.

Sperling, S. (1991) "Baboons with Briefcases vs. Langurs in Lipstick. Feminism and Functionalism in Primate Studies," in M. di Leonardo (ed.) *Gender at the Crossroads of Knowledge: Feminist Anthropology in the Postmodern Era*, Berkeley: University of California Press.

Stanford, C.B. (1991) "Review of *Primate Visions*," *American Anthropologist* 93: 1031–32.

Stanley, L. and Wise, S. (1983) *Breaking Out: Feminist Consciousness and Feminist Research*, London: Routledge and Kegan Paul.

Strum, S.C. (1987) *Almost Human. A Journey into the World of Baboons*, New York: Random House.

—— and Fedigan, L.M. (forthcoming) "Theory, Methods and Women Scientists: What or Who Changed Our Views of Primate Society?," in S.C. Strum and D. G. Lindburg (eds) *The New Physical Anthropology*, Englewood Cliffs, NJ: Prentice Hall.

Tanner, N. (1981) *On Becoming Human*, Cambridge: Cambridge University Press.

Tuana, N. (1989) "The Weaker Seed: the Sexist Bias of Reproductive Theory," in N. Tuana (ed.) *Feminism and Science*, Bloomington: Indiana University Press.

—— (1993) *The Less Noble Sex. Scientific, Religious, and Philosophical Conceptions of Woman's Nature*, Bloomingon: Indiana University Press.

Wasser, S.K. (ed.) (1983) *Social Behavior of Female Vertebrates*, New York: Academic Press.

Wylie, A. (1992) "Reasoning about Ourselves: Feminist Methodology in the Social Sciences," in E. D. Harvey and K. Okruhlik (eds) *Women and Reason*, Ann Arbor: University of Michigan Press.

Zihlman, A. (1978) "Women in Evolution. Part II: Subsistence and Social Organization among Early Hominids," *Signs* 4(1): 4–20.

—— (1981) "Women as Shapers of the Human Adaptation," in F. Dahlberg (ed.) *Woman the Gatherer*, New Haven: Yale University Press, pp. 75–120.

4

MOTHERS, LABELS, AND MISOGYNY

Rebecca Cann

This chapter is a personal exploration of the controversy surrounding the place and time scale for modern human origins, and the meaning (or lack of meaning!) that the concept of race now has for anthropological genetics. My research interests built on the idea that genes from modern people can be used to infer the evolutionary history of ancient populations (Cavalli-Sforza *et al.* 1994), and this gave rise to the hypothesis that all of us shared a common female ancestor, probably an African woman (Cann *et al.* 1987). Controversy about modern human origins re-erupted, in part, from this and additional data gathered by anthropologists and geneticists in the 1980s and early 1990s (Stringer and Andrews 1988; Vigilant *et al.* 1991; Thorne and Wolpoff 1992; Templeton 1993).

WHO OWNS THE PAST?

For several decades prior to the 1980s, one rather prominent view of human evolutionary history was a 3-million-year long straight path leading from an ape-like but fully bipedal African australopithecine ancestor through an archaic human species (*Homo erectus*) with a more expanded brain into anatomically modern people (*Homo sapiens sapiens*). Humans ancestors were thought to have left Africa at least a million years ago when controlled use of fire allowed them to live outside the warm tropics, and many local populations of archaic humans became established on separate continents. Recent redating of fossils from Java may push the initial expansion of human ancestors from Africa back to almost 2 million years ago.

Modern populations of humans were assumed to have some direct biological continuity with the more archaic groups that inhabited the same general area. Separate species of modern humans didn't develop on each continent because migration between groups occurred, and a small level of gene flow united all populations through intermediate links. These links are now nearly extinct, as urban centers and dominant cultures absorb most indigenous peoples. Although minor differences in skin color, hair form, and body shape can be found today among modern humans, everybody eventually invented or shared the same ideas about agriculture and domesticated animals, adopted living conditions that exposed them to a variety of infectious diseases, and acquired the ability to communicate by spoken language.

Under this model of modern human origins, called the "Regional Continuity" model (Thorne and Wolpoff 1992), a molecular biologist might expect to see more DNA sequences shared in common between DNA extracted from a series of fossil humans from China and modern Chinese than between the DNA sequences of modern Chinese and modern Africans. The same should be true of ancient and modern Africans, or ancient and modern Europeans. This model predicts that some genetic divisions between modern people on different continents could be quite deep, with many mutations separating their DNA sequences since they last diverged from a common ancestor. Mutations accumulate with time, and in the absence of continual gene flow to homogenize populations and spread them around, we predict that populations will diverge biologically.

DISCIPLINES IN COLLISON

However, there are alternatives to this scenario, and one is called the "African origin" model (Wilson and Cann 1992). It acknowledges that ancient populations did exist on separate continents, but that most of these populations went extinct without giving most, if any, genes or DNA sequences directly to modern people. This model suggests instead that modern people all stem from a population of archaic humans that originated in Africa, but that spread out from Africa to replace older populations beginning around 200,000–150,000 years ago. Morphological similarities between ancient and modern populations from the same geographic region require a different kind of explanation in this model. It emphasizes the close biological relationships that all modern races and ethnic groups have to each other, rather than drawing attention to minor variations that separate us.

Projection is a strong feature of some arguments between these models, and our heightened ability to detect individual differences visually may lead us to overemphasize the externally visible characters of the human face. The ambiguous nature of our knowledge about our own past fuels further social unease about race and ethnicity that is now expressed in biologically based assumptions (Herrnstein and Murray 1994), themselves having a sordid history (Lane 1994). Even with modern information about biological differences, there is still the danger that we will fall into old patterns of thought and action.

If race is an ever-changing biological entity, as modern genetics has demonstrated (Lewontin 1974), then the fluid nature of human groups will be a constant source of confusion about what race is, even among non-scientists. Owing to the action of natural selection, different genes will show the effects of past history more clearly than others, so even scientists will dispute the major patterns of geographic separation between different populations. Humans need to comprehend patterns that they see in the natural world. The search for a mature understanding of human diversity is akin to the current search for dark matter by physicists and cosmologists, where, "The Greeks said the universe was comprehensible; they did not say it was simple" (Wilford 1994: B8).

DIVERSITY IN A NON-NEUTRAL CONTEXT

Political commentators are sensitive to the possibility that academics have systematically minimized the biological differences between people of different races or ethnic groups in order to push a specific social agenda (Case 1995; Begley 1995). They point to enrichment programs in American education and equal opportunity employment systems as perceived evidence of this social tinkering. Cohort age and west coast urbanization aside (Breslauer 1995), many professional or occupational groups contain racially homogeneous members that might not be predicted from population numbers alone. Biological diversity in modern humans, and the antiquity of the division between different historical populations of hominids, is a legitimate topic for inquiry in anthropology (Groves 1989).

It is my perception that when the discussion of diversity gets too close to us, taking on a female face and black skin, the intensity increases dramatically. Academic platitudes about the need for free and open debate about diversity fail. For example, as a result of speaking about women's genes and human origins for public television, I became bombarded with hate mail from both creationists and various political groups. One family member admonished my parents for my behavior, asking them why I would tell perfect strangers that my ancestors were black when all the family picture albums showed the real truth! After participating in a heated forum on human evolution at a large museum, I was taken aside by a trustee and told that I should learn to respond to hostile questions in a more feminine manner, in order to make my message easier for audiences to digest. The idea of a common African mother, one that inspires poetry (Belle Brown 1991) and drawings (Mankoff 1991), reaches diverse audiences. The power of an unsuspected recent African connection has touched many minds outside of some narrow academic discipline.

ARCHETYPAL WORLDS

Issues of gender and race become readily transparent when writers in the popular press seize on scientific disagreements, portraying early humans as exclusively male, usually with light skin (Lemonick 1994). Although "Lucy" may arguably be the most famous African female of all time (Johanson and Edey 1981), male australopithecines are the more commonly used to illustrate early hominids. Are males, as suggested, just easier to draw? Is it easier to see all that body hair if skin color is light? And why aren't more professionals concerned about these distortions of our biology?

One measure of change I assay each year is the frequency that the phrase "human origins" is used in place of "man's origins," and 1994 was a bad year in this regard. The old linguistic root may imply a gender-neutral term, but I have difficulty accepting the argument that, in English, nothing restrictive is meant or implied by this usage. Choices exist, and they reflect the dominant mood of a discipline. The criticism many female researchers have experienced in physical anthroplogy is clearly directed not just at their work (Haraway 1989). An essay by one senior female anthropologist (Shipman 1995) details the repressive atmosphere of human evolutionary studies she encountered at multiple institutions, from the completion of her PhD at New York University to her decision to leave a faculty job at Johns Hopkins University. It is the most public expression of misery inflicted on a female scientist in this field that I have read.

Male anthropologists have commented about the heated exchanges centered on the evolution of early modern humans (Relethford and Harpending 1994). They take notice of the stridency, questioning its motivation. Criticism rarely remains strictly scientific, but it is usually directed at male and female participants alike. Why then even suspect that a more misogynist force is provoking some of this controversy? I think that the name given to part of the hypothesis about the mitochondrial mother, nicknamed "African Eve," carried deeper connotations that many scientists found objectionable. Biblical references that this name invoked certainly allowed cheap shots about myths and imaginary gardens that invited ridicule or dismissal, but seldom serious consideration. By ridiculing the name, one could forget that the hypothesis was complex, and really contained three separate ideas, namely, that the origin of modern humans was recent, second, that the origin of modern humans was a single event, and third, that the origin of modern humans was ultimately tied to an African population. As long as you could snicker about the term like a dirty joke, the universe of human paleontology would be safe from outside influences.

WHO WAS AFRICAN "EVE"?

"Eve" or "African Eve" was a shorthand term used by the late Allan Wilson to refer to the hypothetical female ancestor that we inferred was the last mother of us all (Cann *et al.* 1987), based on the study of human maternally inherited genes. Phylogenetic trees, the involved cartoons of lines and symbols that connect donors of different continents into a common network of maternal relatives, contain notoriously difficult ideas to portray accurately. For a scientist, there is never just any one tree, but many possible trees. Our problem is that we don't have an exact account, just pieces. Some of the pieces of a phylogeny could fit in multiple places within a big tree, and we struggle to statistically evaluate the goodness of fit for any one piece at any one place. For a historian, however, there is only one true tree, the way evolution actually took place. Without a time machine, we can only approximate this tree. Wilson wanted a general term that would help people remember the importance of the particular human female whose maternal genome started the modern human radiation, and he chose the name "Eve", almost as a joke.

The label "Eve" or "African Eve" that was applied to the recent African origin hypothesis evoked powerful emotional associations that all but overwhelmed normal discourse. All one had to do to start an argument was to say the name Eve. Eyes would roll, tempers would flare, and assumptions would be made. In desperation, we began to search for a different term in order to get around all the irrelevant symbolism this label implied, because just responding to the mistaken assumptions and trying to correct them took so much energy. There were some people who just wanted to fight about it, because, for them, the name symbolized a dilettante approach and all the gross oversimplifications outsiders to anthropology could make about the complexity of modern human evolution. Then again, some people would not abandon the name even though they knew it was provocative, because it dictated an agenda.

> from time immemorial men have thought there is some mysterious essential connection between a thing and the spoken name for it. You could use the name of your enemy, not only to designate him either passionately or dispassionately, but also to exercise a baleful influence.
>
> (Schlauch 1955: 13)

Misrepresenting ideas associated with the term "African Eve" or "Mitochondrial Eve" detracted from the real debate about the complexity of human evolution, compared to other primates (Groves 1989). Would we ever move beyond acknowledging that there was more than a single woman ancestor of humans to an accurate quantification of human population extinction rates? Was there much variation in population continuity across continents, glacial epochs, or cultural stages or would we be forever restating the obvious distance between mythology and archaeology?

The last common ancestor of all modern humans does not have to be the last common maternal ancestor, as genealogists will agree (Shoumatoff 1985), and "Lucky Mom" does not have to belong to any particular species championed at the moment by anyone. However, by asserting that the use of this name was equivalent to the idea of a single female being the sole ancestor of all people (Klein *et al.* 1990), or insisting that one could not base a theory about all of human evolution using neutrally evolving female genes (Wolpoff 1989), the stage was set. The backlash against a recent African origin for all humans was secondary to the backlash against this misrepresented female, whatever species name she is accorded, and wherever her children went later.

Legitimate concern exists over whether the source female was really African, and further studies using large numbers of unlinked genes that are inherited from both parents give the idea of an African radiation overwhelming support (Goldstein *et al.* 1995; Nei 1995). For geneticists, the question of geographic origin is now largely a non-question. They have moved on to debates about the calibration of a mutation rate that would place the origin nearer to 200,000 years ago, or 100,000 years ago. Both dates are consistent with the initial African mother hypothesis. They also now explore the size of the initial expanding population, and the possible movements of population waves through the Middle East or North Africa, reconstructed from gene frequencies and differences between geographically contiguous modern populations.

STEPPING BACK

A feminist perspective gathered by using genes that are traced only through matrilines altered the debate about modern human origins (Wilson and Cann 1992), and brought the role of females back into prominent reconstructions of human evolution. Their inclusion as important factors in the latest stages of hominization are critical because of the behavioral shifts, especially those affecting fertility and completed family size, which took place as modern humans changed their subsistence bases and expanded their ranges into new geographic areas (Soffer 1987; Klein 1992). The African replacement model doesn't provide a mechanism for understanding why some previously successful groups went extinct, and the portrayal of "killer Africans," even in jest, illustrates the difficulty molecular biologists have in taking physical anthropology seriously. A recent introductory textbook contained a sidebox commenting on this question (Stein and Rowe 1993). It stated that there was no evidence of any armed conflict in the fossil record for the period concerned. Such emphasis indicates ignorance of the fundamental concept of reproductive success in producing "biological fitness" for evolution by natural selection, stressing only the male-centered idea of competition! When the question of how population A eventually replaces population B becomes one of demographics and better parenting instead of armed conflict, it is impossible to seriously consider the absence of "total genocide in the fossil record" as sufficient proof that the recent African origin of modern people is wrong.

RECOVERED GROUND

Anthropologists striving to define specific hypotheses about the time scale and geographic place of origin for our recent ancestors have attempted to regain the ground lost by the distracting and inaccurate protrayals of the real issues (Stringer and Brauer 1994). A recent African origin for modern people is really a nested set of ideas about our past. First, all people, no matter what group they now identify with, share descent from a common African gene pool. Second, this gene pool probably existed between 200,000 and 100,000 years ago. Third, waves of anatomically modern humans arose from this ancestral group, but we don't know exactly where this took place. Initially it might have been in Africa, but if the date were 100,000 years ago, the African migrants might have moved into a new homeland adjacent to Africa. Fourth, older populations of humans on other continents were effectively replaced by this newer group, although how and where the replacement started or when it finally stopped is impossible to tell from mitochondrial DNA (mtDNA) data alone.

Previous theories about the origins of human diversity asserted the strict geographic continuity of morphological and hence genetic relationships between all ancient and modern populations of humans, built upon the early work of the anthropologist Carleton Coon (1962). Even though population centers were thought to be relatively isolated, migration between isolates might have allowed them to evolve in parallel fashion on different continents (Thorne and Wolpoff 1992; Frayer *et al.* 1994). This idea alone is contrary to modern systematic views on the origin of mammalian species (Groves 1989), which, when analyzed using explicit criteria, usually show restricted geographic ranges.

Migration of some magnitude might have also spread cultural innovations (Wolpoff 1989), so there was room in the multi-regional universe of ideas for environmental changes affecting human anatomy as well. However, genetically continuous populations require good luck in order to persist for over a million years, with large extended families, open breeding systems, and even sex ratios. This description is one of a population that is homogeneous genetically (at equilibrium), yet modern people are not (Cavalli-Sforza *et al.* 1994). Continuous populations that exchanged migrants should also have spread artifacts and the ideas associated with their production across 12,000 kilometers. Instead, we see no evidence that this occurs until much later (Klein 1992). In the multi-regional hypothesis, local constraints in the production of specific stone or wooden tools biases the archaeological record against such discoveries. Emphasis on extreme bias in tool discovery and production, along with a temporally incomplete record of artifacts, could be just a smokescreen for evading hard questions about the statistical improbability of attaining and sustaining such high migration rates in technologically simple cultures (Majumder 1991).

As a result of recognizing the importance of factors affecting population stability, increased emphasis on the role of demography and human social networks has provided better models for anthropological geneticists. It has also exposed our ignorance about how early populations grew, moved, and evolved (Rogers 1995). Differential female contributions to lifetime reproductive success of offspring and the manipulation of sex ratios are accessible topics in primatology (Cheney and Seyfarth 1990), but more difficult ones for human paleontologists to address because the evidence cannot be observed directly. The time scale (200,000 to 40,000 years before present) under consideration here also taxes our ingenuity, so creative mathematical model-ing (Rogers and Harpending 1992) seems the only alternative to endless speculation, in the absence of DNA from the fossils themselves.

The recent African origin hypothesis does not require that all human genes match the biblical story of creation (one man, one woman), or that all other genetic systems (blood groups, hemoglobin proteins, etc.) be fatally biased in recording past history of human evolution. Nor does it state that all other time periods or non-African populations are uninteresting. It also does not assert that geneticists should ignore morphology or macro-evolutionary processes. Yet, all these ideas have been attributed to it (Stein and Rowe 1993).

These views, associated with a "Straw Eve" (Ayala *et al.* 1994), continue to stimulate attack that allows more posturing, rather than serious exploration of human phylogenetic patterns (Takahata 1993). The gang-trashing of the African "Eve" or Lucky Mother hypothesis can be linked to an insistence that something essential which had been previously ignored, overlooked, or misunderstood was to be learned about our history by concentrating on genes inherited exclusively from women. While a zoologist could write about the many unorthodox perspectives which stemmed from concentrating on mtDNA without causing a stampede of protest (Avise 1991), anthropological geneticists were apparently supposed to keep quiet.

I finally felt compelled to speak about the bias against modern genetic studies of human populations in research funding, in symposium invitations, in publications, and in training a whole new generation of physical anthropo-logists to NSF. The opportunity came when I was asked to review a summary of federally funded anthropological research that was to appear in the now-defunct journal *Mosaic*, a publication highlighting NSF sponsored research. My confidential review was given to both professional anthropologists and to a journalist with no formal training in either anthropology or biology. I later found this incident written up in detail and ridiculed in his book on the controversy surrounding modern human origins (Brown, M. 1990: 238–239). I found myself described as an out-of-control, unbalanced female while my male colleagues were portrayed in more neutral or positive language. Since that time, I have refused to review anthropology proposals for NSF.

AGAINST THE GRAIN

Mainstream human genetics is an essential tool for understanding human evolution and biological variation. For example, mitochondrial genes occupy a central position in the study of human genetics of aging (Arnheim and Cortopassi 1992), but, without exception, all discussions of genetics in anthropology begin with the focus of chromosomal inheritance from two parents. The introduction of non-chromosomal inheritance, where (mtDNA) represents a special case of maternal transmission, appears secondarily as a side issue, as it does in most textbooks in genetics aimed at undergraduates. The order of presentation is thought to be justified by the relative contributions of the genes we inherit, most coming from the nuclear chromosomes. However, the secondary presentation of the topic, introduced only after the student has grasped fundamental principles, belies the interest and effort that currently takes place in the field of molecular genetics.

The first complex genome described at the DNA level was the human mitochondrial one (Anderson *et al*. 1981), and maternally inherited diseases soon acquired a new prominence (Wallace *et al*. 1988; Holt *et al*. 1990). Effective thinking about maternally inherited genes required the invention of a new system of molecular population genetics (Birky *et al* 1989; Slatkin and Hudson 1991). Population dynamics of an effectively neutral, haploid genetic system also led to new insights in parasite–host coevolution, population turnover, cytoplasmic sterility, and mechanisms of mutation (Hartl and Clark 1989). These are hardly marginal issues in evolutionary genetics, or evolutionary biology in general. Still, most courses cram the study of maternally inherited systems into the last week of a semester, if the topic appears at all in a syllabus.

Given this disparity, it is even more important to emphasize that mainstream genetics supports the major features of the mtDNA model of human evolution (Nei and Roychoudhury 1993; Cavalli-Sforza *et al*. 1994; Bowcock *et al*. 1994; Dorrit *et al*. 1995; Nei 1995; Goldstein *et al*. 1995) and is not in conflict with it. Evolutionary biologists fully appreciate the significance of these data for interpreting larger patterns in human phylogeny. Comprehensive studies of the human genome place the deepest division of modern people among groups of humans in Africa, emphasize the diversity which exists in all races and especially that which exists among Africans, and underscore the recent expansion of modern human populations. Criticism of statistical methods used to infer the correct human phylogenetic tree from mtDNA data of modern humans are mathematically valid (Felsenstein 1992), but were and are directed towards designing new methods and using all existing information available to achieve greater confidence that individual branches of the tree are correct. Among the scientists at least, the debate is open, international, and active. This newly stimulated intensity of interest in human phylogeny, on the part of geneticists, is not the sign of a negative contribution to anthropology.

PREMATURE JUDGEMENTS

Given that background, it is puzzling that molecular anthropology, especially the study of human biological evolution using mtDNA, was dismissed by sophisticated authors in a popular introductory textbook as a premature subfield (Stein and Rowe 1993: 466–467). Criticism of a particular method to build gene trees does not constitute proof that a tree is impossible, or even improbable. When phylogenetic trees based on mitochondrial molecules are becoming standard in the field of vertebrate systematics (Hillis and Moritz 1990), the objections raised by anthropologists (and some geneticists) to this development is troubling.

No one hypothesis will perfectly account for all the data, but some hypotheses are preferred because they allow us to see our mistakes faster and discard bad ideas quickly. Some anthropologists have been adept at using this approach and seeing the logical outcome. An example of this was the idea that Neandertals had a 10-month gestation period (reviewed, along with other Neandertal myths, in Trinkhaus and Shipman 1992).

MtDNA trees assist the process of hypothesis rejection when testing ideas about how modern populations are linked to past populations. It is possible to analyze the trees with different methods, and look for patterns of congruence with hypotheses generated from archaeology, from linguistics, and from anatomy. Other methods of building trees which make assumptions different from the much-criticized Phylogenetic Analysis Using Parsimony program (PAUP) (Swofford 1991) still generate an overall African origin pattern. The body of genetic evidence now available, using many unlinked genes in other donor groups, makes it hard to understand how the African origin pattern could be so universal, unless our immediate ancestors were Africans. Without independence of thought and new tools to guide research, anthropology is in danger of becoming even more marginalized among professional biologists than it currently is.

WHY AN ACCURATE VIEW OF HUMAN DIFFERENCES IS ESSENTIAL

If we as professionals do not understand the process by which populations arise, become isolated, and then rejoin or face extinction, what about the educated lay person? Old-new hereditarian views in the popular press allude to genes and racial differences in intelligence, but there is a clear distortion of the message about how modern human populations are different from each other in measurable amounts of DNA sequence change. We can compare the genetic differences between two average humans and two average chimpanzees. The two humans are about 1/25 as different from each other as the two average chimpanzees are from each other (Kocher and Wilson 1991). To me, this trivial amount of genetic change between two humans, taken at random any place on the planet, is a particularly vivid illustration of our recent common ancestry. It might be possible that single mutations in a few genes alter human intelligence, and alleles (alternate forms of genes in a population) might be concentrated in one population or another, for historical reasons. However, no reputable geneticist believes that intelligence is the product of only a few genes, and no evidence currently exists to support the hypothesis that any genetic differences in intelligence have a geographically skewed distribution in modern populations (Lane 1994).

In order to understand the significance of that statement, however, one needs to understand the concept of descent with modification from a common ancestor, and the notion that humans and chimps are very closely related, sharing a common ancestor only 5 to 7 million years ago (Horai *et al.* 1992). Again, maternal genes give us this picture, in great detail. MtDNA mutations between humans and chimpanzees reflect the divergence of populations from a common ancestral species, their separate evolutionary trajectories over time, and the accumulation of new mutations in the now reproductively separate groups of modern humans and modern apes.

This pattern of separation and speciation, however, does not account for the differences between modern human groups. They are not different species, or even subspecies. Instead, anthropological geneticists deduce a pattern of expansion, temporary isolation, and finally waves of lineages arising from common ancestral female lines that mix in largely cosmopolitan populations. The idea that phylogenetic trees in general and the significance of race in particular as a historical artifact should be so clearly misunderstood after so much work is personally discouraging. In reality, the murder trial of a prominent ex-athlete/sportscaster will be the means by which most Americans finally learn what DNA is, and this idea is also profoundly humbling. It exposes certain assumptions about how different we think we really are from each other. How best to proceed?

ONE PLAN FOR THE FUTURE

My motives for continuing to use maternally inherited genes, even in light of the problems they entail, are simple. In contrast to emphasizing biparentally inherited genes, the genes contained in the mitochondria of the cell (mtDNA) are simple and compact. They give one the opportunity to follow the migration of women. This window on modern human variation can be used to study the mating systems of different societies and sex-biased dispersal, but it can also explore the genetic roots of indigenous modern people (Shields *et al.* 1992; Torroni *et al.* 1992; Lum *et al.* 1994). Contrasts between the specific branching patterns of their maternal gene trees, their nuclear gene trees, and their kinship systems will aid us in constructing more realistic hypotheses about how early modern humans spread in tribal groups, assimilating or excluding outsiders as they encountered them. Indeed, better understanding of this principle is crucial to progress in questions concerning the peopling of the Americas (Cann 1994).

The mitochondrial mother gave rise to an unbroken line of female descendants, whose genes we carry in us today. Were there special biological characteristics in these women, and how will we find them? In order to proceed, we need to identify the lineages of humans basal in the mtDNA tree. These lineages of men and women, on different continents, might hold the clues to the transformation of humans from archaic to modern people. Their mtDNA is just a shortcut to identify which lineages, in the modern sea of humanity, might be fruitful to examine in greater detail with the new genetic markers identified as a result of the Human Genome Project.

It is my bias that we will never appreciate morphological variation in the human fossil record until we understand morphological and behavioral variation in modern populations. Variation has genetic correlates. Most genetic systems in animals are complicated because of diploid inheritance and sexual recombination. The haploid, non-recombinant DNA system present in females (Birky *et al.* 1989) allows us to examine human variation at a simple DNA level. These data now tax the mathematical abilities of the best scientists, but computational advances will yield a future where diploid systems can eventually be incorporated into realistic phylogenetic analysis (Hudson 1993).

The long-term evolutionary significance of variation in this system is unresolved at present (Felsenstein 1992), and I think it is unlikely that genes associated directly with mtDNA hold the secret to what triggered the transformation from archaic to modern humans. However, these genes are a molecular roadmap to finding the ones that did. They help us to identify previously neglected geographic centers for archaeological or linguistic research, the modern ethnic groups that share specific, informative regions of the nuclear genome, and by genetic linkage analysis, the anatomical complexes subject to rapid bursts of natural selection. We work with DNA from bone when not prohibited by religious or personal beliefs, and in doing so we will extend the survival of genetic lineages to actual populations in one past (Herrmann and Hummel 1994). Some people might have good cause to feel threatened by these implications. Those who view the fossil record with balance and rigor should not. Instead, they should remember their mothers.

BIBLIOGRAPHY

Anderson, S., Bankier, A.T., Barrell, B.G., de Bruijn, M.H.L., Coulson, A.R., Drouin, J., Eperson I.C., Nierlich, D.P., Roe, B.A., Sanger, F., Schreier, P.H., Smith, A.J.H., Staden, R., and Young, I.G. (1981) "Sequence and Organization of the Human Mitochondrial Genome," *Nature* 290, 457–465.

Arnheim, N. and Cortopassi, G. (1992) "Deleterious Mitochondrial DNA Mutations Accumulate in Aging Human Tissues," *Mutation Research* 275, 157–167.

Avise, J. (1991) "Ten Unorthodox Perspectives on Evolution Prompted by Comparative Population Genetic Findings on Mitochondrial DNA," *Annual Review of Genetics* 25, 45–69.

Ayala, F.J., Escalante, A., O'h Uigin, C., and Klein, J. (1994) "Molecular Genetics of Speciation and Human Origins," *Proceedings of the National Academy of Sciences USA* 91, 6787–6794.

Begley, S. (1995) "Three is not enough," *Newsweek* Feb.13, 67–69.

Birky, C.W., Fuerst, P., and Maruyama, T. (1989) "Organelle Gene Diversity Under Migration, Mutation, and Drift: Equilibrium Expectations, Approach to Equilibrium, Effects of Heteroplasmic Cells, and Comparison to Nuclear Genes," *Genetics* 121, 613–627.

Bowcock, A.M., Ruiz Linares, A., Tomfohrde, J., Minch, E., Kidd, J.R., and Cavalli-Sforza, L.L. (1994) "High Resolution of Human Evolutionary Trees with Polymorphic Microsatellites," *Nature* 368, 455–457.

Breslauer, J. (1995) "Not-So-Clueless," *The New Republic* 213 (10), 22–25.

Brown, C.B. (1991) *Feeling Black*, New York: New Era Poet's Press.

Brown, M. (1990) *The Search for Eve*, New York: Harper and Rowe.

Cann, R.L. (1994) "MtDNA and Native Americans: a Southern Perspective," *American Journal of Human Genetics* 55, 7–11.

—— , Stoneking, M., and Wilson, A.C. (1987) "Mitochondrial DNA and Human Evolution," *Nature* 325, 32–36.

Case, E. (1995) "One Drop of Bloody History," *Newsweek*, Feb.13, 70–72.

Cavalli-Sforza, L.L., Menozzi, P., and Piazza, M. (1994) *The History and Geography of Human Genes*, Princeton: Princeton University Press.

Cheney, D.L. and Seyfarth, R.M. (1990) *How Monkeys See the World*, Chicago: University of Chicago Press.

Coon, C. (1962) *The Origin of Races*, New York: Alfred A. Knopf.

Dorrit, R.L., Akashi, H., and Gilbert, W. (1995) "Absence of Polymorphism at the ZFY Locus on the Human Y Chromosome," *Science* 268, 1183–1185.

Ecoffier, L. and Langaney, A. (1989) "Origin and Differentiation of Human Mitochondrial DNA," *American Journal of Human Genetics* 44, 73–85.

Felsenstein, J. (1992) "Estimating Effective Population Size from Samples of Sequences: Inefficiency of Pairwise and Segregating Sites as Compared to Phylogenetic Estimates," *Genetical Research Cambridge* 59, 139–147.

Frayer, D.W., Wolpoff, M.H., Thorne, A.G., Smith, F., and Pope, G.G. (1994) "Getting it Straight," *American Anthropologist* 96, 424–438.

Goldstein, D.B., Ruiz Linares, A., Cavalli-Sforza, L.L., and Feldman, M.W. (1995) "Genetic Absolute Dating Based on Microsatellites and the Origin of Modern Humans," *Proceedings of the National Academy of Sciences USA* 92, 6723–6727.

Groves, C.P. (1989) *A Theory of Human and Primate Evolution*, New York: Oxford.

Haraway, D. (1989) *Primate Visions*, New York: Routledge.

Hartl, D. and Clark, A.G. (1989) *Principles of Population Genetics*, 2nd edition, Sunderland: Sinauer Associates Inc.

Herrmann, B. and Hummel, S. (1994) *Ancient DNA*, New York: Springer Verlag.

Herrnstein, R. and Murray, C. (1994) *The Bell Curve*, New York: Simon and Schuster.

Hillis, D.M. and Moritz, C. (1990) *Molecular Systematics*, Sunderland: Sinauer Associates Inc.

Holt, I.J., Harding, A.E., Petty, R.K.H., and Morgan-Hughes, J.A. (1990) "A New Mitochondrial Disease Associated with Mitochondrial DNA Heteroplasmy," *American Journal of Human Genetics* 46, 428–433.

Horai, S., Satta, Y., Hayasaka, K., Kondo, R., Inoue, T., Ishida, T., Hayashi, S., and Takahata, N. (1992) "Man's Place in Hominoidea Revealed by Mitochondrial DNA Genealogy," *Journal of Molecular Evolution* 35, 32–43.

Hudson, R.R. (1993) "The How and Why of Generating Gene Genealogies," in N. Takahata and A.G. Clark (eds) *Mechanisms of Molecular Evolution*, Sunderland: Sinauer Associates Inc.

Johanson, D. and Edey, M. (1981) *Lucy*, New York: Simon and Schuster.

Klein, J., Gutknecht, J., and Fischer, N. (1990) "The Major Histocompatibility Complex and Human Evolution," *Trends in Genetics* 6, 7–11.

Klein, R.G. (1992) "The Archaeology of Modern Human Origins," *Evolutionary Anthropology* 1, 5–14.

Kocher, T.D. and Wilson, A.C. (1991) "Sequence Evolution of Mitochondrial DNA in Humans and Chimpanzees," in S. Osawa and T. Honjo (eds) *Evolution of Life*, Tokyo: Springer-Verlag.

Lane, C. (1994) "The Tainted Sources of The Bell Curve," *The New York Review of Books* 41(20) 14–19.

Lemonick, M.D. (1994) "How Man Began," *Newsweek* 143 (11), 80–87.

Lewontin, R. (1974) *The Genetic Basis of Evolutionary Change*, New York: Columbia University Press.

Lum, J.K., Rickards, O., Ching, C., and Cann, R.L. (1994) "Polynesian Mitochondrial DNAs Reveal Three Deep Maternal Lineage Clusters," *Human Biology* 66(4), 567–590.

Majumder, P. (1991) "Recent Developments in Population Genetics," *Annual Review of Anthropology* 20 97–117.

Mankoff, R. (1991) Drawing, *New Yorker*, Nov. 11, 112.

Nei, M. (1995) "Genetic Support for the Out-of-Africa Theory of Human Evolution," *Proceedings of the National Academy of Sciences USA* 92 6720–6722.

—— and Roychoudhury, A.K. (1993) "Evolutionary Relationships of Human Populations on a Global Scale," *Molecular Biology and Evolution* 10(5), 927–943.

Relethford, J.H. and Harpending, H.C. (1994) "Craniometric Variation, Genetic Theory, and Modern Human Origins," *American Journal of Physical Anthropology* 95 (3), 249–270.

Rogers, A.R. (1995) "Genetic Evidence for a Pleistocene Population Explosion," *Evolution* 49(4), 608–615.

—— and Harpending, H.C. (1992) "Population Growth Makes Waves in the Distribution of Pairwise Genetic Differences," *Molecular Biology and Evolution* 9, 552–569.

Schlauch, M. (1955) *The Gift of Language*, New York: Dover.

Shields, G.F., Hecker, K., and Voevoda, M.I. (1992) "Absence of the Asian-Specific Region V Mitochondrial Marker in Native Beringians," *American Journal of Human Genetics* 50, 758–765.

Shipman, P. (1995) "One Woman's Life in Science," *American Scientist* 83, 300–302.

Shoumatoff, A. (1985) *The Mountain of Names*, New York: Simon and Schuster.

Slatkin, M. and Hudson, R. (1991) "Pairwise Comparisons of Mitochondrial DNA Sequences in Stable and Exponentially Growing Populations," *Genetics* 129, 555–562.

Soffer, O. (1987) *The Pleistocene Old World, Regional Perspectives*, New York: Plenum Press.

Stein, P.L. and Rowe, B.M. (1993) *Physical Anthropology*, 5th edition, New York: McGraw Hill.

Stringer, C. and Andrews, P. (1988) "Genetics and the Fossil Evidence for the Origin of Modern Humans," *Science* 239, 1263–1268.

Stringer, C. and Brauer, G. (1994) "Methods, Misreading, and Bias," *American Anthropologist* 96, 416–424.

Swofford, D. (1991) *PAUP: Phylogenetic Analysis Using Parsimony*, Champaign: Illinois Natural History Survey.

Takahata, N. (1993) "Evolutionary Genetics of Human Paleo-Populations," in N. Takahata and A.G. Clark (eds) *Mechanisms of Molecular Evolution*, Sunderland: Sinauer Associates.

Templeton, A.R. (1993) "The Eve Hypothesis," *American Anthropologist* 95, 51–72.

Thorne, A.G. and Wolpoff, M.H. (1992) "The Multiregional Evolution of Humans," *Scientific American* 266(4), 76–83.

Torroni, A., Schurr, T., Yang, C.C., Szathmary, E., Williams, R., Schanfield M., Troup, G., Knowler, W., Lawrence, D., Weiss, K., and Wallace, D. (1992) "Native American Mitochondrial DNA Analysis Indicates that the Amerind and the Nadene Populations were Founded by Two Independent Migrations," *Genetics* 130(1), 153–162.

Trinkaus, E. and Shipman, P. (1992) *The Neandertals*, New York: Vintage, Random House.

Vigilant, L., Stoneking, M., Harpending, H., Hawkes, K., and Wilson, A.C. (1991) "African Populations and the Evolution of Human Mitochondrial DNA," *Science* 253, 1503–1507.

Wallace, D.C., Zheng, X., Lott, M.T., Shoffner, J.M., Hodge, J.A., Kelly, R.I., Epstein, C.M., and Hopkins, C.M. (1988) "Familial Mitochondrial Encephalomyopathy (MERRF): Genetic, Pathophysiological, and Biochemical Characterization of a Mitochondrial DNA Disease," *Cell* 55, 601–610.

Wilford, J.N. (1994) "Astronomy Crisis Deepens as the Hubble Telescope Sees no Missing Mass," *The New York Times*, November 29, B5–B8.

Wilson, A.C. and Cann, R.L. (1992) "The Recent African Genesis of Humans," *Scientific American* 266(4), 68–73.

Wolpoff, M.H. (1989) "Multiregional Evolution: The Fossil Alternative to Eden," in P. Mellars and C. Stringer (eds) *The Human Revolution: Behavioural and Biological Perspectives on the Origins of Modern Humans*, Princeton: Princeton University Press.

5

THE PALEOLITHIC GLASS CEILING

Women in human evolution

Adrienne Zihlman

INTRODUCTION

In November 1993, the cover of *Discover* magazine featured a striking diorama from the new permanent exhibit "Human Biology and Evolution" at the American Museum of Natural History in New York. Walking alone on the African savanna in the shadow of a vast volcano, a naked couple leave their tracks in the white volcanic ash. When I visited the exhibit, I stood for a long time pondering the evocative and unsettling scene. A deep and disturbing message about gender relations was being telegraphed, but what was it? Finally, I realized that the scene represented a modern – "scientific" – version of Adam and Eve's ejection from the Garden of Eden, with a spouting volcano instead of an angel's fiery sword, driving our ancestors into the unknown. In thinking about this message, I wondered, how far during the last three decades have we really come as a discipline in the ways we depict women (and men), and their roles during human evolution?

In pursuing this question, I begin in the 1950s and continue through the 1960s, 1970s and 1980s and discuss how women have been portrayed in reconstructions of human evolution in reference to two recurrent themes: (1) the sexual division of labor tied to subsistence and hunting and a rigid assignment of "women's roles;" (2) the reproductive–social unit affiliated with "monogamy" and parental care and its constraints on female sexuality and reproductive behavior. The role of women in evolution has undergone a number of permutations, but paradoxically, in spite of challenges to the contrary, the outcomes have resulted in little change. By the time we arrive at the 1990s, anthropologists reach a wide audience through textbooks, television specials and museum exhibits where women in evolution are rendered either invisible nonparticipants or as the handmaidens to men in prehistory. Whether or not there is a conscious effort to keep women in their place, these pervasive attitudes impose a "glass ceiling" on our female ancestors, much like the "glass ceiling" that limits the upward occupational mobility of contemporary women both within and outside of the academic disciplines.

THE 1950s: NEW VIEWS OF HUMAN EVOLUTION

Anthropology has long recognized that the human way of life in subsistence and social behavior has changed over time. Only after the arrival of the evolutionary synthesis in the 1940s and the increasing hominid fossil record did adaptation in human evolution become a systematic focus of inquiry (Bowler 1986). The new evolutionary synthesis integrated the mechanisms of evolution – natural selection and migration with mutation and chance – while rejecting completely all aspects of goal-directed change, or orthogenesis. The consolidation of the evolutionary synthesis within anthropology was marked by a symposium "Origin of Man" held at Cold Spring Harbor in 1950. A key participant, Sherwood Washburn, contributed a great deal toward integrating physical anthropology and the study of human evolution within this new framework (Washburn 1951a). Combining the study of living forms with the fossil record and utilizing new research methods, Washburn helped to shift the discussion of human evolution away from descriptive anatomy and toward an analysis of adaptation (Washburn 1951b).

Two papers published in the 1950s illustrate new approaches to human evolution and bear upon this larger discussion about women in evolution. First in addressing early hominid behavior, George Bartholomew, a young zoologist at UCLA, collaborated with Joseph Birdsell, a UCLA physical anthropologist who had participated in the Cold Spring Harbor symposium. Their innovative paper, "Ecology of the Protohominids" (1953), applied ecological concepts from vertebrate zoology to the study of human evolution in general and to the australopithecines in particular. Using comparisons with other mammals, they discussed the advantages of large body size, terrestrial locomotion and the freeing of hands for tool use. In addition, they discussed population spacing and territoriality, population equilibrium and reproductive potential.

Reasoning that the loss of estrus and sexual bonds based on continuing mutual attraction provided a biological foundation, Bartholomew and Birdsell speculated that the protohominids formed relatively stable family groups. In their view, the long-surviving family unit is a central element in human sociality, essential for providing parental care of dependent young, and the mother–offspring bond serves to shape social life. They also pointed out that males are more aggressive and tend to be dominant over females in most situations, especially where force is involved.

Following Raymond Dart's lead (1949), the authors proposed that the australopithecines depended on tools for aggressive interactions and for killing and butchering animals. Australopithecines were believed to hunt in groups much like canids and killer-whales. Similarly to Robert Broom (1950), Bartholomew and Birdsell suggested that sexual dimorphism arose as a product of sexual selection associated with competition between males for females; aggressive behavior associated with hunting and a sexual division of labor were secondarily derived functions of this dimorphism.

In a number of respects the Bartholomew and Birdsell article was forward looking; it pointed to the significance of ecology in studying human evolution and advocated the collection of new kinds of data, utilizing new techniques. On the other hand, the authors' focus on the topics of aggression and hunting, male competition and sexual selection, remains as the central agenda in most human evolutionary reconstructions today. Unfortunately, reconstructions of this type fail to recognize alternatives to aggressive behavior as shaping the course of human evolution.

The second paper from the 1950s of importance to this discussion, "The Evolution of Human Behavior" (Washburn and Avis 1958), combined a nonhuman primate framework with information from recent fossil hominid discoveries and new dating techniques. As a way to assess the direction of change during human evolution, the authors compared monkeys, apes and "man," in such features as reproduction and growth, social groups, special senses, and locomotion. The article is an interesting mix of innovative approaches, while remaining grounded in traditional assumptions about women's and men's roles. For example, Washburn and Avis discuss the human infant's long period of dependency, and note that "devices to help the mother carry the baby" must have evolved early; they also link the slow growth and long dependence of human infants to hunting, tool use, and food sharing by adult males. The authors question whether the australopithecines were hunters as proclaimed by Dart (Washburn and Avis 1958; Washburn 1957) but conclude that the early hominids did supplement their diet with more animal food than apes do. The distinction remains unclear here, as the article ends with this sentence: "Hunting as an important activity ... had three important effects on human behavior and human nature: psychological, social and territorial" (433).

Washburn and Avis, much like Bartholomew and Birdsell before them, perceive sexual receptivity as a determinant of social behavior; continuous female receptivity is viewed as essential to the monogamous family, and, according to the authors, a hallmark of being human. Both articles, among the first to use an evolutionary framework to explore specifics of human social life, do go beyond description to include process. In this regard, they foreshadow topics central to the view of women in evolution. For example, Bartholomew and Birdsell note that pre-stone age wooden implements were probably important but would not survive in the archaeological record, a point that Richard Lee (1968a) would later emphasize in his discussion of women's digging sticks. Emphasizing tool-using origins, Washburn and Avis note that because tropical hunters subsist mainly on vegetable food, "the first tools were probably used to extend the quantity and variety of this (vegetable food) rather than to obtain meat" (1958: 433). Both these points become important for considering women's roles in human evolution.

However, women are not mentioned directly in either ground-breaking article by Bartholomew and Birdsell or by Washburn and Avis. Women are referred to indirectly in two contexts: as mothers carrying their helpless infants and forming long-term ties with offspring, and as sexually receptive and mates for men. The themes that keep women in their place continue and persist in reconstructions of human evolution – that of the monogamous family based on female sexual receptivity, on the one hand, and male dominance and the primacy of male hunting on the other. One might argue that the evolutionary glass ceiling for women was being installed in the 1950s.

THE 1960S: CONSOLIDATION OF MAN THE HUNTER

By the mid-1960s, the study of human evolution was enjoying a windfall of new information due to the rich fossil discoveries of early hominids in Africa and field research on African apes, other nonhuman primates, and savanna mammals. But it was ethnographic information that both formalized the concept of "man the hunter" and provided a means to challenge it.

More than any other publication, the volume *Man the Hunter* (1968) consolidated the ideas initiated in the 1950s about hunting in human evolution. Not long after completing his doctoral field work in southern Africa on the subsistence of Kalahari hunter–gatherers, Richard Lee, together with Irven DeVore, both Washburn students, were approached by Sol Tax, a social anthropologist at the University of Chicago. Tax asked Lee and DeVore to organize a symposium of current research on foraging peoples of the world (Lee and DeVore 1968a). The conference, "Man the Hunter," held in April 1966 convened ethnographers, archaeologists and physical anthropologists. Topics ranged from ecology and economics to social organization and demography. The subsistence of living peoples was discussed along with early hominid dietary reconstruction based on archaeological investigation of the Paleolithic past. The conference focused on a vanishing way of life that reflected the human nomadic past prior to widespread settlement with permanent dwellings, accumulation of possessions, and management of food sources. Several conferees reported that meat in these nomadic societies is the most valued food – the most nutritious and most desirable food – possibly justifying emphasis on this food resource by the researchers.

Reading this volume again nearly thirty years later, I am struck by how rarely women are mentioned in it. The editors recognized women's activities, but women are barely integrated into the ethnographic or evolutionary record. Paradoxically, this volume gave voice to themes leading to the development of two opposing views of human evolution – one highlighting women's roles, the other elevating men and minimizing women. I illustrate this tension with three quotes from the introduction (Lee and DeVore 1968b).

First, a justification for the emphasis on hunting.

It was also generally agreed to use the term "hunters" as a convenient short-hand, despite the fact that the majority of peoples considered subsisted primarily on sources *other than meat* – mainly wild plants and fish.

(Lee and Devore's emphasis, p. 4)

Second, one of the few specific references to women appears in the context of food.

It is also likely that early woman would not have remained idle during the Pleistocene and that plant foods which are so important in the diet of inland hunter-gatherers today would have played a similar role in the diet of early peoples.

(p. 7)

Finally, a justification for the primary emphasis on male roles.

Hunting is so universal and so consistently a male activity that it must have been a basic part of the early cultural adaptation even if it provided only a modest proportion of the food supplies.

(p. 7)

In the volume, papers by Washburn and Lancaster (1968) and Laughlin (1968) focus on hunting and male activities. However, in the same volume, Lee (1968a) provides a contrasting view by recognizing women's roles in the context of human evolution.

Washburn and Lancaster build upon Washburn's previous ideas on the evolution of hunting (Washburn and Avis 1958; Washburn 1960). On the one hand – and this point is often missed – Washburn widened the framework of human evolution by integrating new information on hunting–gathering people with information from ecology, nonhuman primates and the fossil record. But he also reinforced the idea of monogamy, of male food-sharing with females, and a well-defined sexual division of labor. His emphasis on a home base and food-sharing, first discussed in 1958, is further developed here. In this scheme, the single most important factor that shaped human nature was meat procurement, gained by male efforts and shared with their mates. The closing sentence epitomizes the theme: "for those who would understand the origin and nature of human behavior there is no choice but to try to understand 'Man the Hunter'" (Washburn and Lancaster 1968: 303).

In contrast, Lee highlights women's work. His findings were singled out for mention when the volume was reviewed in *Science*: "hunting by males is usually of less significance to subsistence than the foraging after wild plants by females" and "life there is *not* nasty, brutish or short" (Service 1969: 1045). Although Lee only touched upon women's activities, that touch contributed substantially to formulating a place for women in evolution. He brought to the reader's attention an image of women as active, not sitting idly and passively around the Paleolithic hearth. His clear exposition of women's roles in subsistence set a tone, though it stood alone in this volume, when he wrote: "men's and women's work input is roughly equivalent" and "the women provide two to three times as much food by weight as the men" (Lee 1968a: 33). Later he discussed, without mentioning women specifically, the necessity for long-distance travel, and implied that women were mobile, active and involved in subsistence. Lee enumerated women's activities and contributions, rather than pigeon-holing them into monogamous relationships within narrowly defined categories of a sexual division of labor.

Despite Lee's innovative work within mainstream anthropology the catchy phrase "Man the Hunter" had become a rallying-point for the reconstruction of early human behavior. It came to stand for a way of life that placed males center-stage, gave an evolutionary basis for aggressive male behavior and justified gun use, political aggression, and a circumscribed relationship between women and men as a "natural" outcome of human evolutionary history. "Man the Hunter" purported to explain the selective force behind the development of "human" anatomical and behavioral features. It implied that monogamy and a sexual division of labor are ancient and defining human traits. Unfortunately, even though the details of hominid reconstructions have been modified in the subsequent decades, the principle of male centrality and female invisibility has been retained now, as it was then.

THE 1970s: WOMEN SCIENTISTS AND "WOMAN THE GATHERER"

The social climate of the 1970s encouraged questions about women's roles in evolution, about human nature, about whether there is a definable female or male nature, and about the validity of hunting as a defining human activity.

In particular, ethnographic studies on women and children helped remediate stereotypes of females as helpless mothers bonded to and dependent upon males. Patricia Draper's research (1975, 1976), for example, provided further details on the lives of !Kung women under foraging conditions and under new conditions of permanent settlements.

Draper illustrates that, in spite of its low level of technology, a foraging life is complex and women are knowledgeable and autonomous. Gathering, for instance, is not just a matter of picking up and collecting nuts or melons. !Kung women must know where to find food items and in what season they are edible; often women must walk 16 km or more a day, carry a full day's harvest and usually a child, and keep oriented in the bush (Draper 1976). The women pay close attention to tracks of dangerous animals, learn how to deal with each species, and when they return home in the evening, tell the men about potential hunting opportunities. From her firsthand experience, Draper could appreciate the years it takes to integrate the wide range of skills necessary to survive in a foraging and collecting way of life, and how such skills contribute to women's autonomy.

However, the everyday lives of women and children dramatically change with village and sedentary life (Draper 1975). Due to the changing ecological and political situation in southern Africa during the 1960s, some groups of the !Kung gave up a nomadic foraging way of life for one based on the raising of livestock and living in villages with permanent dwellings. What is particularly valuable about this "natural experiment" is that the people living in these two settings came from a population with the same cultural history, geographical location and genetic background. Women, once mobile and autonomous, now spend their time doing household chores, looking after the accumulation of material things, caring for the permanent dwellings and children.

Whereas previously children had no subsistence responsibilities until the teen years, in the sedentary villages young girls become socialized early to help with domestic tasks. Young boys go out to look after the goats and roam widely. Furthermore, the birth interval decreases from the traditional 5 to 3 years (Lee 1972; Howell 1979). Older female children, not caretakers when living as foragers, as villagers become caretakers of younger siblings. By age 5, girls and boys are well socialized into their gender roles and have separate lives. This is in strong contrast to the mixed age and sex play groups observed when the life style is foraging in the bush (Draper 1976). Thus, the relatively egalitarian nature of women's and men's roles and social relationships in a foraging way of life can be overturned in one newly socialized generation. Therefore custom, not nature, makes women sedentary and dependent.

Picking up on and emphasizing the active dimensions of women's lives as did Lee (1968a and b), Sally (Linton) Slocum offered a counter to the mainline hunting thesis: "Woman the Gatherer: Male Bias in Anthropology" (1975). This article, perhaps more than any other, served to catalyze the possibilities of alternatives. Slocum questioned male hunting activities as the primary mode of subsistence and countered with an emphasis on women's gathering activity. She challenged male centrality in social life with findings from primate social behavior studies that revealed female primates with offspring have pivotal roles in social life. In these studies, females, not males, transmit social rank to the offspring. Slocum's paper laid the groundwork for more detailed examination of women's roles in past and present societies.

In the context of this new challenge, Nancy Tanner and I wrote about human origins, utilizing a range of newly emerging information, with the purpose of providing a specific picture of early human social life that incorporated women and children (e.g. Zihlman and Tanner 1974; Tanner and Zihlman 1976; Zihlman and Tanner 1978; Zihlman 1978). We assessed female social life, anatomy, and ecology by incorporating information from living foraging people, fossil hominid record, and findings on wild populations of monkeys and apes. Previously, in order to clarify changes during human evolution, Washburn and DeVore (1961) compared and contrasted savanna baboons with pre-agricultural humans. In addition, in order to speculate about the origin of human scavenging and hunting, Schaller and Lowther (1969) studied lions and hyenas and experimented with scavenging themselves. We contended that chimpanzees served as a better model for a prehominid ancestor than did baboons or carnivores.

Three crucial lines of new data made a compelling case for looking to chimpanzees for potential similarities with prehominid ancestral populations: (1) molecular biology which demonstrates a close genetic relationship between humans, chimpanzees and gorillas; (2) the discovery of fossils which reveals anatomical similarities between chimpanzees and the earliest hominids, and (3) observed behavior from free-ranging chimpanzee studies.[1] Incorporating this range of new information, Tanner and I discussed hominid origins and women's roles utilizing chimpanzee behavior as a working ancestral baseline.

It was in this context of writing about hominid origins and women's roles that Tanner and I questioned hunting. This point is often overlooked, and I underscore it here. For example, Conkey and Williams (1991) have the misconception that our ideas were developed in the context of feminist theory. However, in the early 1970s there was no such theory. Rather, Tanner and I drew on the broad spectrum of data emerging from multiple areas of research that did not support the hunting hypothesis. Incorporating this information, we proposed reasons why women during human evolution must have been active participants in subsistence and several dimensions of social life, in addition to their centrality in reproduction. We contended that, in the earliest stages of human evolution, gathering plant foods entailed technological innovations for collecting, carrying and sharing food; that the large grinding teeth of fossil hominids suggested a diet of plant foods; that hunting emerged in human evolution relatively late, half a million years ago – as compared to human origins at over 3 million years – and emerged from the technological and social foundations established by the gathering of plant foods.

Our views of a sexual division of labor and monogamy departed considerably from those associated with the hunting paradigm. We argued against a rigid sexual division of labor in this earliest stage of human evolution. Alternatively, we argued for flexibility of roles and maintained that it was more likely that all individuals – regardless of sex – performed a wide range of tasks, a contention supported by additional research on foragers (e.g. Peacock 1991; Estioko-Griffin 1985). As noted by Lee and Draper, among foragers men as well as women gather plant foods, and women hunt (Estioko-Griffin and Griffin 1981). Within this flexible system, which is also observed among chimpanzees, activities are likely to vary by age and the reproductive stage of females rather than be somehow intrinsic to being female or male.

Regarding sexuality and reproduction, we questioned monogamy as a human hallmark and alternatively, utilizing newly emerging discussions about sexual selection, conjectured that females chose their mates, facilitated by subtle communication rather than overt morphological signals like sexual swellings. We went on to speculate that females chose friendly males who would share food – in contrast to provisioning or doling out food – a speculation that has some support in recent field studies of chimpanzees. We maintained that the widespread assumption of a pair bond in this early stage of human evolution was a projection back in time to a narrow Western view of marriage and mating, a formulation too rigid to account for the variation that exists cross-culturally.

A further challenge to the hunting hypothesis took the analysis to yet another level beyond the scientific data. In a little-known but innovative article, Perper and Schrire (1977) point out parallels between the interpretation of hunting as propelling humankind into humanity, on the one hand, and the biblical myth of expulsion from Eden, after Eve's eating of the tree of knowledge, on the other. The authors argue that both fates – that of hunting and of the expulsion – were precipitated by an act of eating – meat in the first instance and forbidden fruit in the second. As for the sexual division of labor, the authors note the parallel of male hunting with the biblical story of Eve, who was, as the story goes, created as a helpmeet for Adam. The authors go on to examine closely the archaeological evidence, pointing out that differential decay of materials over time leads to overrepresentation of large animal bones in the archaeological record and loss of organic material. The documentation of the ability of free-ranging baboons to catch and eat meat lies well within the behavioral repertoire of nonhuman primates and is not specific to humans.

As the 1970s drew to a close, questions arose about the evidence to support the early emergence of hunting, and the concept of gathering and hunting became widely recognized. Glynn Isaac (1978), for example, emphasized food-sharing and incorporated gathering with hunting – the idea of the mixed economy – in his model for human evolution. Initially, or so it seemed, reconstructions of human evolution promised to be broadly based, taking into account women's roles along with those of men. In 1978 Glynn Isaac and Richard Leakey organized a symposium "Men and Women in Prehistory." Several participants discussed aspects of gathering and women's activities along with hunting, scavenging and the fossil record. However, the promise of these initial improvements was short-lived. For example, although Owen Lovejoy and Donald Johanson were participants, their subsequent writings ignore altogether the ideas that Jane Lancaster, Glynn Isaac and I presented at the conference about women in evolution (e.g., Lovejoy 1981; Johanson and Edey 1981).

THE 1980s: TRENDS AND COUNTER-TRENDS

Tensions surrounding the role of women in evolution – detectable in the 1960s and becoming overt in the 1970s – turn into well-established and divergent research paradigms in the 1980s. With momentum gained during the 1970s, research and writing on female primates and women flourished in the 1980s and into the 1990s. The role of hunting in human evolution continued to be questioned by some archaeologists. At the same time, however, women's role in gathering was diminished by a new emphasis on scavenging, by attempts to resurrect hunting and by the co-option of gathering into the male behavioral repertoire. In addition, cultural critiques of theories of human evolution and women's roles in evolution appeared during the 1980s.[2]

Long-term studies on free-ranging populations of macaques, baboons and chimpanzees, as illustrated in Linda Fedigan's *Primate Paradigms, Sex Roles and Social Bonds* (1982), challenged the stereotype of female monkeys and apes and addressed major issues regarding female and male behavior. Fedigan questions the sex-stereotypes of male aggression, dominance and alliance, and female passivity. Primate females, as Fedigan observes, demonstrate the ability to take care of themselves and their offspring with little, or even no, help from primate males. Fedigan also notes the power of language in describing differences between the sexes. For example, research terminology encourages the perception of females as passive or inferior to males.

Addressing female energetics and reproduction, Jeanne Altmann (1980) documents the extensive physical investment and behavioral alterations of females in producing and caring for their offspring. Building upon Thelma Rowell's earlier work on the structure of baboon troops and concepts of social dominance (1966, 1974), Barbara Smuts (1985) and Shirley Strum (1987) offer alternatives to the stereotypes of the aggressive, dominating male baboons who control social life. Smuts's discussion of female–male friendships reflects a texturized picture of relationships between the sexes, and Strum emphasizes that it is males' social skills, rather than fighting ability, that secure their position in a new social group. Documenting life histories of female chimpanzees, Goodall (1986) confirms the breadth of female participation in daily social life and species survival.

Ethnographic research continued to provide new perspectives on women's lives. In a now classic work, *Nisa: the Life and Words of a !Kung Woman*, Marjorie Shostak (1981) dramatized women's lives through an "upclose and personal" portrait of a remarkable woman. Nisa emerges as competent, observant, witty and independent. She narrates a rich emotional and social life – growing up, getting married, having children – and surprise! taking lovers. Women in Nisa's society are free to divorce and choose new mates. These revelations alone would be sufficient to negate stereotypic or simplistic notions about monogamy and relationships between women and men in this society or in prehistoric ones.

New directions in ethnographic research not only documented the relationship between subsistence, nutrition and work, but also the relationship between work effort and conception, pregnancy and lactation (e.g., Peacock 1985; Bentley 1985; Panter-Brick 1989). Women, even those with children, hunt quite effectively in some cultures, further challenging what has been touted as a strictly male domain (Estioko-Griffin and Griffin 1981; Estioko-Griffin 1985). These studies, and several others, convey the multi-dimensional reality of women's lives and illustrate the necessity for featuring females in discussions of human evolution (e.g., Tanner 1981; Dahlberg 1981; Zihlman 1981).

During this time archaeological studies produced evidence that served to question the sufficiency of the evidence for an early appearance of hunting in hominid evolution. Through the study of bone accumulations in South African hominid cave sites alleged by Dart (1949) to be the remains of australopithecine hunting, Brain (1981) effectively refuted these claims by demonstrating the bones in question were the remains of carnivore meals. In these same early hominid fossil deposits Brain (1985) later uncovered bone implements with striations which he duplicated experimentally from digging in dry sandy soil. Such implements and their presumed use could support the hypothesis that early hominid subsistence included plant gathering, though this connection was not made directly.

Approaching hunting from another angle, Binford (1981) and Potts (1984) studied the association of animal bones and stone tools in East African hominid sites. They questioned whether these associations sufficiently demonstrated hominid hunting and home bases and alternatively concluded that carnivores, as well as hominids, were agents in accumulating the bones and that these areas were not likely to be hominid home bases. In a review of archaeological sites, Klein (1987) emphasized that, especially in open-air sites near water, human artifacts and animal bones found together may not be functionally related; he concluded that effective human hunting probably did not emerge prior to the later part of the Middle Pleistocene some 200,000 years ago.

Parallel to these studies questioning interpretations about human hunting and home bases, research on the scavenging and butchering of large animals renewed an emphasis on the importance of meat-eating during human evolution (e.g., Bunn 1981; Blumenschine 1986; Shipman 1986). Evidence for such theories emerged, for example, from observations of cut marks and percussion marks on fossil animal bones, characteristics that can be duplicated by stone tools and so presumably made by them. Scavenging as the means to obtain meat is now a major research paradigm for a number of archaeologists. It replaces hunting while dismissing gathering, as illustrated in the following quote:

The direct evidence of early hominid diet allows us to dismiss models of human evolution which do not incorporate meat-eating as a significant component of early hominid behavior.

(Bunn 1981: 577)

A variety of questions might be raised about these interpretations of scavenging and presumed significant meat-eating, for example: the possibility that trampling of bone by large animals may mimic cut marks by stone tools (Beyrensmeyer *et al.* 1986); the overinterpretation of the sample size which derives from a small number of hominid sites and of bones showing cut marks; the differential preservation of large animal bones, pointed out by Perper and Schrire (1977) and Lee (1968b), or the fact that the earliest evidence for cut marks and presumed butchering and scavenging are 2 million years later than is evidence for the earliest hominids themselves, which is the period in which gathering is proposed.

Even granting that the evidence for hominid butchering is unequivocal, and its interpretation that scavenging and meat-eating were of central importance in human evolution, the point here is that this renewed emphasis on butchering and scavenging not only refocuses on meat-eating in human evolution, but draws attention away from the possibility of women's participation in subsistence activities. Eliminating discussion of gendered activities is another, though subtle, way to promote male centrality and to render women invisible in evolutionary reconstructions.

A much-cited article, "The Origin of Man," published in *Science* by Lovejoy (1981) offers another twist to the portrayal of women's roles in evolution in the 1980s; namely, males, not females, gathered plant food. Presented as a new explanation for the origin of hominid bipedal locomotion, Lovejoy reverts to the earlier view of social evolution – sexual division of labor and a pair bond while rejecting the notion that males hunted. His theme develops in the following way. The success of the human species depended upon an increase in hominid population size; this was achieved by a decrease in the interval between births to two years. In order to do this females reduced their mobility, stayed near a home base, and became dependent upon males who provisioned their own mates and offspring. The pair bond, Lovejoy argues, ensured a male's paternity and the male does not invest in offspring not his own.

This view of women in evolution insists on male dominance and male provisioning of immobile, continually breeding, dependent females. Lovejoy's argument stands in contradiction to studies (1) demonstrating that female monkeys and apes and foraging women are mobile throughout all reproductive stages and (2) that the birth interval for foraging women, as for the great apes, lies between 3 and 5 or more years (e.g. Fedigan 1982; Altmann 1980; Draper 1975, 1976; Howell 1979; Shostak 1981). Lovejoy's argument not only ignores the evidence counter to his position but it also suspends the biological and ecological associations for early hominids and sets them up as a special case departing from other primates. This view of human evolution is a reincarnation of the themes from the 1960s of a rigid sexual division of labor and of a pair bond. (See Falk this volume and Zihlman 1995 for further discussion.)

My last example to illustrate the undermining of women in evolution during the 1980s comes from an article in which the authors claim to analyze objectively models of human evolution. Tooby and Devore (1987), adding to Hill (1982) attempt to make a case for the primacy of male hunting, pair bonds and sexual division of labor. In order to resurrect "man the hunter," Tooby and DeVore must first dispel the gathering hypothesis. In order to do so, the authors ignore almost all of the data supporting the hypothesis and dismiss any role for gathering on the grounds that it is merely a feminist counter to hunting (1987: 212). They contend that chimpanzees, rather than baboons, are used to model the prehuman ancestor in the gathering hypothesis because "male dominance is less popular as a research perspective than the putatively more peaceful chimpanzees" (1987: 187); and gathering is "defective because it concentrates only on women" (1987: 192). They do not acknowledge any of the genetic, paleontological, anatomical, behavioral and archaeological evidence supporting an alternative to the hunting hypothesis. Instead they maintain that the "hunting hypothesis has fallen from favor because of feminist revisionism" (1987: 222). Tooby and Devore do give a convincing argument against scavenging, and although praising Lovejoy (1981) for his conclusions about monogamy and male parental investment, a sexual division of labor, and male–male competition, they maintain that hunting behavior best explains these human hallmarks (1987: 226).

These articles and a number of others illustrate the divergent approaches to the place of women in evolution. During the 1980s, the trend to minimize food-gathering by women in evolutionary reconstructions grew. The emphasis on scavenging and invisible females, provisioning of gathered food by males and the resurrection of hunting all contributed to shifting reconstructions of early hominid life away from gathering, crowding out any role for women by presenting no alternatives. Ironically, during this same period information continued to come forth to document the many social and reproductive dimensions of female lives.

THE 1990S: THE GLASS CEILING

The increasing focus on women and female primates has begun to correct the neglect of women in evolution and has helped in the development of a more complete evolutionary record. Although women may now officially be part of human evolution, a mixed message prevails. I have presented a sample of some key articles from the academic/scientific literature to illustrate the significant trends in women's inclusion, or exclusion, in evolution. In this last section, drawing on examples from textbooks, a recent television special and a new museum exhibit, I examine how academic research is translated and presented to a wider audience which includes both the general public and students of evolution. These portrayals, whether consciously or not, undermine the improving status of women as equal players in evolution and at the same time demean the contributions of women as scientists.

Textbooks for introductory biological anthropology courses treat women's roles in a variety of ways, mostly by omitting them altogether. If gathering is mentioned at all, it tends to be dismissed as "a female-centered view" or a feminist reaction to the hunting hypothesis, and hunting, inadvertently or not, is therefore emphasized. Lovejoy is cited frequently as providing the most useful model for hominid evolution. For example, "In spite of its problems, Lovejoy's model remains useful in its effort to link bipedalism with increased fertility and/or survival" (Relethford 1994: 349). In Nelson and Jurmain, Lovejoy provides "a recent comprehensive reconstruction" (1991: 263). In the same 1991 volume, "gathering" is not indexed though "hunting" receives eleven entries. In an effort to update their text, Nelson and Jurmain (1994, sixth edition) discuss "Man, the Hunter; Woman, the Gatherer?" in a specific inset. The "man the hunter" theory is summarized in some detail and acknowledged as male-centered. Although pointing out that the hunting hypothesis does not hold up to analysis, the gathering hypothesis is confusingly presented along with Elaine Morgan's (1972) unscientific aquatic theory of human evolution. The authors leave the impression that all reconstructions of human evolution are culturally bound and therefore are all equally valid/invalid.

A public television series on human evolution aired in early 1994, and the simultaneous publication of its companion text (Johanson et al. 1994) offers a 1990s version of the 1960s view of human evolution. In the 1960s the idea that women were participants in human evolution did not exist at the conscious level. In contrast, in the 1990s the existence of women in evolution is less easily ignored, and therefore their contributions must be denied. I briefly illustrate this point with three examples from Ancestors (Johanson et al. 1994).

Johanson resurrects Owen Lovejoy's 1981 hypothesis about social life and presents it as "a social model for bipedalism's beginnings:"

> In Owen's model, both sexes choose a mate because each has something to offer: the female offers the male a guarantee that his genes pass into the next generation, and the male offers the female a reliable source of food and shared parenting duties. . . . The male could save perhaps half of his mate's time that would otherwise be spent searching for food and could now be devoted toward raising young.

(p. 79)

This translation of Lovejoy – males exchange food with females in return for guaranteed paternity – now has a 1990s spin: efficiency of time use, economics of trade, and the sociobiological emphasis on reproductive success. Consequently, early hominid females are the means for hominid males to achieve their economic and reproductive objectives!

Next, the possibility that early hominids hunted is dismissed. Not surprisingly, for Johanson, scavenging and butchering now hold the answers for explaining early hominid behavior. Rob Blumenschine is featured as "one of the new generation of archaeologists" who is exploring scavenging by studying African carnivore behavior (Johanson *et al.* 1994: 102). This exegesis overinterprets the evidence of cut marks on bones. Scavenging and butchering is presumed to be men's work, and the issue of food gathering is ignored, thereby side-stepping any role for women in evolution.

In a third example, Johanson reviews new research by C.K. Brain at Swartkrans on the possible use of bone tools in obtaining plant foods. (Previously I mentioned Brain's work on bone concentrations in the caves that led to overturning Dart's ideas that the hominids were killer-apes.) In the chapter on "The nutcracker people: *Australopithecus robustus*" Johanson *et al.* (1994) report on Brain's experimental study that duplicates abrasions on some fossil bone fragments. These bone fragments have worn and rounded tips and, when placed under a microscope, show abrasions. Carrying out experiments on other bone fragments, Brain duplicates these abrasions when digging up edible bulbs and tubers common in areas nearby. Brain presents this indirect evidence for hominids utilizing plant foods. However, Johanson dismisses the possible importance of plant foods early in human evolution. He concludes "that robusts may have been using digging sticks and *Homo* may have been using both digging sticks and stone tools" (1994: 166). Therefore, the genus *Homo*, the real human ancestor, is tied to the exploitation of meat and to using stone artifacts. Even if *A. robustus* did gather plant foods – though there is no allusion to this point or to gendered activities – this behavior was important to the species that was a dead end in human evolution!

These examples – scavenging, male provisioning and plant foods as tied to an evolutionary dead end in human evolution – serve as illustrations that discussion of gender, or women's activities, is best avoided, and with that avoidance the idea that women had an active participatory role in human evolution.

My last illustration from the 1990s returns to the new permanent exhibit "Human Biology and Evolution" at the American Museum of Natural History and the companion book *The Human Odyssey* (Tattersall 1993). The exhibit consists of holograms, films, interactive videos, murals and dioramas. Although textual labels do accompany each exhibit, it is the visual images – particularly in the diorama scenes of ancient human life – that carry the impact.

In the exhibit, impressive dioramas depict scenes from the "human fossil record" of *Australopithecus afarensis*, *Homo erectus*, Neandertal and *Homo sapiens*. A large mural displays the life of early hominids. Interestingly, in the text (Tattersall 1993: 91) the male walking in the foreground holds a set of antelope horns, but in the museum's mural, a plant replaces the horns. The old themes, with their typical emphasis on the male hunting and fighting within and between hominid groups, give way to an overall impression of a kinder, gentler hominid history.

This ambiance contrasts with earlier popular books on human evolution. For example, in 1965 the Time/Life *Early Man* by F.C. Howell combined text with visual representations of scenes such as those of australopithecines fighting with hyenas, and a battle between *Australopithecus* and *Homo* at Olduvai. Illustrated chapter titles in the 1965 book read as "The origins of meat-eating" and "A hunter's life." *Homo erectus* is heralded as "A true man at last" and *Homo sapiens*, "A new kind of man." The vegetarian *Paranthropus* individuals depicted by Jay Matternes (in Howell, F.C. 1965) as peaceful collectors of fruits and vegetables became an "evolutionary dead end," presumably becoming extinct because they did not hunt and eat meat – the stance that Johanson *et al.* (1994) adopt in *Ancestors*. In this and other older texts, although hominid women were accorded a condescending nod, there was little room for portraying their part in evolution.

In the new American Museum exhibit, the murals and dioramas carry mixed messages. For example, Jay Matternes's skills return in the mural entitled "Early Human Life Styles." In contrast to his 1965 images, the new exhibit painting emphasizes a peaceful and social atmosphere. It shows a group of adults collecting food on the savanna, youngsters playing, and a female with an infant. The legend below declares, "All higher primates are very sociable and most groups are cemented by the mother–offspring bond. . . . This bond would have stabilized early human groups and also formed the basis for larger kinship networks." But this vital point is lost in the other dioramas – that is, the point that human ancestors, like people today and other primates, live not as isolated adult pairs, but in social groups of all ages and both sexes. Instead, the dioramas give the distinct impression that the social group consists of a pair-bonded female and male – the nuclear family – despite the demurrer under the *Homo erectus* diorama that states, "Placing an adult male and female in this scene is not intended to suggest a nuclear family."

In contemplating these scenes I thought of Diane Gifford-Gonzalez's (1993) study of prehistoric dioramas. Gifford-Gonzalez, along with other scholars, has begun to systematically examine, document and analyze how women are depicted in visual representations in prehistory. An entire symposium at the annual meeting of the American Anthropological Association (1992), "Envisioning the Past: Visual Forms and the Structuring of Interpretations," explored the relationship between power and culture as affected by objects and language in the social constructions of these relationships. In analyzing prehistoric *Homo sapiens* depictions in books, Gifford-Gonzalez (1993) noted that in 88 scenes consisting of 444 individuals, adult males appear in 84 per cent of the scenes and comprise 50 per cent of the individuals. Males are more often portrayed in the foreground, standing, running, walking, hunting, carrying game or firewood, or engaging in ritual activities. Adult females appear in less than 50 per cent of the dioramas and are fewer than 25 per cent of the individuals; they are usually in the background, rarely standing or being physically active, and often are crouching on all fours scraping hides.

The American Museum exhibit provides examples that support Gifford-Gonzalez's findings. For example, the *Homo sapiens* diorama of mammoth-hunters living 15,000 years ago in Mezhirich, Ukraine, depicts three figures. The woman crouches on one knee in the foreground, as she leans to extract frozen meat from the permafrost refrigerator. In contrast, the man stands behind and towers over her, carrying a large horizontal bundle of firewood across his shoulders. The third figure, perhaps a youngster of indeterminate sex, emerges from the bone hut on all fours.

In another diorama, consisting of three Neandertal adults, only the man is standing while using a small tool to sharpen a long stick or spear. A younger woman is seated using her teeth to anchor a hide as she holds and scrapes it – a slightly modified version of what Gifford-Gonzalez (1993, 1995) calls the faceless "drudge-on-the-hide." The older woman is sitting and gesturing at the young woman. One reviewer of the exhibit from the *Washington Post* interpreted this as the mother-in-law giving advice (April 16, 1993). These two dioramas match Gifford-Gonzalez's survey of prehistoric images; the male figure stands tall and dominant while the females sit or kneel in a subservient manner.

The *Australopithecus afarensis* diorama depicts two lone and naked figures presumed to be our earliest ancestors from Laetoli, Tanzania, leaving their footprints in volcanic ash as they walk across the bleak African savanna. This scene troubled me for three quite different reasons. First, this particular representation is supposedly based on scientific evidence, when, in fact, the evidence is anything but conclusive. The male is constructed as considerably taller than the female, denoting that within this single species there is presumably considerable difference in size between the sexes. Within the scientific community, however, there is strong disagreement regarding whether or not the large and small fragmentary fossil specimens found in East Africa really represent female and male members of one species. The collection of fossil bones and teeth may include at least two different kinds of hominids, both of which might be female, or both of which might be male (Falk 1990; Hager 1991; Zihlman 1985).

However, this exhibit supports the "single species hypothesis" as demonstrated by the representation of a tall male, towering over the smaller female. The label below the display attempts to convey scientific accuracy, noting that "These figures are based on fossils attributed to *Australopithecus afarensis*, but although their body proportions are thus presumably accurate, many details of these reconstructions are entirely conjectural." No comment is made on the major assumption that the fossils represent one species. To further convince the viewer of their scientific accuracy, the label continues, "Among the attributes that can only be guessed at are hair density and distribution, skin color, form of the nose and lips and many other features" (Tattersall 1993: 76). The display as a whole misrepresents the scientific climate and therefore misleads non-anthropologists who view the exhibit.

There is a second troublesome issue. In the positioning of the two figures relative to each other, the taller male has his hand and arm firmly enfolding the female's shoulder, a strong nonverbal message. Touch can communicate affection and reassurance, but nonreciprocal touching also expresses power relationships, in which the toucher is perceived as dominant or with higher status than the recipient of the touch (Major 1981). The idea conveyed to the audience is that the more powerful male protects and reassures the frightened and presumed weaker female.

A third issue is the profoundly unsettling way in which the two figures are freeze-framed. Of all of the dioramas and murals in the new exhibit, this one alone gives no indication of the species' way of life; there is no evidence of food, tools, or group social life. The australopithecines are depicted as though they do not belong on the savanna at all, despite the fossil remains preserved at Laetoli along with the footprints indicating that the hominids lived here and were not just passing through. This diorama mirrors Adam and Eve's ejection from the Garden of Eden and illustrates visually how religious beliefs from the Old Testament about relations between Man, Woman and God (or Nature) – a scene depicted repeatedly by the greatest western artists for the past millennium – is now a part of the most up-to-date scientific presentation of human history and evolution.

Because we as a species rely so much on the visual sense, information conveyed visually and nonverbally carries considerable emotional force in interpersonal communication (Henley 1977). Age, sex, body posture, facial expressions, the relationship of figures to each other – all convey universal messages that people grasp instantly and intuitively, though often unconsciously (Mayo and Henley 1981). In conveying to the public an image of the traditional western relationship between the sexes, with men in the dominant positions, women in the submissive positions, the diorama holds a power more effective than words.

SUMMING UP

In conclusion, speculation about early human social life began taking shape in the 1950s. The "Man-the-Hunter" theory prevailed during the 1960s when women's roles in evolution were either off-stage altogether or merely on-stage in supporting roles to men. With the renewed awareness of the 1970s, the question arose, "where are the women?" Through the efforts of scientists, many of whom also happened to be women, females started to take their place on the evolutionary stage. But in spite of a more inclusive perspective – both in terms of women scientists' ideas and women's roles in prehistory presented during the 1970s – these ideas were degraded during the 1980s with the re-emergence of views that omitted women. Here we are now in the 1990s; women and men are in the midst of a backlash against the hard-won gains of women in so many spheres of contemporary life (Faludi 1991), and evolution is no exception. The "Second Sex" continues to be portrayed as the handmaidens of society's male players who, if we are to accept current theories, were out there innovating and making hominid evolution happen. What is particularly ironic is that this back eddy runs counter to the increasingly powerful current of research demonstrating the centrality of women and female primates in social life and the evolutionary process. But the concept of women in evolution remains encased in the glassed-in Old Testament diorama held down by a Paleolithic glass ceiling.

ACKNOWLEDGEMENTS

My thanks to Lori Hager for the invitation to participate in the volume and for our discussions over the years. The paper benefited a great deal from the comments of Melissa Remis, Sheila Hough, Robin McFarland, Jerry Lowenstein, and especially Kim Nichols. I also thank the University of California, Santa Cruz, Committee on Research and the Social Sciences Division Research Committee which has supported my research.

NOTES

1 Beginning in the 1960s with Kortlandt (1962) and Reynolds (1966), several field primatologists emphasized behavioral continuity between chimpanzees and humans and the insights that chimpanzee behavior provides into human evolution (e.g. Teleki 1974; Goodall and Hamburg 1975).
2 During the 1980s, the gathering–hunting debate served as an exemplar for analyzing discourse around gender that was taking place in the wider cultural context, and for raising questions about the place of women scientists, the masculine nature of scientific activity and scientific objectivity (e.g. Keller 1985; Harding 1986; Haraway 1989; Schiebinger 1989). Within anthropology the growing voice of women primatologists and anthropologists (e.g. Hrdy 1981; Small 1984; Fedigan and Fedigan 1989; Lancaster 1989) called attention to gender as an issue in interpreting the human prehistoric past (e.g. Conkey and Spector 1984; Fedigan 1986; Spector and Whelan 1989; Zihlman 1987).

BIBLIOGRAPHY

Altmann, J. (1980) *Baboon Mothers and Infants*, Chicago: University of Chicago Press.
Bartholomew, G.A. and Birdsell, J.B. (1953) "Ecology of the Protohominids," *Amer. Anthrop.* 55: 481–498.

Bentley, G.R. (1985) "Hunter–Gatherer Energetics and Fertility: a Reassessment of the !Kung San," *Human Ecology* 13(1): 79–101.

Beyrensmeyer, A.K., Gordon, K.D., and Yanagi, G.T. (1986) "Trampling as a Cause of Bone Surface Damage and Pseudo-Cutmarks," *Nature* 319: 768–771.

Binford, L.R. (1981) *Bones: Ancient Men and Modern Myths*, New York: Academic Press.

Blumenschine, R.J. (1986) "Carcass Consumption Sequences and the Archaeological Distinction of Scavenging and Hunting," *Journal of Human Evolution* 15: 639–659.

Bowler, P. (1986) *Theories of Human Evolution: A Century of Debate 1844–1944*, Oxford: Blackwell.

Brain, C.K. (1981) *The Hunters or The Hunted: An Introduction to African Cave Taphonomy*, Chicago: Chicago University Press.

—— (1985) "Cultural and Taphonomic Comparison of Hominids from Swartkans and Sterkfontein," in E. Delson (ed.) *Ancestors: the Hard Evidence*, New York: Alan R. Liss, pp. 72–75.

Broom, R. (1950) "The Genera and Species of the South African Fossil Ape-Man," *Amer. J. Phys. Anthrop.* ns 8: 1–13.

Bunn, H.T. (1981) "Archaeological Evidence for Meat-Eating by Plio-Pleistocene Hominids from Koobi Fora and Olduvai Gorge," *Nature* 291: 574–577

Conkey, M.W. and Spector, J.D. (1984) "Archaeology and the Study of Gender," in M. Schiffer (ed.) *Advances in Archaeological Method and Theory* 7: 1–38.

Conkey, M.W. and Williams, S.H. (1991) "Original Narratives: The Political Economy of Gender in Archaeology," in M. di Leonardo (ed.) *Gender at the Crossroads of Knowledge: Feminist Anthropology in the Postmodern Era*, Berkeley: University of California Press, pp. 102–139.

Dahlberg, F. (1981) *Woman the Gatherer*, New Haven: Yale University Press.

Dart, R. (1949) "The Predatory Implemental Technique of *Australopithecus*," *Amer. J. Phys. Anthrop.* n.s. 7: 1–38.

Draper, P. (1975) "!Kung Women: Contrasts in Sexual Egalitarianism in the Foraging and Sedentary Contexts," in R.R. Reiter (ed.) *Toward an Anthropology of Women*, New York: Monthly Review Press.

—— (1976) "Social and Economic Constraints on Child Life Among the !Kung," in R.B. Lee and I. DeVore (eds) *Kalahari Hunter–Gatherers: Studies of the !Kung San and Their Neighbors*, Cambridge, MA: Harvard University Press, pp. 199–217.

Estioko-Griffin, A. (1985) "Women Hunters: the Implications for Pleistocene Prehistory and Contemporary Ethnography," in M.J. Goodman (ed.) *Women in Asia and the Pacific*, Honolulu: University of Hawaii Press, pp. 61–81.

—— and Griffin, P. Bion (1981) "Woman the Hunter: The Agta," in F. Dahlberg (ed.) *Woman the Gatherer*, New Haven: Yale University Press, pp. 121–151.

Falk, D. (1990) "Brain Evolution in *Homo*: the 'Radiator' Theory," *Behavioral and Brain Sciences* 13: 333–381.

Faludi, S. (1991) *Backlash: The Undeclared War Against American Women*, New York: Crown Publishers.

Fedigan, L.M. (1982) *Primate Paradigms: Sex Roles and Social Bonds*, Eden Press, Montreal (reprinted 1992, Chicago: University of Chicago Press).

—— (1986) "The Changing Role of Women in Models of Hominid Evolution," *Annual Review of Anthropology* 15: 25–66.

—— and Fedigan, L. (1989) "Gender and the Study of Primates," in S. Morgan (ed.) *Gender and Anthropology: Critical Reviews for Teaching and Research*, Washington DC: American Anthropological Association, pp. 41–64.

Gifford-Gonzalez, D. (1993) "You Can Hide, But You Can't Run: Representations of Women's Work in Illustrations of Paleolithic Life," *Visual Anthropology Review* 9: 23–41.

—— (1995) "The Drudge-on-the-Hide," *Archaeology* 48(2): 84.

Goodall, J. (1986) *The Chimpanzees of Gombe*, Cambridge, MA: Harvard University Press.

—— and Hamburg, D. (1975) "Chimpanzee Behavior as a Model for the Behavior of Early Man. New Evidence on Possible Origins of Human Behavior," *American Handbook of Psychiatry*, New York: Basic Books.

Hager, L.D. (1991) "The Evidence for Sex Differences in the Hominid Fossil Record," in D. Walde and N. Willows (eds) *The Archaeology of Gender*, Calgary: Archaeological Association, University of Calgary, pp. 46–49.

Haraway, D. (1989) *Primate Visions: Gender, Race and Nature in the World of Modern Science*, London: Routledge.

Harding, S. (1986) *The Science Question in Feminism*, Ithaca: Cornell University Press.

Henley, N. (1977) *Body Politics: Power, Sex and Nonverbal Communication*, New York: Prentice-Hall.

Hill, K. (1982) "Hunting and Human Evolution," *Journal of Human Evolution* 11: 521–544.

Howell, F.C. (1965) *Early Man*, New York: Time/Life.

Howell, N. (1979) *Demography of the Dobe !Kung*, New York: Academic Press.

Hrdy, S.B. (1981) *The Woman That Never Evolved*, Cambridge, MA: Harvard University Press.

Isaac, G. Ll. (1978) "The Food-Sharing Behavior of Protohuman Hominids," *Scientific American* 238: 90–109.

Johanson, D.C. and Edey, M. (1981) *Lucy: The Beginnings of Humankind*, New York: Simon and Schuster.

Johanson, D.C., Johanson, L., and Edgar, B. (1994) *Ancestors: In Search of Human Origins*, New York: Villard Books.

Keller, E.F. (1985) *Reflections on Gender and Science*, New Haven: Yale University Press.

Klein, R.G. (1987) "Reconstructing How Early People Exploited Animals: Problems and Prospects," in M.H. Nitecki and D.V. Nitecki (eds) *The Evolution of Human Hunting*, New York: Plenum Press, pp. 11–45.

Kortlandt, A. (1962) "Chimpanzees in the Wild," *Scientific American* 206: 128–138.

Lancaster, J.B. (1989) "Women in Biosocial Perspective," in S. Morgan (ed.) *Gender and Anthropology: Critical Reviews for Teaching and Research*, Washington DC: American Anthropological Association, pp. 95–115.

Laughlin, W.S. (1968) "Hunting: an Integrating Biobehavior System and its Evolutionary Implications," in R.B. Lee and I. DeVore (eds) *Man the Hunter*, Chicago: Aldine, pp. 304–320.

Lee, R.B. (1968a) "What Hunters Do for a Living, or, How to Make Out on Scarce Resources," in R.B. Lee and I. DeVore (eds) *Man the Hunter*, Chicago: Aldine, pp. 30–48.

—— (1968b) "Comment," in S. Binford and L. Binford (eds) *New Perspectives in Archeology*, Chicago: Aldine, pp. 342–346.

—— (1972) "Population Growth and the Beginnings of Sedentary Life Among the !Kung Bushmen," in B. Spooner (ed.) *Population Growth: Anthropological Implications*, Cambridge, MA: MIT Press, pp. 329–342.

—— (1979) *The !Kung San: Men, Women, and Work in a Foraging Society*, Cambridge: Cambridge University Press.

—— and DeVore, I. (eds) (1968a) *Man the Hunter*, Chicago: Aldine.

—— and DeVore, I. (1968b) "Problems in the Study of Hunters and Gatherers," in R.B. Lee and I. DeVore (eds) *Man the Hunter*, Chicago: Aldine, pp. 3–12.

Lovejoy, C.O. (1981) "The Origin of Man," *Science* 211: 341–350.

Major, B. (1981) "Gender Patterns in Touching," in C. Mayo and N. Henley (eds) *Gender and Nonverbal Behavior*, New York: Springer-Verlag, pp. 15–37.

Mayo, C. and Henley, N. (1981) *Gender and Nonverbal Behavior*. New York: Springer-Verlag.

Morgan, E. (1972) *Descent of Woman*, New York: Stein and Day.

Nelson, H. and Jurmain, R. (1991) *Introduction to Physical Anthropology*, fifth Edition, St Paul: West Publishing Company.

—— (1994) *Introduction to Physical Anthropology*, sixth Edition, St Paul: West Publishing Company.

Panter-Brick, C. (1989) "Motherhood and Subsistence Work," *Human Ecology* 17(2): 205–228.

Peacock, N. (1985) "Time Allocation, Work and Fertility among Efe Pygmy Women of Northeast Zaire," unpublished PhD dissertation, Harvard University, Cambridge, MA.

—— (1991) "Rethinking the Sexual Division of Labor, Reproduction and Women's Work among the Efe," in M. di Leonardo (ed.) *Gender at the Crossroads of Knowledge: Feminist Anthropology in the Postmodern Era*, Berkeley: University of California Press, pp. 339–360.

Perper, T. and Schrire, C. (1977) "The Nimrod Connection: Myth and Science in the Hunting Model," in M.R. Kare and O. Maller (eds) *The Chemical Senses and Nutrition*, New York: Academic Press, pp. 447–459.

Potts, R. (1984) "Home Bases and Early Hominids," *American Scientist* 72: 338–347.

Relethford, J.H. (1994) *The Human Species: An Introduction to Biological Anthropology*, Mountain View, CA: Mayfield Press.

Reynolds, V. (1966) "Open Groups in Hominid Evolution," *Man* 1: 441–452.

Rowell, T.E. (1966) "Forest-Living Baboons in Uganda," *J. Zoology (London)*: 149: 344–364.

—— (1974) "The Concept of Dominance," *Behavioral Biology* 11: 131–154.

Schaller, G.B. and Lowther, G. (1969) "The Relevance of Carnivore Behavior to the Study of Early Hominids," *Southwestern Journal of Anthropology* 25(4): 307–341.

Schiebinger, L. (1989) *The Mind Has No Sex?: Women in the Origins of Modern Science*, Cambridge, MA: Harvard University Press.

Service, E. (1969) "Primitives and Very Primitives," *Science* 164: 1045.

Shipman, P. (1986) "Scavenging or Hunting in Early Hominids: Theoretical Framework and Tests," *Amer. Anthrop.* 88: 27–43.

Shostak, M. (1981) *Nisa: The Life and Words of a !Kung Woman*, Cambridge, MA: Harvard University Press.

Slocum, S. (1975) "Woman the Gatherer: Male Bias in Anthropology," in R.R. Reiter (ed.) *Toward an Anthropology of Women*, New York: Monthly Review Press, pp. 36–50.

Small, M.F. (1984) *Female Primates: Studies by Women Primatologists*, New York: Alan R. Liss.

Smuts, B.B. (1985) *Sex and Friendship in Baboons*, New York: Aldine.

Spector, J.D. and Whelan, M.K. (1989) "Incorporating Gender into Archaeology Courses," in S. Morgan (ed.) *Gender and Anthropology: Critical Reviews for Teaching and Research*, Washington DC: American Anthropological Association, pp. 65–94.

Strum, S. (1987) *Almost Human: A Journey into the World of Baboons*, New York: Random House.

Tanner, N.M. (1981) *On Becoming Human*, Cambridge: Cambridge University Press.

Tanner, N. and Zihlman, A. (1976) "Women in Evolution. Part I. Innovation and Selection in Human Origins," *Signs: Journal of Women in Culture and Society* 1(3, pt. 1): 585–608.

Tattersall, I. (1993) *The Human Odyssey: Four Million Years of Human Evolution*, New York: Prentice Hall.

Teleki, G. (1974) "Chimpanzee Subsistence Technology: Materials and Skills," *Journal of Human Evolution* 3: 575–594.

Tooby, J. and Devore, I. (1987) "The Reconstruction of Hominid Behavioral Evolution through Strategic Modeling," in W.G. Kinzey (ed.) *The Evolution of Human Behavior: Primate Models*, New York: State University of New York Press, pp. 183–237.

Washburn, S.L. (1951a) "The Analysis of Primate Evolution with Particular Reference to the Origin of Man," *Cold Spr. Harb. Symp. Quant. Biol.* 15: 67–77.

—— (1951b) "The New Physical Anthropology," *Trans. NY Acad. Sci.* 13(2): 298–304.

—— (1957) "The Hunters or the Hunted?" *Amer. Anthrop.* 59: 612–614.

—— (1960) "Tools and Human Evolution," *Scient. Amer.* 203(3): 62–75.

—— and Avis, V. (1958) "Evolution of Human Behavior," in A. Roe and G.G. Simpson (eds) *Behavior and Evolution*, New Haven: Yale University Press, pp. 421–436.

—— and DeVore, I. (1961) "Social Behavior of Baboons and Early Hominids," in S.L. Washburn (ed.) *Social Life of Early Man*, Chicago: Aldine, pp. 91–105.

—— and Lancaster, C.S. (1968) "The Evolution of Hunting," in R.B. Lee and I. DeVore (eds) *Man the Hunter*, Chicago: Aldine, pp. 293–303.

Zihlman, A.L. (1978) "Women in Evolution. Part II. Subsistence and Social Organization among Early Hominids," *Signs: Journal of Women in Culture and Society* 4(1): 4–20.

—— (1981) "Women as Shapers of the Human Adaptation," in F. Dahlberg (ed.) *Woman the Gatherer*, New Haven: Yale University Press, pp. 75–120.

—— (1985) "*Australopithecus afarensis*: Two Sexes or Two Species?," in P.V. Tobias (ed.), *Hominid Evolution: Past, Present and Future*, New York: Alan R. Liss, pp. 213–220.

—— (1987) "American Association of Physical Anthropologists Annual Luncheon Address, April 1985: Sex, Sexes and Sexism in Human Origins," *Yrbk of Phys. Anthrop.* 30: 11–19.

—— (1995) "Misreading Darwin on Reproduction: Reductionism in Evolutionary Theory," in F. Ginsberg and R. Rapp (eds) *Conceiving the New World Order*, Berkeley: University of California Press, pp. 425–443.

—— and Tanner, N. (1974) "Putting Women into Evolution," paper presented at the American Anthropological Association, Mexico City.

—— (1978) "Gathering and the Hominid Adaptation," in L. Tiger and H. Fowler (eds) *Female Hierarchies*, Chicago: Beresford Book Service, pp. 163–194.

6

BRAIN EVOLUTION IN FEMALES

An answer to Mr Lovejoy

Dean Falk

A little more than a decade ago, the field of paleoanthropology was visited with a new hypothesis about the role of women in human origins in an article in *Science* entitled "The Origin of Man" (Lovejoy 1981). The reasoning underlying this new hypothesis went something like this: since the origin of hominids may have coincided with that of bipedalism (but not with the beginnings of tool production or brain expansion which occurred later), if one can explain the origin of bipedalism then one will understand the "*sine qua non* of human origin" (*ibid*.: 341). Lovejoy theorized that bipedalism was selected for in males who travelled over increased daily ranges and gathered food to be hand-carried back to female–offspring groups who remained in core areas. Differential selection for bipedalism in males was presumed to be under strong positive selection that resulted in (a) lowered mobility for females and therefore a reduced accident rate in females and their offspring, (b) reduced exposure to predators, and (c) an intensification of parenting behavior. The net result was more and better hominids. According to this view, early hominid females were left not only four-footed, pregnant, hungry, and in fear of too much exercise in a central core area, they were also left "waiting for their man." In other words, western idealized monogamy and the nuclear family were the order of the prehistoric day. Why? According to Lovejoy, this enabled males to travel away from core areas without fretting about the possibility that the calories they retrieved might actually be nurturing someone else's offspring rather than their own. With faithful mates, males could rest assured of their paternity.

All of this scenario building was couched in demographic, comparative ethological, and sociobiological theory. However, one needn't get that technical to realize how weak this particular "just so" story really is. Think of it – a sexually dimorphic terrestrial primate (but one that curiously lacks dimorphism in canines) in whom the females are so fragile that mobility is a threat to mother/offspring survivorship. The females can't walk. They don't have big canines with which to defend themselves. They live in "novel and varied habitats, especially mosaics" (*ibid*.: 347). Although it is well known that severe predator pressure is associated with such habitats, it is never explained how an absence of males from core areas results in reduced exposure to predators in helpless females rather than increasing it. Thus, even at a superficial level, the Lovejoy scenario appears questionable.

The Lovejoy hypothesis may also be viewed at an entirely different level, i.e., as being preoccupied with questions/anxieties about male sexuality. At its most basic level, the hypothesis focuses on the evolution of how men got/get sex. The focal point is on males because it is already known how human females got/get sex. To wit, they "are continually sexually receptive" (Lovejoy 1981: 346) and, ever since those first days when male bipedalism ushered in humanity, females have waited faithfully for their men to return to exercise "copulatory vigilance" (ibid.). Male early hominids, on the other hand, were beset with sexual anxieties as is clear from the worries implied in Lovejoy's article: Will I ever have children? (Yes, if you provide proper nutrition for the mother.) Will my children be healthy? (Sure, if you don't compete with them for food.) Will they be safe? (Yes, as long as they and their mothers don't have to move around too much.) Will I have enough children? (Yes, if you exercise copulatory vigilance and get that interbirth spacing reduced.) How will I know I'm the father? (Because she's pair-bonded with you.) How can I be sure of her love? (Not to worry, she's hooked on your unique epigamic characters.) But I worry that she might like someone else? (She won't – she's monogamous.) Are you sure I won't have to compete with other males for the mother's affections? (No, polygyny is out. You get your own female, they get theirs.) Amazingly, this preoccupation with successful male sexuality was even expressed in a friendly affirmation of the sexual prowess of one of the author's friends. I refer, of course, to documentation of the assertion that "human females are continually sexually receptive" with footnote no. 79 that read "D.C. Johanson, personal communication" (Lovejoy 1981: 346).

But all of this is yesterday's news, right? After all, it's 1997 and nobody believes this stuff anymore. Wrong. Despite a number of reasonable hypotheses about the origins of bipedalism that have been suggested over the past decade and a half, Lovejoy's scenario is still widely invoked. Furthermore, concern with male sexuality continues to be confused with "scientific" endeavors. For example (and to continue a thread), D. C. Johanson of footnote no. 79 writes:

> In a joke that eluded the editors, Owen attributed the assertion in his *Science* article that "human females are continually sexually receptive" to "D. C. Johanson, personal communication," as though I was the *scientific source* for this bit of information; maybe that's why I was nicknamed "the Don Juan of paleoanthropology" by one of my colleagues in a recent book [emphasis mine].
>
> (Johanson, Johanson and Edgar 1994: 80)

The saddest thing about continued promotion of Lovejoy's hypothesis is that the research and substantiated ideas of a number of serious paleoanthropologists and physiologists with alternative hypotheses have not been given the full consideration they deserve. But perhaps I can now offer an alternative model that will be more to the liking of those who accept Lovejoy's basic assumptions?

THE ORIGIN OF HUMANS

Despite the above observations, a number of Lovejoy's basic assumptions derive from standard paleoanthropological and biological theory and these will be incorporated into my own model. For example, my hypothesis will include comparative data for mammals and will also "directly address the few primary differences separating humans from apes" (Lovejoy 1981: 341). My model, like Lovejoy's, will include inferences about causes of humanity that predate the appearance of tools and enlarged brains. Additionally, I will accept that sex differences are more than merely superficial (in fact, I will document it), and even that selection might have occurred differentially on one or both sexes. Because it was so important to the Lovejoy scenario, I have decided to incorporate discussion about how males acquired sexual partners during human evolution. Lovejoy states that "man's most unique character is without question his enormous intelligence" (1981: 347), and I fully agree (and also believe this is true for women). I concur with Lovejoy's statement that intense social behavior was important for the development of human intelligence. In fact, I agree so strongly with these last two points that I must disagree with another point. Although Lovejoy believes that human origins could be sufficiently elucidated by explaining the causes of bipedalism, I do not. After all, all early hominid species were bipedal, but not all of them evolved into humans. The present chapter will therefore focus on brain evolution because it is our brains (or our minds) that make us truly human. If one focuses on brains instead of feet, the evolutionary picture that emerges is quite different from that envisioned by Mr Lovejoy. Indeed, a good deal of evidence suggests that selection may have acted differentially on the brains (intelligence) of males and females. And if this is so, one can easily spin a scenario that favors the latter.

SEX DIFFERENCES IN THE BRAIN

The gross anatomy of the brain differs between men and women. Adult men have on average larger brains than adult women. Across the globe, female brains average 91 per cent (ranging between 88–94 per cent for different populations) of the mean male brain size (calculated from Table 1 of Pakkenberg and Voigt 1964: 298). The average brain size of many series of adult human males is 1,345 grams (*ibid.*), 91 per cent of that mean is 1,222 grams as an estimated average adult female brain size. However, several caveats should to be noted about brain size estimates. Brain weights vary with cause of death and frequently become heavier with postmortem absorption of fluids (*ibid.*). (For example, people of both sexes who hang themselves have relatively heavy brains.) Brain size also varies with age, peaking at approximately 20 years of age in males, in whom roughly 100 grams are lost between the ages of 25 and 70. Brain size may peak at a younger age in human females as is the case for female as compared to male rhesus monkeys (Masters, Falk and Gage 1991) although there are not yet enough data for humans to be conclusive on this point (Pakkenberg and Voigt 1964: 301). Finally, using regression analysis, Pakkenberg and Voigt have determined that "brain weight depends significantly on height, but not on body weight" (1964: 303). Holloway (1980) analyzed the same data set used by Pakkenberg and Voigt but showed that the relationship between brain size and height is significant only for males. On the other hand, Holloway finds the relationship between brain size and body weight to be significant for males but only reaches significance for females between 56 and 65 years of age:

> It is clear that for males, there are relationships between brain and body size that appear very much stronger than they do in female samples. It is tempting to try to offer a uniform explanation, such as more lean body mass in males, or concomitantly, more body fat in females which is not directly innervated.
>
> (Holloway 1980: 117)

In other words, because of extra body fat in females, brain size is not as tightly correlated with body size as is the case for males. Furthermore, since females have extra fat, presumably their ratios of brain size/body size are somewhat decreased compared to those of leaner males.

Despite the above, the bottom line that is usually presented is that men have bigger brains than women. This fact is frequently (sometimes gleefully) quoted. But what does the extra 123 grams in "average" male brains mean? Recently, a PhD student in the author's department (Froese 1997), analyzed and reconciled contradictory results of Ankney (1992), Ho *et al.* (1980), Holloway (1980), and Pakkenberg and Voigt (1964) regarding brain size in adult men and women. Froese found that, for any given body size (be it weight or height), relative brain size (brain weight divided by weight or stature) is indeed larger in males than in females. However, brains scale allometrically, i.e., they are relatively larger in smaller than in bigger people (as is the case with other animals), and the average woman is neither as heavy nor as tall as the average man. As it turns out, the average brain size/body weight ratio is slightly but significantly greater in women than in men (Ho *et al.* 1980; Holloway 1980). (Since females have "extra fat" compared to males, one can't help but wonder how much larger their brains would be relatively speaking if all that "body fat . . . which is not directly innervated" [Holloway 1980: 117] were left out of the equation.) Another way to control for body size is to calculate an index of encephalization (EQ) that expresses actual brain size divided by that expected for a given body size. Holloway found EQ to be slightly higher for 165 women (7.154) than for 165 men (7.145), but not significantly so.

Froese's (1997) results show that the relatively large brains of average females is due to scaling factors associated with smaller bodies, whereas the extra 110–150 grams in male brains may not be attributed to allometry because males have larger brains than females of the same body size. How, then, to explain the larger brains of males? As detailed below, it is likely that certain cognitive specialization evolved differentially (but not exclusively) in men and women, and that these parallel sex differences occur in some other animals. A classic example is visuospatial processing which is generally more developed in males than females of certain species, including *H. sapiens*. Although such abilities are not reflected in higher EQs for human males, they may require more neurological hardware.

How else do brains differ between adult men and women? The neuronal densities of brains of females are significantly higher than the densities of males' brains (Haug 1987). Put another way, although the female brain is about 100–150 cubic centimeters smaller than the male brain, females and males have the same total number of neurons. (When it comes to brain tissue, cubic centimeters of volume are essentially interchangeable with grams of weight.) Interestingly, the density of glial ("helper") cells does not appear to depend on brain size since a difference does not exist between male and female brains (*ibid.*). (Thus, male brains have more glial cells simply because they are larger.) Since the same number of neurons occupy a smaller space (braincase) in females than in males, one wonders what besides glial cells takes up the extra space in males. One possibility that must apparently be ruled out is relatively enlarged ventricles in males since the ventricles appear to be the same size in both sexes (Willerman *et al.* 1991).

In addition to the differences in brain size and density of neurons, there are also a number of sexual dimorphisms in the average sizes of certain anatomical structures of the brain. One dimorphic region of the human brain is an area of the hypothalamus which contains specific centers (nuclei) that are involved in sexual behavior. Two "interstitial" nuclei located in the front part of the hypothalamus that is the principal region for male-typical sexual behavior (i.e., the medial preoptic area) have been shown to be larger on average in men than in women (Allen *et al.* 1989). (The ventromedial nucleus that is important for female-typical sexual behavior is approximately the same size in both sexes.)

Other sexually dimorphic regions of the brain are not so obviously related to sexual behavior. For example, various reports have suggested that the large pathway connecting neurons that course between the right and left sides of the brain, known as the corpus callosum, is larger in women than in men. However, these findings have been controversial (see Witelson and Kigar 1987; Hines 1990 for reviews) and it now appears that the corpus callosum is about the same absolute size in the two sexes. If so, the corpus callosum is relatively larger in women because of their smaller brains (LeVay 1993: 102). Since women and men have approximately the same absolute number of neurons (see above), it makes sense that the pathway connecting similarly positioned neurons in the two hemispheres would also be approximately the same absolute size. The anterior commissure is another smaller, phylogenetically "older" connection between the two hemispheres that is absolutely larger in women than in men (Allen and Gorski 1986). Still another band of fibers that connects the thalami of the two sides (across the third ventricle), the massa intermedia, is present more often in females than in males (Rabl 1958). Interestingly, there is some evidence that males with a massa intermedia may have lower nonverbal IQs than males who lack this structure (Lansdell and Davie 1972).

Still another sexual dimorphism, but one that does not directly involve pathways connecting the two sides of the brain, has been reported for planimetric measurements of the superior surface of the temporal lobe (known as the planum temporale). In most human adults, the left planum is larger than the right (Geschwind and Levitsky 1968). However, of the minority in whom the temporal planes are "reversed" so that the right side is larger than the left, significantly more are women than men (Wada *et al.* 1975). This dimorphism in brain shape goes along with another one: in general, right-handed people tend to have right frontal lobes that project farther than the left frontal lobes (known as a "right frontal petalia") and left occipital lobes that extend farther than their right counterparts ("left occipital petalia") (LeMay 1976). This pattern causes the brain and overlying skull to appear somewhat lopsided. As it turns out, reversals of the typical petalia patterns are more common in women than in men (Bear *et al.* 1986).

The known significant anatomical differences between the "average" brains of adult men and women can easily be summarized: men have brains that are approximately 10 per cent larger than those of women, but women average significantly larger brains relative to body weight because of allometric scaling. Brains of women have a higher density of neurons. Two nuclei of the hypothalamus that are involved in male-typical sexual behavior are larger in men. Three structures that connect the right and left hemispheres of the brain are larger or more frequently present in females. Finally, the normal lopsided shape of the brain is more often reversed in females, as is the typical asymmetry in the relative sizes of the top surfaces of the temporal lobes. What all this boils down to is that, on average, the brains of men and women are "wired" differently. And that relates to cognition.

SEX DIFFERENCES IN COGNITION

As discussed above, converging evidence suggests that, on average, the brains of men and women are wired or "configured" differently. The anatomical differences that have been summarized are relatively dramatic and probably represent superficial correlations of more subtle neurochemical dimorphisms (see below). Since "the mind is just the brain doing its job" (LeVay 1993: 31), it is reasonable to ask whether sexually dimorphic brains manifest dimorphisms in what they "do," i.e., in cognitive abilities. Just as the above discussion of anatomical dimorphisms began with the general (brain size, density of neurons) and moved towards the specific (certain brain regions), the present discussion of cognition will also move from the general (performance on IQ tests) to the specific (dimorphisms in particular abilities).

Recent advances in medical imaging technology have allowed noninvasive determination of the size of the brain and/or its components. When analyzed in conjunction with the imaged volunteers' performances on IQ tests, this new technology provides a powerful tool for examining the relationship between brain size and intelligence (i.e., as defined by conventional tests). For example, in a recent magnetic resonance imaging (MRI) study of 20 high IQ (i.e., > 130 on the Wechsler Adult Intelligence Scale-Revised [WAIS-R]) and 20 relatively low IQ individuals (i.e., score < 103) in which each group was equally divided between men and women, results showed that the high IQ group had greater brain size (corrected for body size) for both sexes (Willerman *et al.* 1991). (Interestingly, average IQ men were significantly taller than high IQ men.) With sexes pooled, the IQ-adjusted brain-size correlation was r=0.51, a significant correlation that is somewhat higher than previous reports because of the use of extreme IQ groups (*ibid.*).

This general finding was confirmed in another MRI study of 37 adult males and 30 adult females (Andreasen *et al.* 1993) whose WAIS-R IQs were within the normal range (the mean full-scale IQ was 116 [SD=14]; the mean performance IQ was 114 [SD=13], and the mean verbal IQ was 114 [SD=15]). IQs did not differ significantly between the sexes. This latter study imaged specific parts of the brain as well as intracranial volume and examined the interaction of their sizes with the three types of IQ scores noted above. Once body size was corrected for, larger brains were again found to be correlated with higher IQs in both sexes. However, among the specific components that were measured, only those constituted of gray matter showed a significant positive correlation with intelligence. This was postulated to reflect a greater number of nerve cells and their dendritic branches.

Gender differences were shown in the pattern and number of correlations between sizes of brain regions and performances on different types of IQ tests (*ibid.*). Specifically, females had significant correlations between verbal IQ and intracranial, cerebellar, cerebral, temporal lobe and hippocampal volumes. (The Wechsler verbal scale traditionally includes tests of information, vocabulary, digit span, comprehension, similarities, and arithmetic.) Men, on the other hand, showed stronger correlations between sizes of brain regions and *performance IQ* and had generally fewer significant correlations overall (*ibid.*). (The Wechsler performance scale includes items such as block design, picture completion, picture arrangement, object assembly, and digit symbol tests.)

Men's and women's brains were shown to age differently in another MRI study of 69 healthy adults ranging in age from 18–80 years (Gur *et al.* 1991). In elderly men, the greatest amount of atrophy was in the left hemisphere whereas in women age effects were symmetric. The authors concluded that men are particularly susceptible to aging effects on left hemispheric functions (described below), whereas women are less vulnerable to age-related changes in mental abilities.

The above findings based on MRI research confirm numerous previous studies which demonstrate that, as populations, men and women test differently for certain abilities that are neurologically lateralized, i.e., subserved more by one hemisphere of the brain than the other (see below and Falk 1992a for review). Some workers have questioned the utility of studying such differences because there is usually massive overlap in the distributions of these traits for the two sexes. In such cases, numerous individuals of the weaker sex (sometimes males, sometimes females depending on the task) outperform many of the stronger sex. However, despite the fact that sex differences are frequently small, they are often statistically significant.

Figure 6.1 shows the traits that are lateralized in most human brains. This diagram represents generalizations that are based upon many thousands of clinical, experimental, and anatomical studies (it should be remembered, however, that there are many individual exceptions). The right hemisphere is associated with global, holistic pursuits. Its visuospatial and mental imaging skills are superb, and it is also associated with musical abilities. It has a noticeably greater role than the left hemisphere in expressing emotions in general as well as in reading them in other people. (The right hemisphere has a special role in processing negative emotions.) It also provides tone of voice and has an edge over the left hemisphere in recognizing faces, in the ability to understand metaphor, and in certain aspects of humor. The left hemisphere, on the other hand, is associated with language functions, skilled movements (e.g., of the right hand), and analytical, time-sequencing processes. This hemisphere is also involved in processing positive emotions.

Given that sexual dimorphism exists in three different pathways that connect the right and left sides of the brain (described above) and that the hemispheres of women may on average be more interconnected, it is not particularly surprising that men and women differ in their "average" performances for certain abilities that are lateralized to one hemisphere more than the other (see Bradshaw and Rogers 1993; Falk 1992a; McGlone 1980 for reviews). Men tend to outperform women on perception and manipulation of spatial relationships, such as mental rotation of figures, map-reading, rod-and-frame test, and remembering positions of numbers. They are also better at left–right discriminations, disembedding figures, and localizing points. Males outperform females in certain areas of mathematics, particularly on

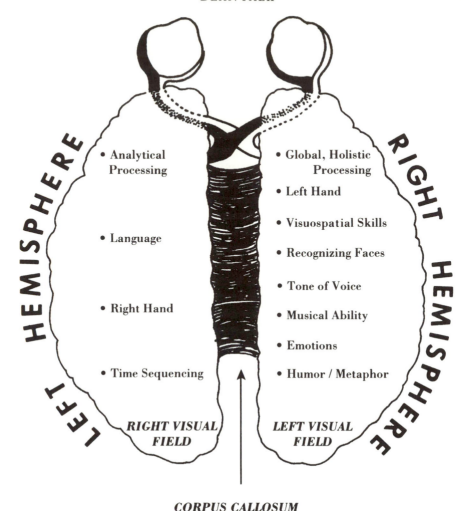

LEFT HEMISPHERE

RIGHT HEMISPHERE

- Analytical
  Processing

- Language

- Right Hand

- Time Sequencing

- Global, Holistic
  Processing

- Left Hand

- Visuospatial Skills

- Recognizing Faces

- Tone of Voice

- Musical Ability

- Emotions

- Humor / Metaphor

*RIGHT VISUAL
FIELD*

*LEFT VISUAL
FIELD*

CORPUS CALLOSUM

6.1 Right and left hemispheres of the brain.

calculus and geometry problems. There is also some indication that males excel at musical composition. Women, on the other hand, outperform males on tests of verbal abilities, including reading comprehension, anagrams, essay-writing, and measures of spoken language. Compared with males, females are also subtly biased for certain emotional skills such as understanding non-verbal body language.

The reader will recall that women more often have "reversals" of certain typical brain shape asymmetries than men (above). This added anatomical evidence that "connectedness" across the hemispheres is sexually dimorphic goes along with a survey which found that females seem to process certain kinds of information with both hemispheres, whereas males tend to rely more on one hemisphere or the other (McGlone 1980). For example, the incidence of aphasia (an inability to understand or use words) after left-hemisphere lesions is at least three times higher in men than in women. This suggests that females may process language more with both hemispheres. Despite this generalization, however, females appear to be more left-hemisphere biased for general motor expression than males, as shown by their greater rightward skill for fine motor tasks such as cursive writing and finger-tapping tasks.

The above findings are based on many hundreds of studies across a diverse spectrum of human activities that entail visuospatial, auditory, musical, motor, emotional, and linguistic skills. Despite the confusion, complexity, and related political issues that abound in the literature, this body of information converges on a clear bottom line: finely shaded but significant sex differences characterize human behaviors. As discussed above, MRI research has shown that the "performance" skills that males excel at are significantly correlated with the sizes of various brain structures (corrected for body size) in males, whereas verbal IQs of females are significantly correlated with corrected sizes of specific parts of their brains (Andreasen et al., 1993). Because of the converging evidence that brains of men and women are on average wired differently, one cannot attribute these dimorphisms exclusively to environmental factors. Although environmental factors are of course crucial for "programing" organisms, one should not discount the importance of the biological machinery itself. Like it or not, what the brain "does" is significantly dependent on how the brain "is." Of all the differences between men and women, the largest is the one in which males are favored for a variety of visuospatial skills (Linn and Petersen, 1985). I believe the fact that males (in an average or statistical sense) are particularly good at reading maps, tracing mazes, and mentally manipulating spatial arrangements, whereas females excel at language skills and decoding social interactions, partially represents the end product of a remarkable evolution in our species.

Numerous studies suggest that differential exposure to sex hormones during prenatal development is responsible for sex differences in cerebral lateralization (Geschwind and Galaburda 1987) and in cognition (Hines 1990). For example, male visuospatial abilities are probably the result of organization during perinatal development by gonadal steroids such as testosterone (Williams and Meck 1991; Bachevalier and Hagger 1991). Hines summarizes other evidence (see Falk 1992a for more) and notes that exposure to low levels of hormones during development is always associated with reduction in male-typical cognitive traits, whereas exposure to high levels of hormones increases these traits:

First, adolescent girls and young women exposed to excess testosterone and other androgens prenatally, because they have a genetic defect called congenital adrenal hyperplasia (CAH), have been reported to show enhanced performance on measures of visuospatial abilities. Second, men exposed to lower than normal levels of androgen from early life, because they have idiopathic hypogonadotrophic hypogonadism, have been found to show reduced visuospatial abilities. Third, women exposed to higher than normal levels of estrogen prenatally, because their mothers were prescribed the synthetic estrogen, diethylstilbestrol (DES), during pregnancy, have been found to show increased language lateralization. Finally, girls and women exposed to lower than normal levels of hormones, because of prenatal ovarian regression associated with the genetic disorder of Turner syndrome, have reduced visuospatial abilities and reduced language lateralization.

This pattern of results may provide convergent evidence for hormonal influences on the development of sex differences in cognition.

(Hines 1990: 54–55)

Even as adults, certain sexually dimorphic lateralized cognitive skills of men and women are influenced by cyclical (menstrual for women, seasonal for men) alterations in levels of hormones (Hampson and Kimura 1988; Chiarello *et al.* 1989). Men apparently perform better at visuospatial tasks in the spring, when presumably their testosterone levels are optimal for such tasks (Gouchie and Kimura 1991), than in the autumn. Women, on the other hand, perform better at some visuospatial tasks such as line orientation judgements during the follicular phases of their menstrual cycles when estrogen levels are rising (Chiarello *et al.* 1989, but see Hampson and Kimura 1988). Apparently, there is a hormonal basis in adults for gender differences in at least some visuospatial skills. As noted above, of all the sexually dimorphic cognitive differences that have been reported, the largest differences exist in visuospatial skills such as mental rotation of geometrical figures (Linn and Petersen 1985). It is also noteworthy that these differences can be detected across the lifespan (*ibid.*).

THE EVOLUTION OF BRAIN LATERALIZATION

Because of the way genes from parents mix and match in their offspring, traits that are selected for in one sex are automatically selected for in the other sex ("sex-linked" traits located on the twenty-third pair of chromosomes are an exception). This would account in large part for the huge overlap in the distributions of sexually dimorphic abilities in men and women. Nevertheless, as outlined above, men "on average" excel at visuospatial tasks whereas women tend to outperform men on verbal tests and decoding social cues. In general, these skills depend upon a highly evolved lateralized primate brain. One way to investigate the evolutionary history behind human visuospatial and verbal (or other) skills is to examine them (and their relationship to sex if known) in other animals and to compare their anatomical substrates across species. A large number of investigations utilizing this "comparative method" on rodents, birds, nonprimate mammals, and primates show that brain lateralization has had a long evolutionary history (Bradshaw and Rogers 1993), and that humans are extremely lateralized compared to other animals, including nonhuman primates (Falk 1992a).

As detailed elsewhere (Falk 1992a), studies of rodents suggest that brain lateralization for visuospatial activities may have originally started in conjunction with preferential circling in one direction or the other. Male and female rats have a slight but significant tendency to circle in opposite directions. Such sex differences in locomotor asymmetries are the rule for a variety of rodent species rather than the exception (Robinson *et al.* 1985). Furthermore, the direction of preferred circling correlates with an asymmetrically high concentration of dopamine deep within the opposite side of the brain in rats (Zimmerberg *et al.* 1974). Although most people are unaware of it, they also have a tendency to circle. People are sexually dimorphic in their preferred directions of circling and there is some evidence that the underlying asymmetry in the dopaminergic systems of humans is even more pronounced than is the case for rats (Bracha *et al.* 1987).

But why circle in one direction if you are a rat or, for that matter, a person? Simply put, if one wanders away, one wanders back to the safety of the nest, if one is a rodent, or full circle back to the starting point, if one is a human who is lost in the woods. At least for the rodent, finding the way back to the nest would be an adaptive trait favored by natural selection. That is, such rodents would live longer and leave more offspring than their conspecifics who lack a "sense of direction." Also, rats who don't have to waste time deciding which way to turn might have an edge over getting away from attackers (Stanley Glick, personal communication).

Voles provide a clue about the possible selective value of enhanced visuospatial skills in males. These small burrowing rodents come in two kinds. Prairie voles from the Midwest United States are monogamous, whereas meadow voles from Pennsylvania are polygynous. Studies based on trapped voles fitted with radio transmitters and then released have shown that male meadow voles travelled far afield during the breeding season in order to mate with as many females as possible (Gaulin and FitzGerald 1988; 1989). However, female meadow voles and monogamous prairie voles of both sexes did not expand their ranging patterns during the mating season. When the voles were subsequently retrapped and tested for visuospatial ability in mazes, only polygynous meadow voles showed consistent male superiority on spatial tasks. This suggests that visuospatial skills evolved in male meadow voles in conjunction with their far-ranging search for mates. That is, voles with good internal compasses travelled further, encountered more mates, and left more offspring. Put simply, research on voles suggests that selection for enhanced visuospatial skills in males of various polygynous species may be related to an earlier evolution (selection) for increased mating opportunities.

Nonhuman primates appear to be lateralized for visuospatial skills. As with humans, the right hemisphere of monkeys has an advantage when discriminating between photographs of faces (Hamilton and Vermeire 1985) and there may be a sexual dimorphism in certain aspects of this ability (Hamilton and Vermeire 1983, 1985). Monkeys also appear to be lateralized for discriminating line orientations (Hamilton and Vermeire 1985) as well as other visuospatial patterns (Jason *et al.* 1984) but, curiously, in a direction that is *opposite* to that of humans (i.e., these tasks are left-hemisphere dominant in monkeys). This is particularly interesting in light of a recent demonstration of mental rotation for visual imagery in baboons, which is the first indication that such capabilities exist in a nonhuman species (Vauclair *et al.* 1993). Again, as was the case for certain visuospatial tasks in monkeys, mental rotation in baboons is lateralized to the left hemisphere rather than the right hemisphere. Monkeys and humans differ in this respect.

As outlined above, the comparative mammalian evidence indicates a very deep time-scale for asymmetries related to visuospatial skills (see Bradshaw and Rogers 1993 for review). Furthermore, there is some evidence which suggests that enhanced visuospatial skills may initially have been selected for in polygynous males in conjunction with finding mates. But what about the evolutionary underpinnings of the verbal abilities that are left- rather than right-hemisphere dominant and relatively enhanced in women? Is there any comparative evidence that social vocalization of one sort or another has had a long evolutionary history or that related skills may have been favored in females? As it turns out, a number of studies show that, like humans, macaque monkeys are left-hemisphere dominant for processing socially meaningful (as opposed to socially neutral) vocalizations (Petersen *et al.* 1978, 1984; Heffner and Heffner 1984, 1986).

Ehret (1987), in a study on the house mouse, suggests that lateralization for processing social vocalizations to left hemispheres may have evolved early in mammals. This study also offers an important clue about the possible selective advantage of this trait in females since the ultrasonic calls emitted by young mice were recognized only by the left hemisphere and evoked maternal caring behavior in mothers. On the other hand, no advantage was detected for either hemisphere in virgin females who were trained to respond to the same ultrasonic calls by conditioning (*ibid.*). Since a calling pup who is displaced from the litter is retrieved to the nest by its mother, lateralization for processing socially meaningful vocalizations in females may have functioned throughout evolution to increase differential survivorship.

To summarize, humans have highly lateralized brains that are the end product of millions of years of evolution. Statistically speaking, each sex excels in certain lateralized skills and there is some evidence that these skills may have contributed to the fitness of our ancestors. That is, enhanced visuospatial skills may have increased breeding opportunities in males, whereas processing social vocalizations may have increased the survivorship of females' offspring. Although evidence is limited, these are reasonable hypotheses in light of the known comparative data.

Of all animals tested, human males (and some females) are relatively adept circlers. Not only do they circle their bodies in preferred directions as they go about their daily business (Bracha *et al.* 1987), but their lateralized brains are proficient at rotating perceived objects in their imaginations (mental rotation tasks)! Furthermore, the fact that baboons and people are lateralized in different hemispheres for mental rotation suggests that brain lateralization continued to evolve with respect to visuospatial tasks during anthropoid (and possibly hominid) evolution. It is also clear that lateralization for processing social vocalizations continued to evolve during hominid evolution since only humans have language as we know it.

A fairly large literature (reviewed above) indicates that "on average" the brains of men and women are connected differently across the hemispheres and that the sexes manifest different patterns of functional lateralization. It is possible that the ongoing development of visuospatial and vocal/communication skills during the evolution of *Australopithecus/Homo* was dramatic and involved reorganization of brain lateralization itself (e.g., with left-hemisphere language functions "displacing" certain visual tasks to the right hemisphere). But what could have driven such evolution?

EARLY HOMINID EVOLUTION

Somewhere around 5.0 million years ago (myr) in Africa, the first hominids diverged from the ancestors of chimpanzees. No one knows for sure why this happened, but it may have been related to the opening of new niches in mosaic habitats. Although the earliest hominids probably continued to sleep in trees, it is likely that they were terrestrial during much of the day. It is generally believed that at the time of divergence hominids had already begun the long evolutionary process of refining bipedalism. (Hopefully, additional discoveries of the oldest known australopithecines [White, Suwa and Asfaw 1994] will eventually shed light on this matter.) Scientists agree that by 2.5 myr at least two kinds of australopithecines (gracile and robust) had evolved. However, they do not agree about *when* australopithecines first speciated into more than one contemporaneous species. Until recently, proponents of "Lucy" (*A. afarensis*) as the mother of us all believed that only one species of hominid lived before 3.0 myr. Although the recent discovery of 4.4-myr-old *A. ramidus* dispels this notion, there is presently no consensus about whether more than one evolving *lineage* of australopithecine is represented before 3.0 myr. I continue to believe that more than one species of australopithecine coexisted long before "Lucy" and that she was not the mother of us all (Falk 1990; Falk *et al.* 1995). At any rate, most paleoanthropologists concur that gracile rather than robust australopithecines gave rise to the genus *Homo*. Some also think that the two types of australopithecines lived in distinctly different niches and that the ancestors of *Homo* spent a good deal of time moving about the sunny open grasslands.

So much for generalizations. A key part of Lovejoy's scenario rests on the assumption that early hominids formed monogamous pair bonds. This assumption weakens, however, in face of comparative primate evidence. Not one species of terrestrial nonhuman primate is monogamous, nor are any of the three great apes. The terrestrialism and sexual dimorphism manifested in fossils of early hominids are usually correlated with polygyny in living primates. Furthermore, 80 per cent of contemporary human societies are not monogamous. (See Hrdy 1981 for review.) Recent research on female sexuality and "female choice" in a number of terrestrial primates suggests that "females embarking upon the human enterprise were possessed of an aggressive readiness to engage in both reproductive and nonreproductive liaisons with multiple, but selected, males" (*ibid*. 176). Indeed, much of the world appears to fear that this might still be the case, as indicated by the universal close observation and control of sexual conduct in women in human communities (*ibid*. 186), not to mention all those male insecurities simmering beneath the surface of Lovejoy's hypothesis. Given these observations, the most reasonable assumption to make about early hominid mating patterns is that they were polygynous.

If early hominids were not monogamous, bipedalism could not have been differentially selected for in males in order to provision their helpless "other halves" as hypothesized by Lovejoy. This raises the question of why bipedalism *did* occur in hominids. Although many interesting ideas have been offered to account for bipedalism (reviewed in Falk 1992a), one of the most synthetic is a physiological theory put forward by Pete Wheeler (1988). According to this theory, protohominids of both sexes had to travel through open country to find patches of food scattered within the mosaic environment. In so doing, they encountered intense solar radiation. Like pygmy chimpanzees, these protohominids were probably capable of a certain amount of bipedalism, i.e. they were preadapted for the eventual development of habitual bipedalism. The earliest hominids were therefore able to minimize the amount of body surface that was directly exposed to damaging solar radiation by walking bipedally so that only the shoulders and top of the head took a direct beating from the rays of the sun when it was overhead. With this shift to bipedalism, a naked skin and associated sweat glands evolved to facilitate increased evaporation. According to Wheeler, these features led to "whole-body cooling" that regulated temperature of blood circulating to (among other regions) the brain, helped prevent heatstroke, and thereby released a physiological constraint on brain size in *Homo*.

Since Wheeler formulated this provocative theory, my own research on the evolution of cranial blood flow has resulted in the "radiator" theory of brain evolution, which supports and complements Wheeler's ideas (Falk 1990; 1992a and b). Although a detailed discussion of this theory is beyond the scope of the present chapter, it should be noted here that fossil and comparative evidence shows that a special network of veins that selectively cool the brain under conditions of hyperthermia evolved in our direct early hominid ancestors. This "radiator" evolved as a correlate of two factors, bipedalism and living in a hot savanna environment, and it released a thermal constraint that previously kept brain size from increasing. Thus, both Wheeler and I view the increase in brain size in *Homo* as a consequence of bipedalism occurring in an environment that selected for certain vascular mechanisms that could regulate brain temperature. These physiological theories are mechanistic. That is, they suggest that the human brain was only able to enlarge after a thermal constraint had been released, but do not identify the behaviors/abilities that were subsequently selected for. That topic is, of course, at the heart of what makes us human.

Whatever its cause, brain size "took off" somewhere around 2.0 million years ago in the genus *Homo*, so much so that by 100,000 years ago (i.e., by the time of Neandertals) brain size had doubled from approximately 700cm^3 to over 1,400cm^3 (Falk 1992b). Since the time of Darwin, there have been many speculations about a possible single cause ("prime mover") of the dramatic increase in brain size (reviewed in Falk 1980). Prime-mover candidates that have been suggested over the years include warfare, work, language, tool production, throwing, hunting, and social intelligence. As one might surmise from this list, more credit for brain evolution has traditionally been given to activities that are typically (but not exclusively) pursued by males (*ibid*. Falk 1992a and b). Although Lovejoy (1981) focused on bipedalism rather than brain evolution as the *sine qua non* of human evolution, he carried on this biased tradition with his hypothesis by stating that bipedalism was selected for exclusively in males.

However, it wasn't bipedalism that made us human (bipedal robust australopithecines never got there), it was our brains. But what does it mean to have a human brain? Put another way, what can a human brain do that a chimpanzee brain cannot? Looking above at the list of potential prime movers, a number of activities that were previously ascribed exclusively to humans are now known to occur in both chimpanzees and humans. Both make war, make tools (e.g., fishing poles), and hunt (Goodall 1986). Like humans, chimpanzees can concentrate on and carry out a task (work). For example, in addition to solving problems under experimental conditions (summarized *ibid*.), chimpanzees can learn how to knap stone tools from human teachers (Toth *et al.* 1993). They can also throw (*ibid*.). That leaves just two candidates, language and social intelligence.

Chimpanzees, like most anthropoid primates, are intensely social. For this reason, I have been reluctant to entertain social (or "Machiavellian") intelligence as a realistic prime mover of human brain evolution (Falk 1992b). Dunbar (1993), on the other hand, argues that the enlarged human neocortex evolved primarily to keep track of multiple social relationships in increasingly enlarged social groups. My colleague Bruce Dudek and I recently analyzed the same sets of data on brain and group size that Dunbar studied and confirmed that larger primates tend to have larger brains and neocortices, and more often live in larger groups (Falk and Dudek 1993). However, which is cause, which is effect, and which relationships are spurious are not questions that can be unambiguously answered from this data set (*ibid*.). Interestingly, Dunbar notes that:

> in human conversations about 60 percent of time is spent gossiping about relationships and personal experiences. Language may accordingly have evolved to allow individuals to learn about the behavioral characteristics of other group members more rapidly than was feasible by direct observation alone.
>
> (Dunbar 1993: 681)

Dudek and I agree with Dunbar's assessment that language is a social phenomenon, and that humans use language to "groom" each other. However, language is used to impart and absorb all kinds of information in addition to that which is social. Thus social intelligence *per se* probably was not the prime mover of human brain evolution. Language was. This is true because, despite the considerable abilities of signing, computer-using, plastic symbol-manipulating, tool-knapping apes, no amount of training has ever resulted in a chimpanzee who could read, write or talk anything like a human does (Falk 1992a). Unlike the brains of other primates, human brains *do* language.

THE EVOLUTION OF WOMEN: AN ANSWER TO LOVEJOY

The comparative neuroanatomical evidence summarized in this chapter allows one to speculate about the brains of the very first hominids. Certainly they were lateralized (Falk 1987). As is the case for at least some rodents and primates, processing of meaningful vocal communications was probably dependent upon left hemispheres. Like Old World rhesus monkeys and baboons, certain visuospatial skills such as the ability to discriminate line orientations or other spatial relationships were probably also left-hemisphere dominant, while others, like recognition of faces, were right-hemisphere dominant. During the course of hominid evolution, two things probably happened with respect to brain lateralization: the left hemisphere expanded its role in processing vocal communications to include language functions (speech, understanding of spoken language, and eventually reading and writing). The right hemisphere, on the other hand, incorporated certain visuospatial tasks that were previously the domain of the left hemisphere (e.g., mental rotation, discriminating the orientation of lines and other shapes). In other words, during hominid evolution, skills at which females excel today (statistically speaking) displaced those at which males excel from the left to the right hemisphere.

If selection acted differentially on the behaviors of male and female hominids, as Lovejoy asserts, then the neuroanatomical and cognitive sexual dimorphisms that exist today in humans, along with the comparative mammalian evidence, suggest that processing of vocal communications was selected for differentially in females at the same time that visuospatial skills were continuing to evolve in males. And why shouldn't the prime mover of human brain evolution be the result of differential selection on females? If a mother mouse recognizes the distress calls of her young with her left hemisphere and is prompted to return that young to the nest, it is not surprising that Old World monkey mothers also recognize distress calls of their young or that they (and the males of their species) process socially meaningful vocalizations of conspecifics with their left hemispheres. The fundamental social unit for even relatively solitary higher primates like orangutans is the mother/offspring pair. It is primarily the *female*'s reading of and responding to social and environmental cues that escort the genes of her offspring into the future. Therefore it is reasonable to speculate that female hominids evolved better abilities than males for reading social cues and communicating with conspecifics, be they one offspring or a whole troop.

In sexually dimorphic primates like baboons, large male body size is viewed as the anatomical reflection of aggression for male–male competition over mates and for defense of the social group (Lancaster 1984). Smaller female body size, on the other hand, is believed to reflect the energy demands for pregnancy and lactation (*ibid.*). In other words, males are built for breeding/defending and females for mothering. Robust australopithecines were clearly sexually dimorphic, and it is generally assumed that gracile australopithecines were too. (Indeed, there is so much variation is so-called *A. afarensis* that it could easily represent more than one dimorphic species.) If our gracile australopithecine ancestors were sexually dimorphic as is true for terrestrial primates today, then it is not surprising that the underlying nervous system of humans is sexually dimorphic in ways that reflect cognitive correlates related to breeding/mothering (i.e., testosterone-mediated visuospatial skills/verbal abilities). As discussed elsewhere (Falk 1980; 1992b), of the various candidates that have been put forward as possible prime movers of brain evolution, language seems to be the most reasonable. If so, then a hypothesis that entails differential selection on females may not be as outlandish as some might suppose, especially if one views language as an outgrowth of selection for "social intelligence" (Dunbar 1993). This is not to say that the slight but significant edge that women have over men in verbal tasks indicates that most men are without wonderful language skills (or that a majority of women lack impressive visuospatial abilities). As already noted, there is huge overlap in the distributions of verbal performance on a variety of tests for the two sexes. However, one cannot discount the possibility that men evolved their loquaciousness "clinging to the apron strings of the women," as suggested by some versions of the "Woman the Gatherer" model (Fedigan 1986: 35).

One thing is for sure. I do not see early hominid males as bipedally bringing home the veggies to helpless, quadrupedally locomoting females and their (his) young. Contrary to Lovejoy (1981), the relatively large bodies of males suggest they were polygynous, competed for mates, and aggressively defended their social groups. It may even be that early hominid males patrolled their borders like modern-day chimpanzees from Gombe (Goodall 1986), i.e. that they sought aggressive encounters with strangers. From this point of view, it is interesting that testosterone is viewed as a major organizer of the developing human brain in males (Geschwind and Galaburda 1987) and that it is correlated with both visuospatial skills and aggression in adults.

At least in my culture, more men than women seem to have an inordinate fascination with warfare and with sports that involve propelling missiles (often balls) at targets (points, holes or spaces). In autumn, when testosterone levels are increasing in men (Dabbs 1990), the visuospatial love of putting balls in specified places merges with aggression during the football season in the US. The lack of sexual dimorphism in early hominid canine size may even indicate that females sexually selected less aggressive males with smaller teeth (Zihlman 1978), and that males were already on their way to sublimating their aggression through male-bonded sports activities. In other words, while she was out gathering food for dinner (kids in tow and no doubt muttering to herself) (Zihlman 1985), he and his buddies were out on the savanna inventing golf.

To summarize, my hypothesis is based on an extensive number of scientific studies that span psychology, zoology, the neurosciences, and recent advances in medical imaging: although brains of males are somewhat larger than those of females of the same body size, the average brain size/body weight ratio of males is significantly smaller because of scaling factors associated with larger bodies (Froese 1997). Brains of males are also characterized by a lower density of neurons. Three structures that connect the right and left hemispheres are, on average, larger or more frequently present in females. As discussed above, a variety of research converges on the conclusion that men's and women's brains are "wired" differently and suggests that these differences form at least part of the substrate for superior average performance on verbal tasks (and assessing social cues) in women versus enhanced scores on visuospatial tests in men. Furthermore, magnetic resonance imaging studies show that, for each sex, the typical cognitive strengths (at least as demonstrated with standardized tests) are significantly correlated with the size of related brain structures. Along other lines, comparative studies on a variety of mammals suggest that the cognitive specialties of men and women are likely to have evolved for reasons to do with classical "reproductive fitness" – i.e. superior visuospatial skills may have first developed in polygynous male ancestors of hominids for finding mates (and the way home) whereas enhanced abilities to interpret vocalizations may have been selected in female ancestors in conjunction with mothering.

The reader may rightfully question whether or not my hypothesis of selective brain evolution is as biased in favor of females as Lovejoy's scenario regarding the origins of bipedalism is towards males. I have written this chapter in order to emphasize that sexual dimorphism in the human brain can no longer be ignored by evolutionary biologists. Indeed, medical imaging technology in combination with cognitive psychological investigations is in the process of revolutionizing our understanding of how brains look and think, and I predict that an increasing amount of evidence will further document the fact that brains of men and women differ, on average, in their wiring. In any event, if one assumes that it is the brain rather than bipedalism that made us human, then my scenario is already supported by a good deal of evidence and is at least plausible.

But I want to add a final caveat. The problem with my interpretation, as with Lovejoy's, is with the assertion that certain skills that may (or may not) have been differentially selected for in one sex were somehow more valuable for the evolution of our species than other advanced abilities (Lovejoy's "*sine qua non* of human origin"). Indeed, it is this line of reasoning that has led some workers (including myself) to choose language as the most likely prime mover of human brain evolution. However, to suggest that certain skills may have been the focus of brain evolution is one thing; to suggest that they alone account for what makes us human is another. Granted, reading and writing are unique human accomplishments. But so are building airplane engines, composing symphonies, and playing football. The reality that men and women, on average, engage in these activities at different levels and frequencies at least partially reflects the fact that lateralized brains of men and women are wired somewhat differently (Falk 1987). In the final analysis, if one believes that our species has benefited from a wide array of enhanced cognitive abilities, then it is best to abandon the assertion that one sex or the other is more "intelligent" or that one sex should take more credit for the unique evolutionary history that made us "human." Agreed, Mr Lovejoy?

BIBLIOGRAPHY

Allen, L. S. and Gorski, R. A. (1986) "Sexual Dimorphism of the Human Anterior Commissure," *Anat. Rec.* 214: 3A.

Allen, L. S., Hines, M., Shryne, J. E. and Gorski, R. A. (1989) "Two Sexually Dimorphic Cell Groups in the Human Brain," *J. Neurosci.* 9: 497–506.

Andreasen, N. C., Flaum, M., Swayze, V., O'Leary, D. S., Alliger, R., Cohen, G.,

Ehrhardt, J. and Yuh, W. T. C. (1993) "Intelligence and Brain Structure in Normal Individuals," *Amer. J. Psychiatry* 150: 130–34.

Ankney, C. D. (1992) "Sex Differences in Relative Brain Size: The Mismeasure of Women Too?" *Intelligence* 16: 329–336.

Bachevalier, J. and Hagger, C. (1991) "Sex Differences in the Development of Learning Abilities in Primates," *Psychoneuroendocrinology* 16: 177–88.

Bear, D., Schiff, D., Saver, J., Greenberg, M. and Freeman, R. (1986) "Quantitative Analysis of Cerebral Asymmetries," *Arch. Neurol.* 43: 598–603.

Bracha, H. S., Seitz, D. J., Otemaa, J. and Glick, S. D. (1987) "Rotational Movement (Circling) in Normal Humans: Sex Difference and Relationship to Hand, Foot and Eye Preference," *Brain Res.* 411: 231–35.

Bradshaw, J. L. and Rogers, L. J. (1993) *The Evolution of Lateral Asymmetries, Language, Tool Use, and Intellect*, San Diego: Academic Press.

Chiarello, C., McMahon, M. A. and Schaefer, K. (1989) "Visual Cerebral Lateralization Over Phases of the Menstrual Cycle: A Preliminary Investigation," *Brain and Cognition* 11: 18–36.

Dabbs, J. M., Jr. (1990) "Age and Seasonal Variation in Serum Testosterone Concentration Among Men," *Chronobiology Int.* 7: 245–49.

Dunbar, R. I. M. (1993) "Co-evolution of Neocortical Size, Group Size and Language in Humans," *Behav. Brain Sci.* 16: 681–735.

Ehret, G. (1987) "Left Hemisphere Advantage in the Mouse Brain for Recognizing Ultrasonic Communication Calls," *Nature* 325: 249–51.

Falk, D. (1980) "Hominid Brain Evolution: The Approach from Paleoneurology," *Yrbk. Phys. Anthropol.* 23: 93–107.

—— (1987) "Brain Lateralization in Primates and its Evolution in Hominids," *Yrbk. Phys. Anthropol.* 30: 107–125.

—— (1990) "Brain Evolution in *Homo*: The 'Radiator' Theory," *Behav. Brain Sci.* 13: 333–81.

—— (1992a) *Braindance*, New York: Henry Holt.

—— (1992b) "Evolution of the Brain and Cognition in Hominids," the 62nd James Arthur Lecture, New York: The American Museum of Natural History.

—— and Dudek, B. (1993) "Mosaic Evolution of the Neocortex," *Behav. Brain Sci.* 16: 701–2.

——, Gage, T. B., Dudek, B. and Olsen, T. R. (1995) "Did More Than One Species of Hominid Coexist Before 3.0 Ma?: Evidence From Blood and Teeth," *J. Hum. Evol.* 29: 591–600.

Fedigan, L. M. (1986) "The Changing Role of Women in Models of Human Evolution," *Ann. Rev. Anthrop.* 15: 25–66.

Froese, N. (1997) "Relative Brain Size in Men and Women: Who Has More Upstairs and Does It Matter?" under review.

Gaulin, S. J. C. and FitzGerald, R. W. (1988) "Home-range Size as a Predictor of Mating Systems in *Microtus*," *J. Mammal.* 69: 311–19.

—— (1989) "Sexual Selection for Spatial-learning Ability," *Animal Behav.* 37: 322–31.

Geschwind, N. and Galaburda, A. M. (1987) *Cerebral Lateralization: Biological Mechanisms, Associations, and Pathology*, Cambridge: MIT Press.

Geschwind, N. and Levitsky, W. (1968) "Left/right Asymmetries in Temporal Speech Region," *Science* 161: 186–87.

Goodall, J. (1986) *The Chimpanzees of Gombe*, Cambridge: Belknap Press.

Gouchie, C. and Kimura, D. (1991) "The Relationship Between Testosterone Levels and Cognitive Ability Patterns," *Psychoneuroendocrinology* 16: 323–34.

Gur, R. C., Mozley, P. D., Resnick, S. M., Gottlieb, G. L., Kohn, M., Zimmerman,

R., Herman, G., Atlas, S., Grossman, R., Berretta, D., Erwin, R. and Gur, R. E. (1991) "Gender Differences in Age Effect on Brain Atrophy Measured by Magnetic Resonance Imaging," *Proc. Natl. Acad. Sci.* 88: 2845–9.

Hamilton, C. R. and Vermeire, B. A. (1983) "Discrimination of Monkey Faces by Split-brain Monkeys," *Behav. Brain Res.* 9: 263–75.

—— (1985) "Complementary Hemispheric Superiorities in Monkeys," *Soc. Neurosci. Abs.* 11: 869.

Hampson, E. and Kimura, D. (1988) "Reciprocal Effects of Hormonal Fluctuations on Human Motor and Perceptual-spatial Skills," *Behav. Neurosci.* 102: 456–59.

Haug, H. (1987) "Brain Sizes, Surfaces, and Neuronal Sizes of the Cortex Cerebri: A Stereological Investigation of Man and His Variability and a Comparison with Some Mammals (Primates, Whales, Marsupials, Insectivores, and One Elephant)," *Amer. J. Anat.* 180: 126–42.

Heffner, H. E. and Heffner, R. S. (1984) "Temporal Lobe Lesions and Perception of Species-specific Vocalizations by Macaques," *Science* 226: 75–6.

—— (1986) "Effect of Unilateral and Bilateral Auditory Cortex Lesions on the Discrimination of Vocalizations by Japanese Macaques," *J. Neurophysiol.* 56: 683–701.

Hines, M. (1990) "Gonadal Hormones and Human Cognitive Development," in J. Balthazart (ed.) *Hormones, Brain and Behaviour in Vertebrates. 1. Sexual Differentiation, Neuroanatomical Aspects, Neurotransmitters and Neuropeptides*, Basle: Karger. *Comp. Physiol.* 8: 51–63.

Ho, K., Roessmann, U., Straumfjord, J. V., and Monroe, G. (1980) "Analysis of Brain Weight: Adult Brain Weight in Relation to Body Height, Weight, and Surface Area," *Arch. Pathol. Lab. Med.* 104: 640–5.

Holloway, R. L. (1980) "Within-species Brain–body Weight Variability: A Re-examination of the Danish Data and Other Primate Species," *Amer. J. Phys. Anthropol.* 53: 109–21.

Hrdy, S.B. (1981) *The Woman That Never Evolved*, Cambridge, MT: Harvard University Press.

Jason, G. W., Cowey, A. and Weiskrantz, L. (1984) "Hemispheric Asymmetry for a Visuo-spatial Task in Monkeys," *Neuropsychologia* 22: 777–84.

Johanson, D., Johanson, L., and Edgar, B. (1994) *Ancestors: In Search of Human Origins*, New York: Villard Books.

Lancaster, J. B. (1984) "Introduction," in M. F. Small (ed.) *Female Primates: Studies by Women Primatologists*, New York: Alan Liss.

Lansdell, H. and Davie, J. C. (1972) "Massa Intermedia: Possible Relation to Intelligence," *Neuropsychologia* 10: 207–10.

LeMay, M. (1976) "Morphological Cerebral Asymmetries of Modern Man, Fossil Man, and Nonhuman Primates," *Ann. N. Y. Acad. Sci.* 280: 349–60.

LeVay, S. (1993) *The Sexual Brain*, Cambridge: MIT Press.

Linn, M. C. and Petersen, A. C. (1985) "Emergence and Characterization of Sex Differences in Spatial Ability: A Meta-analysis," *Child Development* 56: 1479–98.

Lovejoy, C.O. (1981) "The Origin of Man," *Science* 211: 341–50.

McGlone, J. (1980) "Sex Differences in Human Brain Asymmetry: A Critical Survey," *Behav. and Brain Sci.* 3: 215–63.

Masters, A. V., Falk, D. and Gage, T. B. (1991) "Effects of Age and Gender on the Location and Orientation of the Foramen Magnum in Rhesus Macaques (*Macaca mulatta*)," *Amer. J. Phys. Anthropol.* 86: 75–80.

Pakkenberg, H. and Voigt, J. (1964) "Brain Weights of the Dane," *Acta Anat.* 56: 297–307.

Petersen, M., Beecher, M., Zoloth, S., Moody, D., and Stebbins, W. (1978) "Neural

Lateralization of Species-specific Vocalizations by Japanese Macaques (*Macaca fuscata*)," *Science* 202: 324–27.

Petersen, M. R., Beecher, M. D., Zoloth, S. R., Green, S., Marler, P. R., Moody, D. B. and Stebbins, W. C. (1984) "Neural Lateralization of Vocalizations by Japanese Macaques: Communicative Significance is More Important Than Acoustic Structure," *Behav. Neurosci.* 98: 779–90.

Rabl, R. (1958) "Strukturstudien an der Massa Intermedia des Thalamus Opticus," *J. Hirnforsch.* 4: 78–112.

Robinson, T. E., Becker, J. B., Camp, D. M. and Mansour, A. (1985) "Variation in the Pattern of Behavioral and Brain Asymmetries due to Sex Differences," in. S. Glick (ed.) *Cerebral Lateralization in Nonhuman Species*, New York: Academic Press.

Toth, N., Schick, K. D., Savage-Rumbaugh, S. S., Sevcik, R. A. and Rumbaugh, D. M. (1993) "Pan the Tool-maker: Investigations into the Stone Tool-making and Tool-using Capabilities of a Bonobo (*Pan paniscus*)," *J. Archaeol. Sci.* 20: 81–91.

Vauclair, J., Fagot, J. and Hopkins, W. D. (1993) "Rotation of Mental Images in Baboons when the Visual Input is Directed to the Left Cerebral Hemisphere," *Psych. Sci.* 4: 99–103.

Wada, J. A., Clarek, R. and Hamm, A. (1975) "Cerebral Hemispheric Asymmetry in Humans," *Arch. Neurol.* 32: 239–46.

Wheeler, P. E. (1988) "Stand Tall and Stay Cool," *New Scientist*, 12 May: 62–5.

White, T. D., Suwa, G. and Asfaw, B. (1994) "*Australopithecus ramidus*, a New Species of Early Hominid from Aramis, Ethiopia," *Nature* 371: 306–312.

Willerman, L., Schultz, R., Rutledge, J. N. and Bigler, E. D. (1991) "*In vivo* Brain Size and Intelligence," *Intelligence* 15: 223–28.

Williams, C. L. and Meck, W. H. (1991) "The Organizational Effects of Gonadal Steroids on Sexually Dimorphic Spatial Ability," *Psychoneuroendocrinology* 16: 155–76.

Witelson, S. F. and Kigar, D. L. (1987) "Neuroanatomical Aspects of Hemisphere Specialization in Humans," in. D. Ottoson (ed.) *Duality and Unity of the Brain, Proceedings of an International Symposium at the Wenner-Gren Center*, Stockholm, May 29–31, 1986, New York: Macmillan, pp. 466–95.

Zihlman, A.L. (1978) "Women in Evolution, Part II: Subsistence and Social Organization among Early Hominids," *Signs* 4(1): 4–20.

—— (1985) "Gathering Stories for Hunting Human Nature," *Fem. Studies* 11: 364–77.

Zimmerberg, B., Glick, S. D. and Jerussi, T. P. (1974) "Neurochemical Correlate of a Spatial Preference in Rats," *Science* 185: 623–25.

7

A POUND OF BIOLOGY AND A PINCH OF CULTURE OR A PINCH OF BIOLOGY AND A POUND OF CULTURE?

The necessity of integrating biology and culture in reproductive studies

Susan Sperling and Yewoubdar Beyene

Nowhere is the polarization within anthropology between biological and cultural schools more distinct than in the study of human reproduction. Recipes for major reproductive events vary, not only in relative proportions ("to a pound of biology add a pinch of culture"), but in the ingredients themselves ("leave out biology altogether.") Reductionist approaches in evolutionary biology ignore the power of culture to shape the body and its functions, while cultural theorists too often deny the relevance and variety of bodily phenomena. But the ovary and its functions are shaped by evolution, culture, and the ecologies in which individuals develop, offering insights into the exquisite intertwining of biology and cultural practice.

Since the mid-1970s a particular postulation of biological ultimate causality, sociobiology, has dominated many studies of human evolution; these have been widely disseminated in scholarly and popular discourses (Hamilton 1964; Hrdy 1981; Kitcher 1985; Sperling 1991; Trivers 1972; Wilson 1975). Sociobiologists view behavior and biology through the lens of kin selection, asking questions about how observed structures and behaviors increase the fitness of individuals and their close relatives, maximizing their chances of contributing genes to future generations. The roots of sociobiology lie in nineteenth- and early-twentieth-century arguments about whether natural selection operates at the group or individual level. Evolutionists like Darwin, Haldane, and Wynne-Edwards believed that traits may be selected for because they are advantageous for populations (Darwin 1859; Haldane 1932; Wynne-Edwards 1962), while sociobiologists contend that selection occurs only at the level of the individual. They have made two key assertions: that all-important social behaviors are genetically controlled, and that natural selection of the genome is caused by a set of specific adaptive mechanisms (kin selection) that produce behaviors which maximize an organism's ability to contribute the greatest number of genes to the next generation.

Hamilton's theory of kin selection (1964) is based on the concept that the fitness of an organism has two components: fitness gained through the replication of its own genetic material by reproduction, and "inclusive fitness" gained from the replication of copies of its own genes carried in others as a result of its actions. According to this theory, when an organism behaves "altruistically" toward related individuals, it is also benefiting itself, by increasing the fitness of relatives and therefore their likelihood of contributing shared genes to future generations. Thus genes are viewed as being selected for because they contribute to their own perpetuation, regardless of the organism of which they are a part. This paradigm has often led sociobiologists to speculate about the ultimate cause (reproductive advantage) of human reproductive characteristics from mate choice and marriage patterns to menopause.

Sociobiology has influenced both academic and popular discourses about human evolution over the last decades (Kitcher 1985; Sperling 1991). The reasons for this are varied and include its appeal to certain political perspectives and the continuing public curiosity about animal and human behavior. Most recently this perspective has informed a new popular literature of "evolutionary psychology" in articles in popular magazines like *Time* and *Psychology Today*, and in books like *The Moral Animal* by science writer Robert Wright (Furlow and Thornhill 1996; Wright 1994).

The epistemological issues raised by sociobiology's reductionist assertions of ultimate causality have been widely debated in a number of critiques (Fausto-Sterling 1985; Kitcher 1985; Oyama 1985; Sperling 1991). Sociobiology's popular literature posits that complex behaviors have simple genetic roots. But the association of biology with the invariant is a mistake: complex traits arise in a variety of ways, not just through natural selection of particular genotypes. Other things shape behavior besides genes and shape it in important ways for the organism in question. In many species only females show parenting behaviors, whereas males are always aggressive or indifferent towards infants (Oyama 1985). But this difference is not determined only by genes or hormones; parental caretaking is a developmental behavioral response in females, who are always present at the time of birth. Males develop some of the same caretaking patterns, such as posturing for nursing, when exposed to newborn young (Oyama 1985). From an evolutionary point of view, new behaviors may develop and persist in a population either because of changes in the average genotype by natural selection or by enduring changes in the environment in which the average genotype develops. Gould and Vrba (1982) illuminate problems with this limiting adaptationist model, limning the ways that characteristics may represent historically contingent processes rather than natural selection.

As biologist Susan Oyama (1985) points out, an ant larva may develop into a worker or a queen, depending on nutrition, temperature, and other variables, just as a male rodent may exhibit nurturant behaviors when exposed to certain stimuli. Control does not flow only from the gene outward. To understand the much more complex developmental sequences involved in the acquisition of human reproductive characteristics and behavior requires developmental studies in different cultural, ecological, and historical settings (Ellison 1990; Konner and Shostak 1986; Konner and Worthman 1980; Lee 1972, 1979).

There is much more to understanding the development of reproductive characteristics than retrospectively hypothesizing their adaptive functions, although clearly adaptation is one factor among many to be considered. This does not imply that natural selection is a minor force: a significantly maladaptive trait (one which consistently reduces reproductive fitness) is unlikely to persist over time in populations, unless balanced by some other strong reproductive advantage. Nor should the fundamental role played by evolution in determining reproductive structures and behaviors be under-estimated. However, evolution and ultimate causality cannot help us under-stand the complexity and variation within our own and other species in many reproductive events, which are reflective of changing proximate environ-mental and ecological factors, and cultural realities.

In comparison to evolutionary studies of reproduction, focused studies of human reproduction by cultural anthropologists are relatively new. Cultural studies have viewed reproductive practices as the cultural regulation of the body through marriage patterns, birthing and child-rearing patterns, the cultural meanings and management of reproduction. Up to the 1960s tradi-tional scholarship in this area focused on culturally variable beliefs, norms and values surrounding reproductive behavior (Ford 1964; Mead 1928). As more women took part in the field, studies of the structural and cultural dynamics that affect women as recipients or consumers of health care became important (Jordan 1983; Kay 1982; MacCormack 1982; Browner and Sargent 1990.) Since the 1970s the analysis of reproduction has been greatly enriched by the encounter between feminism and anthropology, in which women's reproductive experiences are analyzed as sources of power and subordination (Ginsberg and Rapp 1991.) These studies have had a major impact on current popular discourse about pregnancy, birth, and motherhood.

Studies of the medicalization of women's reproductive experiences in western culture have expanded into studies of the increasing role of repro-ductive technologies in every aspect of women's lives. These draw attention to the political economy of reproductive health, noting powerful economic circumstances that affect access to prenatal and postnatal care, among other disenfranchisements (Boone 1988; Johnson and Snow 1982; Lazarus 1988, 1990; E. Martin 1987; McClain 1985; Poland 1988; Rapp 1988, 1991).

This approach provides a valuable contribution to the understanding of constraints on women's autonomy in health matters, but has left biological issues out of the equation. Cultural anthropological studies of childbirth or reproductive health have focused solely on political, cultural and social factors, avoiding biology and ignoring ecological variables such as climate, nutrition, disease and other environmental factors known to affect reproduction. The body is universalized in cultural studies and its systematic interactions within the social and physical environment are ignored.

Such studies have understood the body itself as a cultural construct without reference to its physiological responses. This perspective has been particularly acute since the 1980s, when many cultural anthropologists rejected the possibility of empiricism and explanation in favor of interpretation (Townsend and McElroy 1992). The exclusion of the body's role reflects in part a reaction to the reductionism of much current evolutionary biology; there has been an understandable distrust on the part of many cultural anthropologists of the "biologizing" of human behavior by neo-social Darwinists. But this is throwing out the baby with the bathwater: the variability and plasticity of human biology are always germane to reproductive studies.

Human reproductive phenomena always take place within a cultural context in which their meanings are culturally constructed. Given our unique propensity for employing the body's rich potential as a symbolic medium, it is not surprising that a great variety of meanings are derived and expressed through important reproductive life-cycle events (Beyene 1989). For example, symbolic elaborations of menstruation, childbirth and menopause are an important component of human social organization (Beyene 1989; Lock 1993; Brown and Kerns 1985; Skultans 1988). But the body and its physiological mechanisms as they interact with cultural practices have been left out by most cultural theorists, as well as most evolutionists. Notable exceptions to this are the important studies of the San of southern Africa (despite some reductionist spinoffs which have erroneously represented the San as the "universal" food-forager and "type specimen" for the hominid past) which provide insight into the interlocking nature of biology, culture and ecology (Bentley 1985; Konner and Shostak 1986; Konner and Worthman 1980) and among Efe women of Zaire (Ellison *et al.* 1986; Ellison 1990). These studies show some of the variation in reproductive experiences among populations of our species and that few aspects of women's reproduction are universal or unified experiences.

The biology of reproduction is always mediated through widely ranging fertility experiences. This has relevance to Western biomedicine, in which reproduction is understood as a series of universal biological events common to all humans regardless of the cultural and ecological context. This biomedical model relies on a set of endemic Western beliefs based on recent

Western cultural reproductive patterns. Where high fertility and prolonged lactation are the norm, menstrual cycling may be relatively uncommon and its loss unremarkable to the physical and social body (Beyene 1989; Anderson 1983; M.C. Martin *et al*. 1993). By contrast in the West, phenomena such as premenstrual syndrome and menopausal symptoms (i.e., hot flashes) are a major focus in women's health care. The limited ethnocentric view of Western biomedicine has important ramifications for clinical practice in a pluralistic society in which not all women share the same reproductive history. As Western biomedicine is exported to the rest of the world through "well-meaning" development projects, this issue is particularly acute.

A potential strength of medical anthropology in studying reproductive health is that it is situated to bridge these gaps in data and theory, working as it does in all three of these realms (biology, culture and biomedicine). Broader insights may be gained by studying the life course as continually subject to changing social and ecological environments, and the way in which these interact with human biology.

NONHUMAN PRIMATES

Biological anthropologists have viewed certain human reproductive characteristics as crucial to the hominid transition and as unique adaptations in our species (Fedigan 1986; Hrdy 1983; Isaac 1978; Lovejoy 1981; Washburn and Lancaster 1968; Zihlman and Tanner 1978). When human reproductive biology is viewed within the larger context of primate evolution, major physiological reproductive changes are not impressive between our species and other higher primates, particularly those most closely related to us. Rather what we see is the plasticity of the primate reproductive system within differing ecological and social contexts (Bernstein 1976; Fedigan 1982; Smuts 1987).

There is interspecific variation among nonhuman primates in the timing and expression of major female reproductive events. These include menarche, the onset of sexual receptivity and proceptivity, the existence or lack of sexual swelling around the perineum of the female, the existence or lack of birth seasonality in a group, conception, pregnancy, lactation, and menopause (Koyama *et al*. 1992; Jurke 1996; Torii *et al*. 1996; Michael and Zumpe 1993; Helvacioglu *et al*. 1994). The physiological template upon which these variations play is the primate menstrual cycle, a complex set of neuroendocrine events producing mid-cycle ovulation, whether or not copulation has occurred, and the shedding of the uterine endometrium at approximately 25–35 day intervals, in the absence of conception (Timiras 1974). The menstrual cycle is unique to the primates; other female placental mammals have a variety of systems controlling ovulation (rabbits, for instance, are reflex ovulators, releasing ova when copulation occurs). Although the selective advantages of the menstrual cycle, as compared to other reproductive systems in female mammals, are not readily apparent, we can be sure that it worked well enough to be sustained by numerous species over 65 or so million years of primate evolution.

In *Primate Paradigms* (1982) Fedigan reviews much of the data available from the first twenty years of post-World War II field and laboratory studies on primate reproductive behavior. Numerous studies have confirmed the relative independence of primate sexual behavior from strictly hormonal control (Beach 1965; Nadler 1994; Nigi *et al.* 1990). Primate reproductive behavior is subject to socioenvironmental factors, displaying a wide variety of patterns that defy neat phylogenetic analysis. For instance, there are significant differences between the sexual behavior of both subspecies of chimpanzees, gorillas and orangutans that do not relate to their respective evolutionary relationships to our species. Hormonal and behavioral states appear closely correlated in gorilla reproductive behavior, somewhat less so in chimps, and least of all in orangutans (Rowell 1972; Nadler 1975).

The primate menstrual cycle is one part of an enormously varied and complex set of developmental, physiological and behavioral characteristics responsible for primate reproductive patterns. Male endocrine physiology, including fluctuations in testicular size in response to social and ecological variables (Enomoto *et al.* 1995; Michael and Zumpe 1993) must also be considered an important factor in the reproductive behavior of primate groups, although it rarely has been (Fedigan 1982; Rowell 1972).

Human females share the basic physiology of the menstrual cycle with nonhuman primates, with fluctuations of estrogen and progesterone producing mid-cycle ovulation. But what of the cessation of hormonal cycling at menopause? Although until recently many evolutionary anthropologists viewed menopause as a uniquely human phenomenon, it is now clear that menopause is probably quite widely distributed among the approximately 200 members of the primate order, given that females survive long enough to reach old age. Captive data show that female nonhuman primates of a number of species undergo irregular and lengthened menstrual cycles, lower estrogen levels and cessation of reproductive viability as they age (Walker 1995; Takahata *et al.* 1995; Koyama *et al.* 1992). The pattern of vaginal bleeding and alterations in serum hormone profiles of macaques in the third decade of their lives are similar to those described in perimenopausal and postmenopausal women (Hogden *et al.* 1977). Aged captive chimpanzees cease ovulation completely (Gould *et al.* 1981; Graham *et al.* 1979; Small 1984). Recent improvements in data collection on the hormonal status of free-ranging primates will make it easier to determine how common menopause is in a variety of species given that animals survive to old age (Stavisky *et al.* 1995; Shideler *et al.* 1995). Thus the differences in important reproductive characteristics emerge as relative rather than absolute between our species and other primates, calling into question evolutionary postulates of "uniquely human" reproductive "adaptations" such as "the loss of estrus" (see Power and Aiello this volume).

Social factors may also influence ovarian function in nonhuman primates. Altmann *et al.* (1987) found that in a population of baboons (*Papio cyno-cephalus cynocephalus*) daughters of high-ranking females underwent puberty as much as a year earlier than those of low-ranking mothers, and conceived their first infants earlier as a result.

Primatologists have noted an inverse relationship between group size and female fertility, positing food competition and access as causative factors (Altmann and Altmann 1987). Differences in demographics between populations of the same species are often striking in primates and may frequently relate to chance events affecting small groups, for instance a series of births altering significantly the sex ratio of a small group will change social behavior in important ways (Altmann and Altmann 1987).

Upon the basic template of the primate menstrual cycle great variation is played out in reproductive life-history patterns. At the extremes, adult female mouse lemurs (*Microcebus murinus*) are reproductively viable at about one year and produce up to two litters of two or three offspring each year. At the other extreme, the gorilla (*Gorilla gorilla gorilla*) female produces a single offspring every four to five years, and does not breed until about ten years old (Harvey *et al.* 1987). Such differences have probably evolved partly as adaptations for exploiting different ecological niches. Other factors in the evolutionary histories of species must be considered. As Gould and Vrba point out (1982) some characteristics of organisms are "exaptations" (or traits "coming along for the ride"). Such traits are not selected for, but are secondary results that occur when other structures or behaviors are selected for. It is possible, for instance, that monthly shedding of the uterine endometrium is an exaptation; not particularly adaptive, but rather a consequence of features of the menstrual cycle under selective pressure.

Some important elements of reproductive life history in primates appear to be roughly correlated with body size: sexual maturity, gestation length, lactation interval, and life-span are longer in larger primate species (Harvey *et al.* 1987). In addition, a significant relationship exists between some important reproductive life-history events and brain size among primates and other mammals (Sacher 1982). Ultimately, maturation of the nervous system may be an important factor because the brain is an energetically expensive organism. Life-history studies across several nonprimate phyla suggest that animals who have relatively slow prenatal development, or produce relatively large young, are also those that wean and mature relatively late in life (Sacher 1982).

In terms of the timing of major reproductive life-cycle events, gorillas and chimpanzees, genetically the most closely related primates to our own species, share many similarities with humans. This is not surprising since we have an approximately 98 per cent chromosomal likeness with the African apes, and fossil and genetic evidence strongly suggest a time of divergence from a common ancestor of only 5 to 7 million years ago (Cronin 1986). Free-ranging chimpanzees experience menarche between age 10–11.5 and first birth typically two years thereafter (Eaton *et al.* 1994). The duration of lactation per birth is 3–4 years with frequent nursing. A completed family size of five offspring is typical. This suggests a pattern very similar to that of some human foragers (Eaton *et al.* 1994).

MODERN HUMANS

Although as primates we share basic reproductive patterns with other members of the order, human reproductive experiences are profoundly culturally influenced. Over the last several decades a number of important studies have looked at the relationships between cultural and ecological parameters (menarche, menstruation, menopause, age at marriage, subsistence patterns, lactation patterns, nutrition, energy output, disease) and reproductive physiology (Beyene 1989; Martin 1993; Campbell and Wood 1994; Ellison 1990, 1994; Ellison *et al.* 1986; Knodel 1983; Konner and Worthman 1980; Howell 1987; Newman 1985; Wood 1989). Moreover, reproductive patterns have altered historically in our own and other cultures. A few centuries ago the reproductive patterns of many individuals in Western societies resembled those of certain nonindustrial societies (Short 1994). Although change occurs in all societies, the change in reproductive patterns with the introduction of postindustrial technologies and their consequences has been dramatic; its impact on women's bodies cannot be overestimated.

For example, cross-cultural studies reveal that the prolonged, frequent and continuous pattern of menstrual cycles of women in contemporary postindustrial Western societies are anomalous. In nonindustrialized societies, female life cycles have typically been characterized by late menarche, frequent pregnancies, and prolonged lactation that suppresses menstrual cycles (Anderson 1983; Harrell 1981). This has implications for theory and practice by calling into question, for example, the use of exogenous hormones patterned after this unusual situation (Anderson 1983; Short 1994).

When put in cross-cultural perspective, the unusual nature of the long gap between menarche and social adulthood which characterizes the contemporary West is evident. In the US the median age for the onset of menarche is 12.8 years, while the median age at marriage is 20.8 years. In many nonindustrialized societies, the median age at menarche is much later, around 17 years, and often closely coincides with social adulthood and marriage (Eveleth 1986). The average age of menarche in many of the world's societies as late as 1940 was typical of that found among living foragers, such as the San and Efe (in 1940 the age of menarche in rural China was 17.1 years and 16 years in the nineteenth-century West). In most cultures, the onset of menarche is considered to be the chief index of readiness for marriage, which typically follows soon thereafter. First birth is on the average two years following menarche, with three to four years of lactation creating an ovulation interval. With this pattern of hiatus in ovulation of three to four years following birth, combined with "late" menarche and "early" onset of menopause (relative to the west), the average family size of surviving offspring seems to be about five children in many populations (Howell 1987; Konner and Worthman 1980; Wood *et al.* 1985, 1990; Worthman *et al.* 1993). The total number of menstrual cycles most women in such societies have experienced in a lifetime amounts to approximately 4 years (or 48 cycles).

By contrast, average family size in much of the postindustrial west is 2.5 children. Breast-feeding may not occur at all or occur only on a limited basis (Short 1994). There is evidence that relatively high nutritional availability induces ovulation shortly after the birth of an infant and delays the onset of menopause, which occurs typically in a woman's early fifties (Short 1994). Many women in these settings thus experience approximately thirty-five years of ovulatory cycles, a pattern seemingly unheralded in nonindustrial human or nonhuman primate reproduction. The hormonal milieu of modern Western women over the life cycle is thus dramatically different from that of most female primates.

As with the experience of menstruation, the timing of menopause also varies between and within populations. The average age for onset of menopause for Western industrialized women is 51 years, while it is between 42 and 43 years for many women from nonindustrialized societies (Gosden 1985; Gray 1976; Leidy 1991; Treloan 1974; WHO 1981). Cross-cultural studies indicate that in some cases menopause is unmarked either biologically or socially (Beyene 1989), in contrast to the postindustrial western pattern.

Not only physiological manifestations but also cultural meanings of menopause differ between and within societies (Lock 1993). In contrast to Western biomedical assumptions about women's experience of menopause, studies by anthropologists have noted that the onset of menopause may bring greater social freedom, enhanced sexual pleasure and greater status for women in many cultures. This may be particularly true where fertility is high and access to reliable birth control is limited for much of the woman's adult life (Beyene 1989; Brown 1982; Skultans 1988).

Such studies illustrate some of the proximate mechanisms affecting menopausal experience such as life-style changes (Lau and Cooper 1993), parity (Murphy *et al.* 1994), and nutrition (Beall 1987), which have been hypothesized to affect bone loss and fracture rate in pre- and postmenopausal women. While the precise biological mechanisms involved in these relationships are not always clear, progress continues to be made in this area (Beall 1987; Gosden 1985; Murphy *et al.* 1994). Reproductive events cannot be separated from the ongoing life course, and therefore there is a need for life-history approaches in considering the timing and experience of menopause and bone loss leading to osteoporosis. Taking a life-span approach involves considering a woman's history within the context of cultural, social, and environmental experiences. Chronically elevated estradiol levels may exacerbate the physical transitions of menopause. For example the Maya, whose exposure to estradiol throughout reproductive life is much lower than women in postindustrial settings, have an absence of hot flashes and other menopausal symptoms common in the West (Beyene 1989 and M. C. Martin *et al.* 1993).

Theoretical models and clinical practices in Western biomedicine have not encompassed this variation in experience. The historically recent reproductive patterns of Western women exemplify the extreme plasticity of the body in response to changing cultural practices, and are a distinct departure from many previous patterns as current western cultural practices have profoundly affected the timing of the reproductive clock. With few exceptions, bio-medicine has largely ignored these historical changes in reproduction: the focus is an ovary that exists in a constantly stimulated hormonal environment, cycling for 35 years or more, and producing both eggs and ovarian hormones. It has universalized this pattern in the belief that it characterizes all women regardless of fertility history and cultural practices.

We see the clinical implication of this model dramatically expressed in the current treatment of menopause and the etiology of osteoporosis and cardiovascular illness as "estrogen-deficiency disease." At the same time, recent research suggests that some reproductive carcinomas result from a surplus of gonadal steroids over the life span, viewing the reduction in age of reproductive maturity as a risk factor for breast and perhaps prostate cancers (Eaton *et al.* 1994; Short 1994). Altered physical activity, fertility patterns, and breast-feeding practices related to changed workloads and new techno-logies also increase the risk of reproductive cancer (Bernstein *et al.* 1994), as do diet, including reduced fiber and increased fat intake (Adlecrentz 1990; Rische *et al.* 1994). Changes in lifetime exposure to gonadal steroids foster these health risks: gonadal activity has increased not only in lifetime duration but also in level of hormonal output in women (Ellison *et al.* 1993).

Biomedical interventions as currently conceived may reset an already disrupted clock, perpetuating the unusual pattern of constant ovarian cycling found in the postindustrial West (Voda 1993; Short 1994). Yet there are no easy solutions to the issue of exogenous hormone use given the state of current research and clinical models, nor can we, or should we, turn the clock back to past reproductive patterns which have no viability in the context of worldwide cultural change. But hormonal regimes that attempt to mimic an anomalous constantly cycling pattern should be questioned as the means to address postmenopausal osteoporosis and cardiovascular risk.

Studying human reproduction within the context of the extreme plasticity of primate bodies and behaviors leads away from reductionist postulations of ultimate causality: that reproductive experience is either "culturally constructed" or "biologically invariable." Anthropologists must study the highly contingent processes that are responsible for individual and group variation over the life-span. When genes or cultural norms are reified as "ultimate causes" the complexity of biocultural interactions in human reproduction is obscured. Anthropologists can resituate the ovary within a body that is itself situated in evolutionary biological, cultural, ecological, and political economic realms.

BIBLIOGRAPHY

Adlecrentz, H. (1990) "Western Diet and Western Diseases: Some Hormonal and Biochemical Associations," *Scandinavian Journal of Clinical and Laboratory Investigation*, Suppl. 50: 3–23.

Altmann, J., Altmann, S.A., and Hausfater, G. (1987) "Determinants of Reproductive Success in Savannah Baboons *(Papio cynocephalus)*," in T.H. Clutton-Brock (ed.) *Reproductive Success*, Chicago: University of Chicago Press.

Anderson, P. (1983) "The Reproductive Role of the Human Breast," *Current Anthropology* 24 (1): 24–45.

Beach, F. (ed.) (1965) *Sex and Behavior*, New York: Wiley.

Beall, C.M. (1987) "Nutrition and Variation in Biological Aging," in F.E. Johnston (ed.) *Nutritional Anthropology*, New York: Liss.

Bentley, G.R. (1985) "Hunter–Gatherer Energetics and Fertility: A Reassessment of the !Kung San," *Human Ecology* 13(1): 79–109.

Bernstein, I.S. (1976) "Dominance, Aggression, and Reproduction in Primate Societies," *Journal of Theoretical Biology* 60: 459–472.

Bernstein, L., Henderson, B.E., Hamisch, R., Sullivan-Halley, J., and Ross, R.K. (1994) "Physical Exercise and Reduced Risk of Breast Cancer in Young Women," *Journal of the National Cancer Institute* 86: 1403–1408.

Betzig, L.L., Borgerhoff Mulder, M., and Turke, P.W. (eds.) (1988) *Human Reproductive Behaviour*, Cambridge: Cambridge University Press.

Beyene, Y. (1989) *From Menarche to Menopause: Reproductive Lives of Peasant Women in Two Cultures*, Albany, NY: SUNY Press.

Biberoglu, K.O., Yildez, A., and Kandermir, O. (1993) "Bone Mineral Density in Turkish Postmenopausal Women," *International Gynecology & Obstetrics* 41: 153–157.

Boone, M. (1988) "Social Support for Pregnancy and Childbearing among Disadvantaged Blacks in an American Inner City," in K. Michaelson (ed.) *Childbirth in America: Anthropological Perspectives*, South Hadley, MA: Bergin and Garvey.

Brown, J.K. (1982) "Cross-Cultural Perspective on Middle-Aged Women," *Current Anthropology* 23: 143–156.

—— and Kerns, V. (1985) *In Her Prime: A New View of Middle-Aged Women*, South Hadley, MA: Bergin and Garvey.

Browner, C.H. and Sargent, C.F. (1990) "Anthropology and Studies of Human Reproduction," in T.M. Johnson and C.F. Sargent (eds.) *Medical Anthropology: Contemporary Theory and Method*, New York: Praeger, pp. 215–229.

Campbell, B. (ed.) (1972) *Sexual Selection and the Descent of Man 1871–1971*, Chicago: Aldine.

Campbell, K.L. and Wood, J.W. (1994) *Human Reproductive Ecology: Interactions of Environment, Fertility, and Behavior*, Annals of the New York Academy of Sciences: 709.

Crews, D.E. (1993) "Biological Anthropology and Human Aging – Some Current Directions in Aging Research," *Annual Review of Anthropology* 22: 395–423.

Cronin, J.E. (1986) "Molecular Insights into the Nature and Timing of Ancient Speciation Events: Correlates with Paleoclimate and Paleogeography," *South African Journal of Science* 82: 83–85.

Cronk, L. (1991) "Human Behavioral Ecology," *Annual Review of Anthropology 1991* 20: 25–53.

Dahl, J.F. (1991) "Monitoring the Ovarian Cycles of *Pan troglodytes* and *Pan paniscus* – a Comparative Approach," *American Journal of Primatology* 24 (3–4): 195–209.

Darwin, C. (1859) *On the Origin of Species by Means of Natural Selection*, London: John Murray.

Delvoye, P., Demacy, M., and Deloyne-Desnoeck, J. (1977) "The Influence of the Frequency of Nursing and of Previous Lactation Experience on Serum Prolactin in Lactating Mothers," *Journal of Biosocial Science* 9: 447–451.

DeVore, I. (ed.) (1965) *Primate Behavior: Field Studies of Monkeys and Apes*, New York: Holt, Rinehart and Winston.

Dittus, W. (1975) "Population Dynamics of the Toque Monkey, *Macacca sinica*," in R.H. Tuttle (ed.) *Socioecology and Psychology of Primates*, The Hague: Mouton.

Draper, P. (1989) "African Marriage Systems: Perspectives from Evolutionary Ecology," *Ethology and Sociobiology* 10: 145–169.

Dunbar, R.H. (1987) "Demography and Reproduction," in B. Smuts, D. Cheney, R. Seyfarth, R. Wrangham, and T. Struhsaker (eds.) *Primate Societies*, Chicago: University of Chicago Press.

Eaton, S.B, Pike, M.C., Short, R.V., Lee, N.C., and Trussell, J. (eds.) (1994) "Women's Reproductive Cancers in Evolutionary Context," *Quarterly Review of Biology* 69: 353–367.

Ellison, P.T. (1990) "Human Ovarian Function and Reproductive Ecology: New Hypotheses," *American Anthropologist*, 92: 933–952.

—— (1994) "Breastfeeding and Fertility," in K.A. Deltwyler and P. Stuart-Macadam (eds.) *Breastfeeding: A Biocultural Perspective*, New York: Aldine.

——, Parter-Brick, C., Lipson, S.F., and O'Rourke, M.T. (1993) "The Ecological Context of Human Reproduction," *Human Reproduction* 8: 2240–2258.

——, Peacock, N.R., and Lager, C. (1986) "Salivary Progesterone and Luteal Function in Two Low-Fertility Populations of Northeast Zaire," *Human Biology* 58: 473–483.

Enomoto, T., Matsubayashi, K., Nagato, Y., and Nakano, M. (1995) "Seasonal changes in Spermatogenic Cell Degeneration in the Semeniferous Epithelium of Adult Japanese Macaques (*Macaca fuscata fuscata*)," *Primates*, vol. 36 (3): 411–422.

Eveleth, P. (1986) "Timing of Menarche: Secular Trends and Population Differences," in J.B. Lancaster and B. Hamburg (eds.) *School-Age Pregnancy and Parenthood: Biosocial Dimensions*, Hawthorne NY: Aldine de Gruyder.

Fausto-Sterling, A. (1985) *Myths of Gender: Biological Theories about Women and Men*, New York: Basic Books.

Fedigan, L.M. (1982) *Primate Paradigms: Sex Roles and Social Bonds*, Montreal: Eden Press.

—— (1986) "The Changing Role of Women in Models of Human Evolution," *Annual Review of Anthropology* 15: 25–66.

Ford, C.S. (1964) *A Comparative Study of Human Reproduction*, New Haven, CT: Human Relations Area Files.

Ford, K. and Huffman, S. (1980) "Nutrition, Infant Feeding and Post-Partum Amenorrhea in Rural Bangladash," *Journal of Biosocial Science* 20: 461–469.

Furlow, F. and Thornhill, R. (1996) "The Orgasm Wars," *Psychology Today* (Jan.), pp. 42–46.

Ginsburg, F. and Rapp, R. (1991) "The Politics of Reproduction," *Annual Review of Anthropology* 20: 311–343.

Goldman, N., Westhoff, C.F, and Paul, L.E. (1987) "Variations in Natural Fertility: The Effect of Lactation and Other Determinants," *Population Study* 41: 127–146.

Gosden, R.G. (1985) *Biology of Menopause: the Causes and Consequences of Ovarian Aging*, New York: Academic Press.

Gould, K.G., Flint, M. and Graham, C. (1981) "Chimpanzee Reproductive Senescence: A Possible Model for Evolution of Menopause," *Maturitas* 3: 157–166.

Gould, S.J. and Vrba, E. (1982) "Exaptation: A Missing Term in the Science of Form," *Paleobiology* 8: 4–15.

Graham, C. (1981) "Menstrual Cycle Physiology of the Great Apes," in C.E. Graham (ed.) *Reproductive Biology of the Great Apes: Comparative and Biomedical Perspectives*, New York: Academic Press.

—— , King, O.R., and Steiner, R.A. (1979) "Reproductive Senescence in Female Nonhuman Primates," in D. Bowden (ed.) *Aging in Nonhuman Primates*, New York: Van Nostrand Reinhold.

Gray, R.H. (1976) "The Menopause: Epidemiological and Demographic Considerations," in R.J. Beard (ed.) *The Menopause*, Baltimore: University Park Press.

Haldane, J.B.S. (1932) *The Causes of Evolution*, London: Longmans, Green.

Hamilton, W.D. (1964) "The Genetical Evolution of Social Behavior, I and II," *Journal of Theoretical Biology* 7: 1–52.

Haraway, D. (1989) *Primate Visions: Gender, Race, and Nature in the World of Modern Science*, New York: Routledge.

Harrell, B. (1981) "Lactation and Menstruation in Cultural Perspective," *American Anthropologist* 83: 796–823.

Harvey, Paul H., Martin, R.D., and Clutton-Brock, T.H. (1987) "Life Histories in Comparative Perspective," in B. Smuts, D. Cheney, R. Seyfarth, R. Wrangham and T. Struhsaker (eds.) *Primate Societies*, Chicago: University of Chicago Press.

Heistermann, M., Finke, M., and Hodges, J.K. (1995) "Assessment of Female Reproductive Status in Captive-Housed Hanuman Langurs (*Presbytis entellus*) by Measurement of Urinary and Fecal Steroid excretion Patterns," *American Journal of Primatology* 37(4): 275–284.

Helvacioglu, A., Aksel, S., Yeoman, R.R., and Williams, L.E. (1994) "Age-Related Hormonal Differences in Cycling Squirrel Monkeys (*Samiri boliviensis boliviensis*)," *American Journal of Primatology* 32 (3): 207–213.

Hogden, G.D., Goodman, A.K., O'Conner, A., and Johnson, D.K. (1977) "Menopause in Rhesus Monkeys: Models for Study in the Human Climacteric," *American Journal of Obstetrics and Gynecology* 127: 581–584.

Howell, N. (1987) *Demography of the Dobe !Kung*, New York: Academic Press.

Hrdy, S.B. (1981) "'Nepotists' and 'Altruists': The Behavior of Old Females among Macaques and Langur Monkeys," in P. Amoss and S. Harrell (eds.) *Other Ways of Growing Old*, Stanford: Stanford University Press.

—— (1983) "Heat Lost," *Science 83* (October): pp. 73–78.

—— (1987) "Patterning of Sexual Activity," in B. Smuts, D. Cheney, R. Seyfarth, R. Wrangham and T. Struhsaker (eds.) *Primate Societies*, Chicago: University of Chicago Press.

Isaac, G.L. (1978) "The Food-Sharing Behavior of Protohuman Hominids," *Scientific American* 238(4): 90–106.

Johnson, S.M. and Snow, L.F. (1982) "Assessment of Reproductive Knowledge in an Inner-City Clinic," *Social Science and Medicine* 16: 1657–1662.

Jordan, B. (1983) *Birth in Four Cultures: A Cross-Cultural Study of Childbirth in Yucatan, Holland, Sweden, and the U.S.*, Shelborne VT: Eden Press.

Jurke, M.H. (1996) "Behavioral and Hormonal Aspects of Reproduction in Captive Goeldis Monkeys (*Callimico goeldii*) in a Comparative Evolutionary Context," *Primates* 37(Jan.) 1: 109–116.

Kaufman, F.R., Xu, Y.K., Ng, W.G., Silva, P.D., Lobo, R.A., and Donnell, G.N. (1989) "Gonadal Function and Ovarian Galactose Metabolism in Classic Galactosemia," *Acta Endocrinologica* 120: 129–133.

Kay, M. (ed.) (1982) *Anthropology and Human Birth*, Phila.: F.A. Davis.

Kitcher, P. (1985) *Vaulting Ambition: Sociobiology and the Quest for Human Nature*, Cambridge, MA: MIT Press.

Knodel, J. (1983) "Natural Fertility: Age Patterns, Levels and Trends," in R.A. Bultatao and R.D. Lee (eds.) *Determinants of Fertility in Developing Countries*, New York: Academic Press.

Konner, M. and Shostak, M. (1986) "Timing and Management of Birth among the !Kung: Biocultural Interaction in Reproductive Adaptation," *Cultural Anthropology* 2(1): 11–28.

Konner, M. and Worthman, C. (1980) "Nursing Frequency, Gonadal Function and Birth Spacing among !Kung Hunter–Gatherers," *Science* 207: 788–791.

Koyama, N., Takahata, Y., and Huffman, M.A. (1992) "Reproductive Parameters of Female Japanese Macaques: Thirty Years of Data from the Arashiyama Troops, Japan," *Primates* 33 (Jan.) 1: 33–47.

Lau, E.M.C. and Cooper, C. (1993) "Epidemiology and Prevention of Osteoporosis in Urbanized Asian Populations," *Osteoporosis International*, supp. 1: 23–26.

Lazarus, E.S. (1988) "Poor Women, Poor Outcome: Social Class and Reproductive Health," in K. Michaelson (ed.) *Childbirth in America: Anthropological Perspectives*, South Hadley MA: Bergin and Garvey.

—— (1990) "Falling Through the Cracks: Contributions and Barriers to Care in Prenatal Clinics," *Medical Anthropology Quarterly* 12: 269–87.

Lee, R.B. (1972) "Population Growth and the Beginnings of Sedentary Life among the !Kung Bushmen," in B. Spooner (ed.) *Population Growth: Anthropological Implications*. Cambridge, MA: MIT Press, pp. 329–342.

—— (1979) *The !Kung San: Men, Women and Work in a Foraging Society*, Cambridge: Cambridge University Press.

—— and DeVore, I. (eds) (1968) *Man the Hunter*, Chicago: Aldine.

—— and Lancaster, J. (1965) "The Annual Reproductive Cycle in Monkeys and Apes," in I. DeVore (ed.) *Primate Behavior: Field Studies of Monkeys and Apes*, New York: Holt, Rinehart and Winston.

Leidy, L. (1991) "The Timing of Menopause in Biological and Sociocultural Context: A Lifespan Approach," PhD thesis, Albany: State University of New York.

Lock, M. (1993) *Encounters with Aging: Mythologies of Menopause in Japan and North America*, Berkeley: University of California Press.

Lovejoy, C.O. (1981) "The Origin of Man," *Science* 211(4480): 341–350.

McClain, C.S. (1985) "Why Women Choose Trial of Labor or Repeat Caesarean Section," *Journal of Family Practice* 21(3): 210–216.

MacCormack, C.P. (1982) *Ethnography of Fertility and Birth*, New York: Academic Press.

MacMahan, B. and Worcester, J. (1966) "Age at Menopause: United States 1960–1962," *National Center of Health Statistics*, Series 11(19).

Martin, E. (1987) *The Woman in the Body*, Boston: Beacon.

Martin, M.C., Block, J.E., Sanchez, S.D., Arnaud, C.D., and Beyene, Y. (1993) "Menopause Without Symptoms: The Endocrinology of Menopause among Rural Mayan Indians," *American Journal of Obstetrics and Gynecology* 100: 1837–1845.

Mayer, P.J. (1982) "Evolutionary Advantages of the Menopause," *Human Ecology* 10: 477–493.

Mead, M. (1928) *Coming of Age in Samoa*, New York: William Morrow.

Michael, R.P and Zumpe, D. (1993) "A Review of Factors Influencing the Sexual and Aggressive Behavior of Macaques," *American Journal of Primatology* 30(3): 213–241.

Murphy, S., Khaw, K.T., May, H., and Compston, J.E. (1994) "Parity and Bone

Mineral Density in Middle-Aged Women," *Osteoporosis Journal* 4(3): 162–166.

Nadler, R.D. (1975) "Laboratory Research on Sexual Behavior of the Great Apes," in C.E. Graham (ed.) *Reproductive Biology of the Great Apes*, New York: Academic Press.

—— (1994) "Walter Heape and the Issue of Estrus in Primates," *American Journal of Primatology* 33(2): 38–87.

Newman, F.L. (ed.) (1985) *Women's Medicine: A Cross-Cultural Study of Indigenous Fertility Regulation*, New Brunswick: Rutgers University Press.

Nigi, H., Hayama, S.I., and Torii, R. (1990) "Copulatory Behavior Unaccompanied by Ovulation in the Japanese Monkey (*Macaca fuscata*)," *Primates* 31 (Apr.) 2: 243–250.

Oyama, S. (1985) *The Ontogeny of Information: Developmental Systems and Evolution*, Cambridge: Cambridge University Press.

Poland, M. (1988) "Adequate Prenatal Care and Reproductive Outcome," in K. Michaelson (ed.) *Childbirth in America*, South Hadley, MA: Bergin and Garvey.

Rapp, R. (1988) "Chromosomes and Communication: The Discourse of Genetic Counseling," *Medical Anthropology Quarterly* 2(2): 143–157.

—— (1991) "Constructing Amniocentesis: Maternal and Medical Discourses," in F. Ginsberg and A. Tsing (eds.) *Uncertain Terms: Negotiating Gender in American Culture*, Boston: Beacon Press.

Riley, M.W. (1979) *Aging from Birth to Death: Interdisciplinary Perspectives*, Boulder, CO: Westview.

Rische, H.A., Jain, M., and Marrett, Z.D. (1994) "Dietary Fat Intake and Risk of Epithelial Ovarian Cancer," *Journal of the National Cancer Institute* 86: 1409–1415.

Rowell, T. (1972) *The Social Behaviour of Monkeys*, Middlesex, England: Penguin Books.

Sacher, G.A. (1982) "The Role of Brain Maturation in the Evolution of the Primates," in E. Armstrong and D. Falk (eds.) *Primate Brain Evolution*, New York: Plenum Press.

Shideler, S.E., Munro, C.J., and Taylor, R. (1995) "Urine and Fecal Sample Collection on Filter Paper for Ovarian Hormone Evaluations," *American Journal of Primatology* 37(4): 305–315.

Short, R.V. (1994) "Human Reproduction in an Evolutionary Context," in K.L. Campbell and J.W. Wood (eds.) *Human Reproductive Ecology*, Annals of the New York Academy of Sciences 709: 416–425.

Skultans, V. (1988) "Menstrual Symbolism in South Wales," in T. Buckley and A. Gottlieb (eds.) *Blood Magic: The Anthropology of Menstruation*, Berkeley: University of California Press, pp. 137–160.

Small, M.F. (1984) "Aging and Reproductive Success in Female *Macacca mulata*," in M.F. Small (ed.) *Female Primates: Studies by Women Primatologists*, New York: Alan R. Liss.

Smuts, Barbara B. (1987) "Gender, Aggression, and Influence," in B. Smuts, D. Cheney, R. Seyfarth, R. Wrangham, and T. Struhsaker (eds.) *Primate Societies*, Chicago: University of Chicago Press.

Sperling, S. (1991) "Baboons with Briefcases vs. Langurs in Lipstick: Feminism, Functionalism, and Sociobiology in the Evolution of Primate Gender," in M. di Leonardo (ed.) *Gender at the Crossroads of Knowledge: Feminist Anthropology in the Postmodern Era*, Berkeley: University of California Press.

Stavisky, R., Russell, E., Stallings, T., and Smith, E.O. (1995) "Fecal Steroid Analysis of Ovarian Cycles in Free-Ranging Baboons," *American Journal of Primatology* 36 (4): 285–297.

Takahata, Y., Koyama, N., and Suzuki, S. (1995) "Do the Old Aged Females Experience a Long Post-Reproductive Lifespan: The Cases of Japanese Macaques and Chimpanzees," *Primates* 36 (Apr.) 2: 169–180.

Tiger, L. and Fowler, H. (eds.) (1978) *Female Hierarchies*, Chicago: Beresford.

Timiras, P. (1974) *Developmental Physiology and Aging*, New York: Macmillan.

Torii, R., Abbot, D.H., and Nigi, H. (1996) "Morphological Changes of the Ovary and Hormonal Changes in the Common Marmoset (*Callithrix jacchus*)," *Primates* 37(Jan.) 1: 49–56.

Townsend, P.K. and McElroy, A. (1992) "Toward an Ecology of Women's Reproductive Health," *Medical Anthropology* 14: 9–34.

Treloan, A.E. (1974) "Menarche, Menopause and Intervening Fecundability," *Human Biology* 46(1): 89–107.

Trivers, R. (1972) "Parental Investment and Sexual Selection," in B. Campbell (ed.) *Sexual Selection and the Descent of Man: 1871–1971*, Chicago: Aldine.

Voda, A.M. (1993) "A Journey to the Center of the Cell: Understanding the Physiology and Endocrinology of Menopause," in J.C. Callahan (ed.) *Menopause: A Midlife Passage*, Bloomington: Indiana University Press.

Walker, M.L. (1995) "Menopause in Female Rhesus Monkeys," *American Journal of Primatology* 35(1): 59–71.

Washburn, S.L. and Lancaster, C.S. (1968) "The Evolution of Hunting," in R. B. Lee and I. DeVore (eds.) *Man the Hunter*, Chicago: Aldine.

Watanabe, K., Mori, A., and Kawa, M. (1992) "Characteristic Features of the Reproduction of Koshima Monkeys, *Macaca fuscata fuscata*: A Summary of 34 Years of Observation," *Primates* 33(Jan.) 1: 1–32.

Wilson, E.O. (1975) *Sociobiology: The New Synthesis*, Cambridge, MA: Belknap Press at Harvard.

Wood, J.W. (1989) "Fecundity and Natural Fertility in Humans," *Oxford Review of Reproductive Biology* 11: 61–109.

—— (1990) "Fertility in Anthropological Populations," *Annual Review of Anthropology* 19: 211–242.

—— (1994) "Nutrition and Reproduction: Why Demographers and Physiologists Disagree About a Fundamental Relationship," in K.L. Campbell and J.W. Wood (eds.) *Human Reproductive Ecology: Interactions of Environment, Fertility, and Behavior*, Annals of the New York Academy of Sciences, pp. 416–425.

—— , Lai, D., Johnson, P.L., Campbell, K.L., and Maslor, I.A. (1985) "Lactation and Birth Spacing in Highland New Guinea," *Journal Biosoc. Sci.* 17: 57–79.

World Health Organization (1981) *Research on the Menopause*, Technical Report Service no. 670, Geneva: WHO.

Worthman, C.M., Jenckins, C.L., Stalling, J.F., and Lai, D. (1993) "Attenuation of Nursing-Related Ovarian Suppression and High Fertility in Well-Nourished, Intensively Breastfeeding Annele Women of Lowland Papua New Guinea," *Journal of Biosoc. Sci.* 25: 425–443.

Wright, R. (1994) *The Moral Animal*, New York: Pantheon.

Wynne-Edwards, V.C. (1962) *Animal Dispersion in Relation to Social Behaviour*, New York: Hafner.

Zihlman, A. and Tanner, N. (1978) "Gathering and the Hominid Adaptation," in L. Tiger and H. Fowler (eds.) *Female Hierarchies*, Chicago: Beresford, pp. 163–194.

8

FEMALE PROTO-SYMBOLIC STRATEGIES

Camilla Power and Leslie Aiello

How did humans become the unique symbolic culture-bearing species that we are? One of the most exciting challenges for paleoanthropology is to understand this extraordinary event. Few convincing arguments have been put forward to explain the evolution of symbolic cognition on a Darwinian basis; no theory has ventured predictions which are testable against symbolic data from both the archaeological and the ethnographic records.

Modern paleoanthropology dates from the 1966 "Man the Hunter" conference (Lee and DeVore 1968). Among the hunter–gatherer ethnographers, primatologists, paleontologists and archaeologists present, a consensus emerged that the evolution of humans was the evolution of the hunter–gatherer adaptation. At the time, evidence for the basic elements of the hunter–gatherer lifestyle – centered on food-sharing and a home base – was identified early in the fossil and archaeological record (Isaac 1971). A unilinear, gradualist model developed which proposed co-evolution of increasing amounts of meat in the hominid diet, increasing levels of co-operation between males in the hunt, and the development of cognition, language, and symbolic culture on that basis.

Inspired by the rise of feminist consciousness in the 1970s, women scientists challenged the overt sexism of this account by advancing the parallel model of "Woman the Gatherer" (Tanner 1981). Invaluable for switching attention to female strategies, "Woman the Gatherer" arose at a time when the newly emergent discipline of sociobiology was offering the prospect of a female-centered methodology for evolutionary accounts (cf. Haraway 1989). Among primatologists in particular, selfish-gene thinking focused attention on conflicts between male and female reproductive strategies, thereby highlighting female priorities of foraging and reproduction. Sociobiology discredited so-called "coat-tails" theories of human evolution (cf. Fedigan 1986), according to which traits were predominantly selected for in males, with females hanging on for the ride.

But for clarifying the question of symbolic cultural origins, "Woman the Gatherer" had the same limitations as "Man the Hunter." Neither model recognized or identified as a problem the uniquely human phenomenon of symbolic culture. Implicitly, both assumed that symbolic communication such as language was necessarily "better," and was so obviously an advantage for organizing social life that any sufficiently encephalized hominine (australopithecine and *Homo*) would generate and use it.

However, symbolic speech is not necessarily better than a primate gesture/call system. It has costs as well as benefits, and would be useless to evolving humans lacking other elements of symbolic culture (Knight 1996). In the tradition of Durkheim (1965 [1912]), symbolic anthropologists (cf. Rappaport 1979) have stressed the interdependence of speech and ritual. Symbolic speech is a set of cryptic mutual references to morally authoritative constructs (Knight *et al.* 1995). As they speak, humans trigger acts of identification of such constructs. But speech is powerless to implant and replicate those constructs throughout a community of speakers in the first place. A construct such as "God," for example, must first be emotively experienced – and the only possible medium for this is ritual. Collective ritual action is the source of those shared, morally authoritative symbolic constructs without which speech could have no force.

If speech and ritual are so interdependent, then any theory of speech origins must simultaneously account for the emergence of ritual action. Using neo-Darwinian methodology, which describes the process of evolution through cost-benefit analyses of short-term fitness payoffs to individuals, how can we explain the ritual domain? What selection pressures would have led individuals to engage with displaced and imaginary constructs, endeavoring to share those constructs with others? What would have been the immediate benefits promoting an interest in illusions?

Among the unique attributes of modern humans are symbolic culture manifested in language, ritual and art, and a sexual division of labor, with distribution and exchange underwritten by ritual taboos and myth (Chase 1994). Also unique in its overall combination of features is the human female reproductive cycle. We will advance a Darwinian model which links female reproductive strategies to the emergence of symbolism and the sexual division of labor. Essentially, the hypothesis proposed here is that symbolism emerged as a set of deceptive sexual signals aimed by female kin coalitions at their mates to secure increased male reproductive investment (cf. Krebs and Dawkins 1984; Knight *et al.* 1995).

FEMALE SEXUAL SIGNALS

The modern human female reproductive cycle is characterized by concealed ovulation and loss of estrus implying the capacity for sexual receptivity at any point of the cycle. These features have regularly been implicated in accounts of the emergence of monogamy with male provisioning including hunting (e.g Lovejoy 1981; Hill 1982; Stoddart 1986). It is worth reviewing some of the scenarios depicting exchange of economic resources for sexual favors. Both Lovejoy and Hill highlighted continuous sexual receptivity as a necessary component. Lovejoy (1981) argued for this in a monogamous context, the male bringing food "home" to his mate and offspring; the more sexually desirable she was, the more he would be motivated to obtain and return with food. This led to selection for such "attractive" characteristics as breasts, buttocks, smooth skin, etc. By contrast with this nuclear family scenario, Hill (1982) modelled a promiscuous and competitive trade of sex for meat. Males would be motivated to bring meat to estrus females. This led to selection on females to extend estrus throughout the cycle – "sham estrus" – leading to the continuous receptivity pattern of humans. Other theorists have noted the problem of female receptivity in relation to hunting behavior (e.g. Lancaster 1975). Stoddart (1986) pointed out that estrus, and particularly olfactory cues of fertility, would have disrupted hunting. Given reliable cues to ovulation, males who stay back at camp rather than go out hunting would have excellent chances of fertile sex. In these circumstances no male would expend energy to hunt. According to Stoddart, this problem necessitated suppression of such olfactory signals.

Models such as these linked levels of male energetic investment with female sexual signals. Lovejoy and Stoddart assumed, rather than explained, a male parental instinct and tendency to provision offspring – that is, a level of male investment radically differentiating hominines from extant nonhuman primates. Hill, a sociobiologist premising his model on conflicts of interest between the sexes, did not make that assumption. But it is not clear how long-term male investment would be generated on the basis of short-term promiscuous exchange.

Why link levels of male investment with female reproductive signals at all? We must posit some such link because of the energetic problems posed by encephalization in the hominine line. As the brain became larger in human evolution, mothers bore the escalating reproductive costs of producing large-brained infants. Female reproductive fitness would increasingly depend on securing greater and more reliable reproductive investment from males. Because it is females who primarily bear the costs of reproduction, we must suppose that females drove this process through sexual selection, their reproductive signals functioning as prime mechanisms for gaining greater investment from males. Our major piece of evidence for the evolution of these features is the modern human female reproductive cycle itself.

As females came under pressure to meet the costs of encephalization, one logical strategy is to reward more attentive "investor" males, and to punish or undermine would-be philanderers. A philandering male maximizes his reproductive fitness by fertilizing as many females as possible. He achieves this by reducing the time he spends searching for each fertile female, and the time he spends with her to ensure impregnation. The human female appears well designed to waste the time of philanderers by withholding accurate information about her true fertility state.

Concealment of ovulation and loss of estrus is a deterrent to a male philandering strategy because it deprives males of any reliable cue by which to judge whether a female is likely to have been impregnated. The longer a male must remain with one female to ensure fertilization in any breeding season, the smaller are his chances of fertilizing another (Dunbar 1988: 160). These features are not unique to humans as against other primates (Hrdy 1981: 158). However, in some species with apparently concealed ovulation, males may be able to track female cycles through olfactory cues (e.g. cotton-top tamarins, Ziegler *et al.* 1993). Studies of variation in human ejaculates (Baker and Bellis 1993: 880) confirm that men are unable to track women's peri-ovulatory periods. Ovulation in women is well concealed from male partners.

Alexander and Noonan (1979) argued that through concealment of ovulation and continuous receptivity alone, males would have been forced into prolonged consortships. Even in multi-male group contexts, pair-bonds would have been reinforced, and hence males would have had greater confidence in paternity, leading to greater parental investment. Against this, Hrdy (1981) proposed that concealment/continuous receptivity among primates correlates with promiscuity, females needing to deprive males of information about paternity, so reducing risks of infanticide. These hypotheses are not mutually exclusive. While ovulation may initially be concealed to counter infanticide risk, once present this trait could be exapted to serve a female strategy of increasing male investment (see Sillén-Tullberg and Møller 1993).

Another key means of thwarting philanderers is reproductive cycle synchrony. Knowlton (1979) formulated a general model of synchrony as a strategy by the sex which invests most in offspring to secure greater parental investment from their mates. If females synchronize their fertile moments, no single male can cope with guarding and impregnating any group of females. He must concentrate his efforts on one female at a time. The evolutionary effect is to bring more males into the breeding system.

Synthesizing Alexander and Noonan's argument on ovulatory concealment with Knowlton's synchrony model, Turke (1984, 1988) was the first to focus on "ovulatory synchrony" in hominine mating systems. He argued that ovulatory concealment (with continuous receptivity) functioned to draw males into longer consortships by depriving would-be philanderers of accurate information about fertility. A pattern of ovulatory synchrony in local populations had the further effect of thwarting male attempts to philander. This drove the ratio of sexually active males to females in groups towards one-to-one. Sustained male/female bonds on a one-to-one basis led to greater paternity confidence, and greater inclination on the part of males to invest in offspring.

Equal sex ratios can only be guaranteed by extreme reproductive synchrony, with local females synchronizing all reproductive events – ovulation, conception, gestation, birth, lactational amenorrhea and return to fecund cycling. In these conditions, to maximize fitness, males have no alternative but to invest in current partners. However, such a strategy would be costly to females in populations with high infant mortality, and would be virtually impossible to sustain where females were using sexual receptivity to bond with males (Arthur 1994). But a seasonal form of synchrony, restricting most female fecund cycles to a certain period of the year, would incur minimal costs to synchronizers, and would still function to counter male attempts to philander.

Seasonal ovulatory synchrony with continuous receptivity would effectively ensure at least as many males in breeding groups as fecundable females. But it would not prevent males from deserting lactating females in favor of cycling females. Where a degree of synchrony was an important female strategy for undermining male philandering, we would predict minimizing of any signal that divulged information about prospective fertility. If synchrony is not going to be perfect, then the least females can do is not advertise the fact.

But one reproductive signal has been amplified in the course of human evolution – menstrual bleeding which is unusually profuse in women (Profet 1993). Signalling is not a primary function of menstruation, which occurs in other primates and a wide range of species. But once ovulation was concealed and estrus was lost in the human lineage, menstruation would have taken on significance as a cue. It is not an accurate indicator of fertility, because it occurs at the non-fertile time of the cycle. But it is a good indicator of impending fertility. Because menstruation would have been the only cue which gave males positive information about female reproductive condition, we would expect that hominine males came under selection pressure to respond to it. Since it is not accurate about timing of fertility, the information is not very useful for philanderers. Menstruation should make a female attractive to males who are prepared to wait around and mate-guard. Given concealment of ovulation, males lack information about when to bring mate-guarding to an end. So the male who responds to menstrual cues must spend plenty of time with the female to increase his chances of paternity.

This implies that menstrual bleeding functioned as a mechanism of attracting extra male attention, procuring mating effort. But the signal does not necessarily secure genuine parental effort from males. Once a female was pregnant, she risked losing male attention to other menstruating females in the vicinity. Can the problem of the giveaway menstrual signal be resolved to uphold a synchrony strategy which would secure a level of paternal investment in the offspring?

One logical possibility is that, within kin coalitions, non-menstruating females "cheated" by "borrowing" the blood of a menstrual relative. Confusing the information available to males by showing the same reproductive signal at the same time, coalition members could then retain both the attractions of menstruation as an indicator of impending fertility, and the advantages of synchrony for maximizing male parental investment.

On this basis, we would expect females, within kin coalitions, to manufacture synchrony of signals whenever a member was actually menstruating –

a strategy we term "sham menstruation." We might then expect them to resort to cosmetic means – blood-coloured pigments that could be used in body-painting – to augment their "sham" displays. We expect the earliest instances of such cosmetic elaboration of menstrual signals to have occurred among archaic *Homo sapiens* as females experienced reproductive stress owing to the increasing costs of encephalization (see below, pp. 162–5).

Such coordinated body-painting at menstruation would function as advertising for extra male attention. Provided females maintained solidarity within their menstrual coalitions, even if males were aware of which females were actually menstruating, they would not be able to use the information. If males attempted to fight for access to a particular female, they would encounter resistance from female relatives, and there would be no fitness benefit since the menstrual female would not be immediately fertile. As a result, males would maximize fitness by continuing to invest in current partners rather than by targeting menstrual females.

The "sham menstruation" model gives a basis for describing behavioral adaptations that prefigure symbolic and ritual activity. A signal that originally belonged to an individual, and was capable of extracting energy from males on a one-to-one basis, would become collectivized and amplified among a coalition of females, broadcasting information of critical importance which males could not afford to ignore. This means that the female coalition would now have a powerful signal for manipulating males. To the extent that some females who were not imminently fertile pretended to be, the signal would be deceptive. Unlike nonhuman primate tactical deception, which is always on an egocentric and individualistic basis (Byrne and Whiten 1988), in this case the deception would be incipiently sociocentric, maintained by a collective. As such, it represents a vital step towards sustaining an imaginary construct and sharing that construct with others – that is, dealing with symbols.

So long as female deceptive displays remained situation-dependent, constrained by the local incidence of biological menstruation, they would not be fully symbolic but tied to here-and-now contexts. Symbolic cultural evolution would take off when cosmetic displays involving use of pigment and body painting were staged as a default, a matter of monthly, habitual performance, irrespective of whether any local female was actually menstruating. Once such regularity had been established, women would effectively have created a communal construct of "Fertility" or "Blood" – no longer dependent on its perceptible counterpart. Ritual body-painting within groups would repeatedly create, sustain, and recreate this morally authoritative construct. Such repeated ritual – which is energetically costly – must be linked to the level, regularity, and kind of male provisioning effort it engenders. We therefore expect that data interpretable as evidence for regular female ritual performance, such as abundant red pigment, will correlate with the onset of a symbolically structured sexual division of labor.

Our model rests on the value of menstruation as a signal of impending fertility to attract and retain male support. But, no matter how amplified, the signal would not motivate males to embark on long-distance, logistic hunts or foraging expeditions; on the contrary, it should promote mate-guarding. Sham menstruation would function to mobilize male mating effort in contexts of area-intensive foraging, where there were sufficient gatherable resources in the vicinity. It is consistent with fairly similar foraging strategies between the sexes where females travel with males for hunting of no more than small to medium game. However, for females burdened with increasingly dependent offspring, one of the key means to alleviate reproductive stress would be to reduce activity levels, especially energetic costs of travel (Prentice and Whitehead 1987). In a study of activity levels among Efe hunter–gatherer women of different ages and reproductive status, Peacock found that "pregnant and lactating women curtail the performance of strenuous work activities in comparison with cycling women" by travelling shorter distances and carrying lighter backloads (Peacock 1991: 350–351).

The sexual division of labor entails differentiation of roles in food procurement, with logistic hunting of large game by males, co-operation and exchange of products. Our hypothesis is that symbolism arose in this context. To minimize energetic costs of travel, coalitions of women began to invest more heavily in home bases. To secure this strategy, women would have to use their attractive, collective signal of impending fertility in a wholly new way: by signalling refusal of sexual access except to males who returned "home" with provisions. Menstruation – real or artificial – while biologically the wrong time for fertile sex, is psychologically the right moment for focusing men's minds on imminent hunting, since it offers the prospect of fertile sex in the near future. Once amplified menstrual displays signalled "no" to males, "ritual" and "taboo" in forms known among hunter–gatherers would have been established. Coalitions of women who had already been artificially manipulating information divulged to males, and engaging in a level of collective deception, would have had the preadaptations necessary to construct such a signal of "no sex" or "taboo."

MENSTRUATION IN HUNTER–GATHERER ETHNOGRAPHY

Hunter–gatherer ethnography documents a cross-cultural linkage between observance of menstrual taboos, hunting success, lunar periodicity and normative beliefs in menstrual synchrony (see Knight *et al.* 1995). Behavioral menstrual synchrony is well documented in human groups (McClintock 1971; and see Graham 1991; Weller and Weller 1993). The human female is well designed for widespread cycle synchrony across a population because the average length of her menstrual cycle corresponds to the mean lunar synodic period at 29.5 days (Gunn *et al.* 1937; McClintock 1971; Vollman 1977; Cutler *et al.* 1980). The average length of gestation at 266 days is a precise multiple of the lunar synodic period (Menaker and Menaker 1959; and see Martin 1992: 263–264).

The model asserts that periodic female inviolability should be discernible as a focus of early ritual traditions. Menstrual taboos satisfy this condition, being sufficiently widespread and invariant to indicate extreme antiquity (Knight 1991: 374ff.). Recurrent among southern African San hunter–gatherer groups are the related beliefs that (a) a man should not hunt while his wife is menstruating (Biesele 1993: 93); (b) he should not have sex while his wife is menstruating (Shostak 1983: 239); or (c) he should not have sex if he is about to go out hunting large game (Biesele 1993: 196). This implies that ideally hunting should follow menstruation which initiates periodic sex abstinence. Associated with this are beliefs in women synchronizing their periods (see Shostak 1983: 68), both with each other, and with the moon. The Hadza of Tanzania and the San both link menstruation to dark moon (see Knight et al. 1995). To this day, the most productive form of hunting among these groups is nocturnal ambush hunting over game trails leading to waterholes, practiced in the dry season (Crowell and Hitchcock 1978; Hawkes et al. 1992). This is necessarily restricted to the moonlight nights between first quarter and full moon. The major religious ceremony of the Hadza, the epeme dance, takes place each dark moon (when women are normatively menstruating) and is held to be vital for hunting luck (Woodburn 1982: 191, and pers. comm.). Among widespread San groups, the distribution indicating considerable antiquity for the practice, a girl's release from her first menstruation cere- mony would be timed for the appearance of the new moon (see Knight et al. 1995). The picture that emerges from the African ethnography is of a sequence of ritual and taboos associated with menstruation around dark moon, preceding and motivating collective, logistic hunting in the period when maximum nocturnal light is available to hunters, towards full moon.

In Khoisan ethnography, cosmetic application of pigment is found regul- arly, and is linked both to menstrual ritual and hunting performance. Among the /Xam (the extinct southern San), a girl emerging from menarcheal seclusion would give all the women of her band lumps of hematite (a very bright red ochre) to dress their cloaks and decorate their faces (Hewitt 1986: 284). A Zu/'hoasi maiden has an ochre design painted on her face, and she adorns the young men with ochre to protect them from accidents while hunting (Lewis-Williams 1981: 51). Similar practices involving real blood, red plant pigments or red ochre are reported for most other San groups (see Knight et al. 1995).

Worldwide in the rock art of hunter–gatherer cultures, representations of ritual power centered on female reproductive signals – menstruation and menstrual synchrony – appear prominently. Examples of such paintings and engravings (Figure 8.1) are found in the European Upper Paleolithic (Marshack 1975), the southern African Later Stone Age (Solomon 1992; Garlake 1987), and Aboriginal Australia (Wright 1968).

8.1 Images of women from the rock art of hunter–gatherer communities: (a) European Upper Paleolithic, Lalinde, Middle Magdalenian, redrawn after Marshack (1975); (b) San, Zimbabwe, Later Stone Age, redrawn after Garlake (1987: fig. 78); (c) Pilbara region, Western Australia, redrawn after Wright (1968: fig. 845).

THE FOSSIL AND ARCHAEOLOGICAL EVIDENCE

This model argues that human symbolism and cognition emerged as a consequence of the increased costs of reproduction borne by the female resulting directly from the energetic costs of encephalization. But what evidence of these major changes in female reproductive strategy is there in the fossil record for human evolution? Behavioral and cognitive evolution leaves little tangible evidence of the stages through which the model takes us. But one feature available in the fossil record enables us to infer when females would be expected to have come under pressure to alter their reproductive strategies. This is the pattern of brain size increase over the course of human prehistory. Measurements of cranial capacity allow us to estimate the increased costs of reproduction resulting from encephalization, and hence when females would have required increased paternal investment. At that stage, we expect females to resort to cosmetic manipulation of signals – sham menstruation – to artificially maintain synchrony. The establishment of a fully symbolic sham menstruation strategy, involving regular ritual, should be evidenced by abundant utilization of red pigment in the archaeological record. This should be associated with evidence for a sexual division of labor, with heavier investment in home bases.

When brain size for the available hominine fossils is plotted against time (Figure 8.2) it is immediately apparent that there are two periods of rapid increase in absolute brain size in the fossil record. The first of these marks the evolution of early *Homo*, and particularly *Homo ergaster*, while the second is an exponential increase which gets under way with the appearance of archaic *Homo sapiens*. Between the time of *Homo habilis* and about 300,000 years ago there is little significant increase in brain size (Rightmire 1981; but see Leigh 1992).

A large brain size itself would be expected to have placed little increased metabolic demand on adult individuals. Even though brain tissue is metabolically very expensive and humans brains are just over 1 kilogram larger than would be expected for an average placental mammal of our body weight, our basal metabolic rates are no greater than would be expected. Intestinal tissue is also metabolically very expensive, and humans compensate for their relatively large brain sizes by having correspondingly small guts (Aiello and Wheeler 1995). Although the evolution of the large brain in the hominines did not necessarily put the adults under an increased energetic strain to maintain this large brain size, it did require them to adopt a higher quality diet. Only a high quality, easy to digest diet is compatible with relatively small (and energetically cheap) digestive systems. High quality diets do, however, have their own energy costs. They require larger foraging areas (Clutton Brock and Harvey 1977; Milton and May 1976) and correspondingly increased levels of total energy expenditure in foraging (Leonard and Robertson 1992).

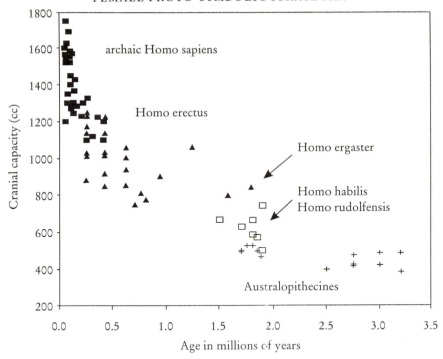

8.2 The relationship between brain size (in cubic centimeters) and time. Archaic *Homo sapiens* includes anatomically modern humans, and Neandertals as well as other archaic *H. sapiens* such as Kabwe and Petralona (data from Aiello and Dean 1990).

Supporting a larger brain, then, required a more costly foraging strategy. For females, this greater energetic stress would have been compounded by the increased reproductive costs involved in the production of larger-brained infants. Smith (1989, 1991) has pointed out very clearly that adult brain size is highly correlated with the age of eruption of the first permanent molar tooth (M1). The larger the adult brain size, the more delayed is the eruption of M1 and the longer is the period of infancy and childhood. In humans the eruption of the M1 takes just about twice as long as it does in the chimpanzee (Aiello and Dean 1990) and the period of dependency on the mother would be correspondingly lengthened. Added to this is the fact that the human infant is born in a more altricial, or less developed, state than is the chimpanzee infant and would be correspondingly more dependent on the mother for a longer period of time (Martin 1990). Furthermore, Foley and Lee (1991) have argued that up until the age of 18 months a human infant is on average about 8.7 per cent more energetically costly than a chimpanzee infant and this is due solely to the high costs of the growth and maintenance of the unusually large human brain. This is reflected in the higher mass specific metabolic rates of human infants in comparison to human adults and gives an indication of the increased energetic demand a human infant would make on its mother during its early years of life.

These analyses compare modern humans and chimpanzees. Earlier hominines with smaller brain sizes than are found in modern humans would have been expected to be under less reproductive stress. Foley and Lee (1991) have estimated that early *Homo* females, living during the long period of apparent stasis in the evolution of brain size (see Figure 8.2), would have been under reproductive stress particularly during the first year after parturition and would have been forced to begin to alter their reproductive strategies (see also Leonard and Robertson 1992).

During this long period of stasis there is nothing in the archaeological record that would suggest sham menstruation or any human-like symbolic or cognitive ability, or for that matter significantly greater paternal investment in the offspring to help lighten the energetic load on the female. Even the reduction in sexual dimorphism that is characteristic of *Homo* in relation to the australopithecines need not imply a move away from inter-male competition for mates towards a more human-like mating strategy (Aiello 1996; McHenry 1994, 1996). Reduction in sexual dimorphism does not need to be explained solely, or even primarily, by a decrease in male body size, as would be implied by these changes in male mating strategy; rather it could be explained by an increase in female size. Such an increase in size would confer on her an essential thermoregulatory advantage in the more open savanna habitat occupied by these hominines (Wheeler 1992). It could also have helped to offset some of the reproductive costs of larger brains by helping her to move more efficiently over larger foraging ranges and also to reduce the cost of carrying dependent offspring. It may have had a further distinct reproductive advantage since the cost of lactation tends to be relatively lower in a larger-bodied animal than in a smaller-bodied one (Martin 1984).

We suggest that the increased energetic costs of the first phase of brain expansion that culminated in the appearance of *Homo ergaster* and *Homo erectus* were met at least in part by the increase in female body size. Another feature that may also have been important at this stage was development of the considerable fat stores that are characteristic of human females, one of the primary functions of which would be to subsidize the energetic costs of lactation, particularly during periods of relative food shortage (Prentice and Whitehead 1987). We would expect that females came under pressure to conceal ovulation and extend receptivity during this period, both to gain greater attention and more food-sharing from males, and to reduce risks of infanticide by males (cf. Hrdy 1981).

This period could be termed the pre-symbolic stage of hominid evolution. It is important to realize that it also would have been characterized by pre-adaptations to the later development of human cognition that would not have been present in other primates. Of particular importance here are the pre-adaptations to human vocal communication. Dunbar (1992, 1993; Aiello and Dunbar 1993) has proposed that language is a direct result of selection for large group size, a factor that he also implicates in the evolution of brain size. He views language as a means of facilitating social bonding which would allow an individual to reduce its social time budget by simultaneously servicing multiple social relationships. In larger groups this would be a distinct advantage over one-to-one grooming behavior in that vocally based social bonding would free a greater proportion of time for other essential activities, such as foraging and feeding. In the earlier stages of this transition as envisaged for early *Homo*, and particularly *Homo ergaster* and *Homo erectus*, this enhanced vocal "grooming" need not have had a symbolic content. Rather, it may simply have resembled the group chattering found today in gelada baboons (Richman 1976, 1978, 1987; Dunbar 1993) which would express mutual interest and commitment and also instill a sense of social cohesion and well being.

Therefore, during this intermediate period in human evolution, our ancestors would have lived a life with no parallel among either extant humans or nonhuman primates. They would have walked on two legs, lived in larger groups in more open environments, incorporated more high quality foods, and particularly animal-derived food, in their diets, had reduced sexual dimorphism, and relied more on vocal communication (Aiello 1996). It is also possible, although there is no direct evidence, that concealed ovulation with accentuated menstrual bleeding may have functioned to secure greater mating effort from males. What is important to realize, however, is that hominines at this stage of evolution were highly successful and that all evidence indicates that this lifestyle lasted for well over 1 million years.

We believe that the appearance of human cognition is associated with the second phase of brain expansion which would have placed mothers under increasing reproductive stress from about 300,000 years ago. It is at this period that our model predicts the beginnings of sham menstruation. In the early stage of the process, sham menstruation would be situation-dependent, triggered by local incidence of real menstruation. At the later stage, correlating with the onset of a sexual division of labor, sham menstruation would form the basis of a fully symbolic ritual tradition of dance and body-painting comparable with modern ethnographic examples and designed to construct elaborate taboos. The first stage would involve a lesser degree of planning; female coalitions may have relied more on biodegradable materials such as animal blood and plant pigment for cosmetic use. Hence, we would predict only occasional traces of utilized ochre. By contrast, the fully cultural strategy implies greater regularity of performance and foresight in planning and organizing rituals. In this context, we expect regular and abundant ochre use.

The archaeological record suggests that archaic *Homo sapiens* was the first hominine to use iron oxides. There are fewer than a dozen known instances of ochre usage predating the Upper Pleistocene and the majority of these occur in the Late Acheulian and early Middle Stone Age (MSA) in sub-Saharan Africa (see Power and Watts 1996). Beginning with the African MSA2a (possibly from as early as 140,000 BP, the height of the Penultimate Glacial), there is evidence of regular and widespread ochre use, while in MSA2b cave and rockshelter assemblages (from *c.*110,000 BP), ochre has become ubiquitous. The scale of ochre use in southern Africa from the MSA2 onwards is unparalleled elsewhere until the Eurasian Upper Paleolithic. Strong reds occur earliest and massively predominate; black pigments are used very rarely, despite their availability (Knight *et al.* 1995). Functional uses for ochre (e.g. in treatment of hides) were then, and remain today, subordinate to ritual and symbolic uses (Watts n.d.; Knight *et al.* 1995). The use of red ochre in Africa contrasts markedly with the picture in Europe before the Upper Paleolithic. The amount of pigment found in French Middle Paleolithic sites is considerably less, and black manganese predominates (Couraud 1991). It seems that most Neandertal pigment use occurred during the late Mousterian (60–34,000 BP). Only during the Chatelperronean, when Neandertals are believed to have been in contact with modern humans, is there a significant increase in amounts of red ochre.

Archaeological evidence for the sexual division of labor during this period remains inconclusive. Stringer and Gamble (1993) argue for the foundation of a "modern" behavioral repertoire, including sexual division of labor, by anatomically modern humans in the phase 60–40,000 BP. Their evidence for this is primarily the greater structuring of "campsites." But southern African MSA cave and rockshelter sites already show structuring similar to that found in the Holocene (since the end of the Pleistocene) (Deacon 1992; Henderson 1992). Grindstones, a processing facility indicative of planning depth, are also found in MSA sites (see Knight *et al.* 1995).

There are no grounds for inferring differences of technological or hunting ability between Neandertals and early anatomically modern humans. Both were equally capable of hunting prime age adults of medium, and sometimes larger, body size (Klein 1989; Stiner 1993). But the point at issue is not hunting ability as such. Rather it is the distribution of the product which matters. Trinkaus (1993) interprets the morphology of Neandertals and early anatomically modern humans to suggest that there may have been greater division of labor by age and possibly sex among Levantine early moderns compared with Neandertals. There is also a high level of stress and trauma in Neandertal skeletons (Trinkaus 1992) and an apparently unusually high level of young adult mortality (Trinkaus 1995).

Therefore, the evidence as it stands is not inconsistent with an incipient symbolic organization of the sexual division of labor, associated with regular ritual use of red pigment, at the period of the emergence of anatomically modern humans. Archaic *Homo sapiens* outside Africa may have utilized context-dependent sham menstruation. But it appears to be in Africa that this strategy was raised to the level of habitual performance (cf. Soffer 1992), establishing the first ritual and symbolic tradition. Reproductive success is strongly correlated with female survivorship, particularly in the young adult years. It is possible that, faced with the escalating energetic stress associated with large brain size, Neandertal females did not alter their reproductive strategies in the same way that early anatomically modern females did. As a result, they may have experienced greater reproductive stress, higher levels of morbidity, and lower infant survivorship. We feel that the novel strategies suggested here would have relieved reproductive stress on young, fertile females. Furthermore, this could have been a significant factor in the rapid population increase at the transition to the Upper Paleolithic (and Later Stone Age) that has been postulated on the basis of both genetic and craniometric data (Harpending *et al.* 1993; Relethford and Harpending 1994). We propose that by this stage anatomically modern females had consummated a strategy of using sham menstrual ritual to secure systematic provisioning from males.

CONCLUSION

We have advanced a sociobiological model for the evolution of symbolism and cognition, premised on the observation that encephalization would have placed hominine females under considerable reproductive stress. Modern human female reproductive characteristics, such as concealed ovulation, the tendency to ovulatory synchrony, and accentuated menstruation acting as a "flag" of imminent fertility would have functioned in ancestral populations as mechanisms for raising levels of male investment. A female coalitionary strategy of cosmetic manipulation of menstrual (imminent fertility) signals – sham menstruation, or artificial synchrony – would effectively form a pre-adaptation to ritual. Collective, deceptive sexual signalling by females exercised a proto-symbolic capacity for sustaining and referring to shared imaginary constructs. A fully symbolic strategy was consummated when women constructed taboos on menstrual signals to motivate male logistic hunting, thereby establishing the sexual division of labor. Modern hunter–gatherer ethnography, and the fossil and archaeological records for human evolution, are compatible with this model.

ACKNOWLEDGEMENTS

The authors would like to thank Lori Hager for inviting us to contribute to this volume. Robin Dunbar, Chris Knight, and Paul Turke have been very helpful with comment and criticism on early drafts for this chapter. We also thank Catherine Arthur for discussions on her modelling of female reproductive synchrony, Ian Watts for extensive discussions concerning his analysis of the southern African ochre record, and Peter Wheeler for discussions on the thermoregulatory and energetic constraints on the hominines.

BIBLIOGRAPHY

Aiello, L. C. (1996) "Hominine preadapations for language and cognition," in P. Mellars and K. Gibson (eds.) *Modelling the Early Human Mind*, Cambridge: McDonald Institute Monograph Series, pp. 89–99.

—— and Dean, M. C. (1990) *An Introduction to Human Evolutionary Anatomy*, London: Academic Press.

—— and Dunbar, R. I. M. (1993) "Neocortex size, group size, and the evolution of language," *Current Anthropology* 34: 184–193.

—— and Wheeler, P. (1995) "The expensive tissue hypothesis: the brain and the digestive system in human and primate evolution," *Current Anthropology* 36: 199–221.

Alexander, R. D. and Noonan, K. M. (1979) "Concealment of ovulation, parental care, and human social evolution," in N. Chagnon and W. Irons (eds) *Evolutionary Biology and Human Social Behavior*, North Scituate, MA: Duxbury Press, pp. 436–453.

Arthur, C. (1994) "Synchrony in human evolution: a female reproductive strategy," unpublished MSc thesis, University of London.

Baker, R. R. and Bellis, M. A. (1993) "Human sperm competition: ejaculate adjustment by males and the function of masturbation," *Animal Behavior* 46: 861–885.

Biesele, M. (1993) *Women Like Meat. The Folklore and Foraging Ideology of the Kalahari Ju/'hoan*, Johannesburg and Indiana: Witwatersrand University Press.

Byrne, R. and Whiten, A. (1988) *Machiavellian Intelligence. Social Expertise and the Evolution of Intellect in Monkeys, Apes and Humans*, Oxford: Clarendon Press.

Chase, P. G. (1994) "On symbols and the Palaeolithic," *Current Anthropology* 35(5): 627–629.

Clutton-Brock, T. H. and Harvey, P. H. (1977) "Species differences in feeding and ranging behavior in primates," in T. H. Clutton-Brock (ed.) *Primate Ecology: Studies of Feeding and Ranging Behavior in Lemurs, Monkeys and Apes*, New York: Academic Press, pp. 557–579.

Couraud, C. (1991) "Les pigments des grottes d'Arcy-sur-Cure (Yonne)," *Gallia Préhistoire* 33: 17–52.

Crowell, A. L. and Hitchcock, R. K. (1978) "Basarwa ambush hunting in Botswana," *Botswana Notes and Records* 10: 37–51.

Cutler, W. B., Garcia, C. R., and Krieger, A. M. (1980) "Sporadic sexual behavior and menstrual cycle length in women," *Hormones and Behavior* 14: 163–172.

Deacon, H. (1992) "Southern Africa and modern human origins," *Philosophical Transactions of the Royal Society of London*, Series B, 337: 177–184.

Dunbar, R. I. M. (1988) *Primate Social Systems*, London and Sydney: Croom Helm.

—— (1992) "Neocortex size as a constraint on group size in primates," *Journal of Human Evolution* 22: 469–493.

—— (1993) "Co-evolution of neocortex size, group size, and language in humans," *Behavioral and Brain Sciences* 16: 681–735.

Durkheim, E. (1965 [1912]) *The Elementary Forms of the Religious Life*, New York: Free Press.

Fedigan, L. M. (1986) "The changing role of women in models of human evolution," *Annual Review of Anthropology* 15: 25–66.

Foley, R. A. and Lee, P. C. (1991) "Ecology and energetics of encephalization in hominid evolution," *Philosophical Transactions of the Royal Society of London* 334: 223–232.

Garlake, P. (1987) *The Painted Caves. An Introduction to the Prehistoric Art of Zimbabwe*, Harare: Modus Publications.

Graham, C. (1991) "Menstrual synchrony: an update and review," *Human Nature* 2 (4): 293–311.

Gunn, D. L., Jenkin. P. M., and Gunn, A. L. (1937) "Menstrual periodicity: statistical observations on a large sample of normal cases," *Journal of Obstetrics and Gynecology of the British Empire* 44: 839.

Haraway, D. (1989) *Primate Visions: Gender, Race and Nature in the World of Modern Science*, New York and London: Routledge.

Harpending, H. C., Sherry, S. T., Rogers, A. R., and Stoneking, M. (1993) "The genetic structure of ancient human populations," *Current Anthropology* 34: 483–496.

Hawkes, K., O'Connell, J. F., and Blurton-Jones, N. G. (1992) "Hunting income patterns among the Hadza: big game, common goods, foraging goals and the evolution of the human diet," *Philosophical Transactions of the Royal Society of London*, Series B, 334: 243–291.

Henderson, Z. (1992) "The context of some Middle Stone Age hearths at Klasies River Shelter 1B: Implications for understanding human behaviour," *South African Field Archaeology* 1: 14–26.

Hewitt, R. L. (1986) *Structure, Meaning and Ritual in the Narratives of the Southern San*, Hamburg: Helmut Buske Verlag (Quellen zur Khoisan-Forschung 2).

Hill, K. (1982) "Hunting and human evolution," *Journal of Human Evolution* 11: 521–544.

Hrdy, S. B. (1981) *The Woman That Never Evolved*, Cambridge, MA: Harvard University Press.

Isaac, G. Ll. (1971) "The diet of early man: aspects of archaeological evidence from lower and middle Pleistocene sites in Africa," *World Archaeology* 21: 278–299.

Klein, R. (1989) "Biological and behavioural perspectives on modern human origins in southern Africa," in P. Mellars and C. Stringer (eds) *The Human Revolution*, Edinburgh: Edinburgh University Press, pp. 529–546.

Knight, C. D. (1991) *Blood Relations: Menstruation and the Origins of Culture*, New Haven and London: Yale University Press.

—— (1996) "Darwinism and collective representations," in J. Steele and S. Shennan (eds) *The Archaeology of Human Ancestry: Power, Sex and Tradition*, London: Routledge, pp. 331–346.

—— , Power, C., and Watts, I. (1995) "The human symbolic revolution: a Darwinian account," *Cambridge Archaeological Journal* 5(1): 75–114.

Knowlton, N. (1979) "Reproductive synchrony, parental investment and the evolutionary dynamics of sexual selection," *Animal Behavior* 27: 1022–1033.

Krebs, J. R. and Dawkins, R. (1984) "Animal signals, mind-reading and manipulation," in J. R. Krebs and N. B. Davies (eds) *Behavioural Ecology: An Evolutionary Approach*, Oxford: Blackwell Scientific Publications, pp. 380–402.

Lancaster, J. (1975) *Primate Behavior and the Emergence of Human Culture*, New York: Holt, Rinehart and Winston.

Lee, R. and DeVore, I. (eds) (1968) *Man the Hunter*, Chicago: Aldine.

Leigh, S. (1992) "Cranial capacity evolution in *Homo erectus* and early *Homo sapiens*," *American Journal of Physical Anthropology* 87: 1–13.

Leonard, W. R. and Robertson, M. L. (1992) "Nutritional requirements and human evolution: a bioenergetics model," *American Journal of Human Biology* 4: 179–195.

Lewis-Williams, J. D. (1981) *Believing and Seeing: Symbolic Meanings in Southern San Rock Paintings*, London: Academic Press.

Lovejoy, C. O. (1981) "The origin of man," *Science* 211: 341–350.

McClintock, M. K. (1971) "Menstrual synchrony and suppression," *Nature* 229: 244–245.

McHenry, H.M. (1994) "Behavioural ecological implications of early hominid body size," *Journal of Human Evolution* 27: 77–87.

—— (1996) "Sexual dimorphism in fossil hominids and its socioecological implications," in J. Steele and S. Shennan (eds) *The Archaeology of Human Ancestry: Power, Sex, and Tradition*, London: Routledge, pp. 91–109.

Marshack, A. (1975) "Exploring the mind of Ice Age Man," *National Geographic* 147 (1): 64–89.

Martin, R. D. (1984) "Scaling effects and adaptive strategies in mammalian lactation," *Symposia of the Zoological Society of London*, 51: 87–117.

—— (1990) *Primate Origins and Evolution*, London: Chapman and Hall.

—— (1992) "Female cycles in relation to paternity in primate societies," in R. D. Martin, A. F. Dixson and E. J. Wickings (eds) *Paternity in Primates: Genetic tests and theories*, Basel: Karger, pp.238–274.

Menaker, W. and Menaker, A. (1959) "Lunar periodicity in human reproduction: a likely unit of biological time," *The American Journal of Obstetrics and Gynecology* 77: 905–914.

Milton, K. and May, M. L. (1976) "Body weight, diet and home range in primates," *Nature* 259: 459–462.

Peacock, N. (1991) "Rethinking the sexual division of labor: reproduction and women's work among the Efe," in M. di Leonardo (ed.) *Gender at the Crossroads of Knowledge: Feminist Anthropology in the Postmodern Era*, Berkeley: University of California Press, pp. 339–360.

Power, C. and Watts, I. (1996) "Female strategies and collective behaviour: the archaeology of earliest *Homo sapiens sapiens*," in J. Steele and S. Shennan (eds) *The Archaeology of Human Ancestry: Power, Sex and Tradition*, London: Routledge, pp. 306–330.

Prentice, A. M. and Whitehead, R. G. (1987) "The energetics of human reproduction," *Symposia of the Zoological Society of London* 57: 275–304.

Profet, M. (1993) "Menstruation as a defense against pathogens transported by sperm," *Quarterly Review of Biology* 68(3): 335–386.

Rappaport, R. A. (1979) "The obvious aspects of ritual," in *Ecology, Meaning and Religion*, Berkeley: North Atlantic, pp. 173–221.

Relethford, J. H. and Harpending, H. C. (1994) "Craniometric variation, genetic theory and modern human origins," *American Journal of Physical Anthropology* 95(3): 249–270.

Richman, B. (1976) "Some vocal distinctive features used by gelada monkeys," *Journal of the Acoustic Society of America*, 60: 718–724.

—— (1978) "The synchronisation of voices by gelada monkeys," *Primates* 19: 569–581.

—— (1987) "Rhythm and melody in gelada vocal exchanges," *Primates* 28: 199–223.

Rightmire, G. P. (1981) "Patterns in the evolution of *Homo erectus*," *Paleobiology* 7: 241–246.

Shostak, M. (1983) *Nisa: the Life and Words of a !Kung Woman*, Harmondsworth: Penguin.

Sillén-Tullberg, B. and Møller, A. P. (1993) "The relationship between concealed ovulation and mating systems in anthropoid primates: a phylogenetic analysis," *American Naturalist* 141: 1–25.

Smith, B. H. (1989) "Dental development as a measure of life history in primates," *Evolution* 43: 683–688.

—— (1991) "Dental development and the evolution of life history in Hominidae," *American Journal of Physical Anthropology* 86: 157–174.

Soffer, O. (1992) "Social transformations at the Middle to Upper Palaeolithic transition: the implications of the European record," in G. Braüer and F. H. Smith (eds) *Continuity or Replacement. Controversies in Homo Sapiens Evolution*, Rotterdam and Brookfield: Balkema, pp. 247–259.

Solomon, A. (1992) "Gender, representation and power in San ethnography and rock art," *Journal of Anthropological Archaeology* 11: 291–329.

Stiner, M. (1993) "Modern human origins – faunal perspectives," *Annual Review of Anthropology* 22: 55–82.

Stoddart, D. M. (1986) "The role of olfaction in the evolution of human sexual biology: an hypothesis," *Man* 21: 514–520.

Stringer, C. and Gamble, C. (1993) *In Search of the Neanderthals: Solving the Puzzle of Human Origins*, London: Thames and Hudson.

Tanner, N. M. (1981) *On Becoming Human*, Cambridge: Cambridge University Press.

Trinkaus, E. (1992) "Paleontological perspectives on Neandertal behavior," in M. Toussaint (ed.) *Cinq millions d'années, l'aventure humaine*, ERAUL 56, pp. 151–176.

—— (1993) "Femoral neck-shaft angles of the Qafzeh-Skhul early modern humans, and activity levels among immature Near Eastern Middle Palaeolithic hominids," *Journal of Human Evolution* 25: 393–416.

—— (1995) "Neandertal Mortality Patterns," *Journal of Archaeological Sciences* 22(1): 121–142.

Turke, P. W. (1984) "Effects of ovulatory concealment and synchrony on proto-hominid mating systems and parental roles," *Ethology and Sociobiology* 5: 33–44.

—— (1988) "Concealed ovulation, menstrual synchrony and paternal investment," in E. E. Filsinger (ed.) *Biosocial Perspectives on the Family*, Beverly Hills and London: Sage Publications, pp. 119–136.

Vollman, R. F. (1977) *The Menstrual Cycle*, New York: Knopf.

Watts, I. (n.d.) "The origins of symbolic culture: the southern African Middle Stone Age and Khoisan ethnography," PhD thesis, University of London, in prep.

Weller, L. and Weller, A. (1993) "Human menstrual synchrony: a critical assessment," *Neuroscience and Biobehavioural Reviews* 17: 427–439.

Wheeler, P. E. (1992) "The thermoregulatory advantages of large body size for hominids foraging in savannah environments," *Journal of Human Evolution* 23: 351–362.

Woodburn, J. (1982) "Social dimensions of death in four African hunting and gathering societies," in M. Bloch and J. Parry (eds) *Death and the Regeneration of Life*, Cambridge: Cambridge University Press, pp. 187–210.

Wright, B. (1968) *Rock Art of the Pilbara Region, North-West Australia*, Canberra: Australian Institute of Aboriginal Studies.

Ziegler, T. E., Epple, G., Snowdon, C. T., Porter, T. A., Belcher, A. M., and Küderling, I. (1993) "Detection of the chemical signals of ovulation in the cotton-top tamarin, *Saguinus oedipus*," *Animal Behavior* 45: 313–322.

9

MOBILIZING IDEOLOGIES
Paleolithic "art," gender trouble, and
thinking about alternatives
Margaret W. Conkey

INTRODUCTION[1]

A few years ago I attended a small rock art conference in South Africa, which focused almost exclusively on the rich and complex rock art repertoire of that country. One evening, we took our boxes of wine back to the conference room to watch videos, including a recently released video about Lascaux – the famous painted Ice Age cave in southwestern France – a video that had been made as part of the commemoration of the 50 years' celebration of Lascaux's discovery in 1940. After the video, my South African colleague – and perhaps one of the most important voices in rock art research today – David Lewis-Williams, asked me to say a few things about the current state of research in Paleolithic art. The room went hush, and I was struck by the rapt attention to, if not veneration of, the topic. As David pointed out later, I could have gone on and on . . . What is it that has generated such awe and interest, such engagement in and mystique of these few hundred caves and rock-shelters, clustered in what is today southern France and northern Spain? Having just spent almost four weeks traipsing about in some of the most magnificent countryside I have ever been in, observing only a handful of what must be more than 100,000 painted rock art sites in South Africa, I was perplexed that for these researchers there was still such reverence for the "decorated" caves of Ice Age Europe.

What has it been about these visual images that has captivated not only archaeologists but, of course, the public? What is it about the ideas, ideologies and prehistories that the images have mobilized for us that has seduced us? In just a nine-month period in 1954, there were 43,000 visitors to Lascaux; no wonder they had to close it due to deteriorating internal conditions. In a Glyn Daniel history of archaeology (1967), he has a chapter on "Discovery and Decipherment," which are themselves still the (only thinly veiled) *raisons d'être* of archaeology. Here he recounts what he calls the paramount discoveries, the discovery stories that are perpetuated as our disciplinary anchors: the Schliemanns at Troy, and Paleolithic art caves in the late nineteenth century; King Tut's tomb and the royal cemetery at Ur in the early twentieth century.

Over and over again, one hears the stories of the famous children and their role in the discoveries of Paleolithic art – little Maria Sautuola being awestruck by the "bulls" on the ceiling of Altamira (in 1879: "Papa, Papa, toros!"); the three sons of Count Henri Begouen exploring the caves of the Volp River in the French Pyrénées, and finding the preserved clay bison at Le Tuc d'Audoubert (1912), and their later exploration of unknown galleries and crevices to discover the magnificent engravings and so-called "Sorcerer" of Les Trois Frères (1914); and last, but not least, there are the four schoolboys of Montignac, France, who supposedly – as the story goes, though it's not quite that way – followed their dog, Robot, down a hole to encounter the majesty of imagery at Lascaux (1940). No doubt these stories with their youthful, untrained heroes and heroines who happen upon some of the "wonders" of the world add to the discovery allure of archaeology, which today has been taken up by such unlikely and self-constructed "media-heroes" as Indiana Jones and Don Johanson.

To probe fully into the ways in which "Paleolithic art"– as we have labelled it – has both mobilized certain ideologies in the present about "the past" and has, as well, been used to infer the ideologies and expressions of the Paleolithic makers and users is obviously a complex, rich, and fascinating topic, which I cannot begin to cover here. For the purposes of this chapter, I attempt only three things: first, in a general consideration of how visual images "work" in the structuring of interpretation how the imagery of and about "Paleolithic art" illustrates (*sic*) several issues. Second, I will examine aspects of one particular "class" of Paleolithic images – the so-called "Venus" figurines – to elaborate on the ways in which the imagery of and about "Paleolithic art" has been and still is deployed in constructing the relationships of the present with the past, especially in the negotiation of difference, including difference(s) of gender. And third, I will begin a consideration of the challenging concerns that require us to consider alternatives: what then, given our critiques, do we want in our imagery of the past?

THE IMAGERY OF "PALEOLITHIC ART" AND THE STRUCTURING OF INTERPRETATION

There are at least two broad categories of imagery that deal with Paleolithic art; first, there is the illustration of the so-called "art" itself – in photographs and drawings. As well, there are the reconstructions (by nineteenth- and especially twentieth-century artists) of the making and (much less frequently) of the "using" or "viewing" of the imagery. And there is, of course, the inter-relationship of the two: what images, for example, are most frequently portrayed as images, and which images and objects are those represented in artists' reconstructions? Interestingly enough – but perhaps not surprisingly – none of the more "serious" textbooks on Paleolithic art (e.g., Leroi-Gourhan 1965, 1982; Ucko and Rosenfeld 1967; Sieveking 1979; Bahn and

Vertut 1988; Delporte 1990) use any of the reconstructions. The one exception is in Pfeiffer's book (1982: 21), which illustrates only one reconstruction, but as an historical document; namely, the 1870 lithograph (Figuier 1870: Figure 68) depicting the three "artists at work" (see also Hadingham 1979: 198). The most abundant source of artists' reconstructions – other than the famous Burian book (Augusta and Burian 1960), which has seven of Paleolithic art – are popular science and archaeology journals (e.g., *National Geographic, Natural History, Archaeology*) and books (e.g., *The Emergence of Man* or Time-Life series); encyclopedias; and especially children's books, which is perhaps expectable. These reconstructions are, however, regularly used in public lectures and introductory archaeology courses; many (perhaps especially the Burian ones [Augusta and Burian 1960]) have become familiar icons of and for "Life in the Upper Paleolithic" (a mere (!) 25–30,000-year time bloc).

Although these artists' reconstructions don't feature explicitly in the professional literature – and this includes almost all introductory archaeology and anthropology texts that almost always feature at least one or two images or objects of Paleolithic art – they are extremely informative about – if not "bring to life" and "make real" – preconceptions, assumptions, theoretical positions, and interpretations that underlie and/or are promoted by the written texts that do not use the reconstructions (Moser 1993, 1992a, b; Gifford-Gonzalez 1993; Moser and Gamble, in press). But despite the fact that these reconstructions are primarily in the more popular genres, it is usually the case in archaeology that the relationship between the present and the past is most exposed precisely at that interface between professional archaeologists and the public, precisely in those arenas of archaeology – such as these journals and children's books – that are in the wider public and popular domain. Although I will not here engage in a systematic analysis of these reproductions (see, for example, Gifford-Gonzalez 1993), I will use them as they illustrate various points.

One of the more interesting aspects of the visual treatments of "Paleolithic art" is how the images of and about the "art" have contributed to our constructions and definitions of art. Our interpretations and visual treatments of Paleolithic art can inform a great deal on what we think about the western art system and about art, more generally. What is crucial here is the fact that the category, art, is an historically contingent concept, with its own history that involves very specific conceptual and definitional transformations. Certain general changes in, for example, what "activities" comprise the "fine arts" (cf., Kristeller 1964; Michel 1886) crystallized in the very years that the painted Paleolithic caves were being discovered and that their authenticity (as veritable productions of Ice Age hunter–gatherer "savages") was being debated and ultimately accepted (in 1902). It is at this time that easel painting and the novel, in particular, emerged as "especially developed and valorized" (Murray 1991: 19–20) as the premier of the "fine arts". In light of this (and other factors) it is not so surprising, on the one hand, that it was *not* the engraved and incised images of the Paleolithic on bone and stone (known as portable art, found in stratigraphic contexts as early as the 1860s) that challenged the evolutionarily inclined late nineteenth-century nouveau-archaeologists, but the polychrome paintings on cave walls. The portable art, the crafts of carving, were more readily accepted, whereas the sometimes polychrome and "naturalistic" paintings in cave "galleries" were unlikely products of distant beings who had barely been admitted into the human family. On the other hand, we are not surprised to note that – even before (as in the oft-reproduced 1870s lithograph, Figure 9.1), and especially after, the discovery of the painted and engraved walls – the "cave artists" are depicted as if they were easel painters of the nineteenth and twentieth centuries!

9.1 A lithograph that seems to have first appeared in 1870 (Figuier 1870), which depicts an Ice Age artist working on the engraving of a plaquette as if it were propped up on an easel. Note that this lithograph was made some nine or more years prior to the "discovery" of the first cave paintings (Altamira, 1879), but during the time when painting was considered the most elevated of the arts. (Reprinted with acknowledgement of the copyright of Figuier, 1870.)

As Murray points out (1991: 9), "art" has been, in our sociohistorical circumstances of the last centuries, an "honorific title (after Becker 1982: 37) that, when bestowed, grants special status to an object or performance, and often by association, to those acknowledged as its creators." Given that "art" is not a category or distinct concept in many (if not most) ethnographically studied groups, and given that "art" – and whatever (variable) attributes this implies – is not inherent in any given object or image, but is produced, what is interesting are the ways in which the visual *treatments* of the Paleolithic imagery have facilitated, if not allowed, our making the materials and images *into* "art." It is through *our* acts of (interpretive) power and *our* acts of (re)production that the materials and images have become "Paleolithic art." It is "art by appropriation," for we have not only appropriated it for framed living-room pictures, postcards, posters, and reproductions (I have a key chain with a lifesize replica of the "Venus of Willendorf," bought for me by an archaeology colleague at the site), but we have made much of it into "our" kind of art: the caves are described as having "galleries" (why not passageways or corridors?), and the vocabulary for discussion is often in our terms, such as "naturalism," "schematism," "perspective" (e.g., Lorblanchet 1992). But even without the vocabulary, the re-presentation of the images conforms to certain parameters of our "art": individual objects are displayed in museums and in texts as separate and neutral objects, often on velvet backdrops and suspended in "neutral" space; perforated objects are displayed as necklaces with a very modern and western symmetry, when we don't even know if they were suspended, much less as-necklace.

The reproductions promote a view of either the-artist-as-individual-master or the artist-as-specialist-with-helpers; thus, a hierarchy in the social production of imagery is conveyed. This is most obviously described by Breuil as "pupils" for the "specialists" in the text that accompanies his 1949 watercolors for children. Not surprisingly, the hierarchy is familiar, based on specific attributes of sex and age: it is women and/or children, in particular, who "service" the specialists – by grinding pigments, by adding details to the main image. In groups of all adult males, the hierarchy is by age: see Burian's illustration (Augusta and Burian 1960: Plate 44) of the young boys holding the lamps for the adult male painter, or Breuil's (1949: 68–69) white-haired "master" sculptors being supplied with pigments. As the caption reads on another reconstruction of cave painting: "Assisted by an apprentice holding an oil lamp and another preparing pigments, a Cro-Magnon artist paints a horse on a cave wall" (Prideaux *et al.* 1973: 27).

One needs no training in visual analysis to notice that the artists are inevitably and always males; in a quite thorough study of dozens and dozens of reconstructions of the making of Paleolithic imagery, only two females as painters/artists are known, and both are in publications that are quite obscure to the archaeological world: one (Figure 9.2, commissioned by myself!) was to accompany the article on Paleolithic art in a youth edition of *Science Year,*

9.2 A pictorial reconstruction of painting a cave wall, which is unusual in that a woman is shown to be actively involved in the actual painting process (using some sort of a moss tampon-style application, which has been documented). The reconstruction was done to accompany a short article for *Science Year 1988*, (Conkey 1988), reporting on the show at the American Museum of Natural History, "Dark Caves, Bright Visions."

1988 (Conkey 1988); the other in a children's book, in French, where the illustrator is a woman (Véronique Ageorges in Ageorges and de Saint-Blaquant 1989). Of course, it is amazing that cartoonists "got" the problem a long time ago, and have often explicitly reminded us of the blatant bias. In two different cartoons, both with two women painting cave walls, in one a woman turns to the other and says: "You don't suppose the men are going to get credit for this, too?"; and in the other a woman is asking: "Doesn't it strike you as weird that none of the great artists have ever been men?" I wish the famous Gorilla Girls – a "bunch of masked avengers [who] fight sexism and racism in the art world, with facts [and] humor ... " (Gorilla Girls 1995) – would take on the world of Paleolithic art as depicted in contemporary archaeology.

Nowhere has the debate over the gender of the Paleolithic "artist" been more transparent than with the implied sex/gender of the creator of the famous so-called "Sorcerer" image at Les Trois Frères for a (October, 1988) special issue of *National Geographic*. The original artist's drawing, done in collaboration with a North American male anthropological archaeologist of the Paleolithic, made it a possibility – if you look at it quite closely – that the image-maker could have been female. The drapery over the torso, with its slit down the sides and concomitant shading, allowed the possibility for there to be female breasts. Just before the issue went to press, a senior (male) editor stopped the presses over this "unacceptable" image. After consulting a prehistorian – not an ethnographer or ethnologist – as an authority on whether there was any ethnographic evidence for female high–status artists/shamans – and armed with the (ethnographically naive) reply that it was "unlikely" – the senior editor demanded the scene be re-drawn and published accordingly. As re-drawn, there is no side slit in the bodice and there is little possibility of inferring that the artist could be a female, although in a generous admission, enough ambiguity remains in the figure – who faces the wall being decorated, while wearing an antlered headdress – that one could perhaps argue that it still "might be" taken as ambiguous enough to be a female. However, there is an extensive corpus of representations of image-making from over the decades that has consistently and repetitively told us otherwise. Whether about our society or others – even some 15,000 years ago – the senior editor is reported to have said that "our" audience (*National Geographic*'s circulation is second only to *TV Guide*) will not accept (or approve of) a woman in either role – "master" artist or shaman. The implication is clear: if this Paleolithic imagery is "art," it is to be "art" as we understand it and as we construct it in the western art system (for a powerful and to-the-point reminder of the gender/race issues of contemporary art, see Gorilla Girls 1995).

And, of course, it is a particular notion of "art" that is preferred. Given that there are at least two somewhat competing perspectives of "art," as discussed below, it seems as if the Paleolithic images are treated and re-presented as much closer to the more traditional nineteenth- and twentieth-centuries' view of art as embodying the aesthetic. This modern view (emergent since the seventeenth century) establishes "art" as the making of things (or performances) that "have significant form and beauty" (Murray 1991: 7). This has been contested by the view that directs attention to the social matrix from which aesthetic expression and "art" (in the sense defined above) emerge and are produced. That is, "art" is anything so designated by people or institutions granted such authority within a society (cf., e.g., Alpers 1983; Bourdieu 1984; Baxandall 1985; Becker 1982; Williams 1977, 1983; Wolff 1981).

Murray (1991) reminds us how these definitions have become categories (though not mutually exclusive), and how they have "served since the advent of Modernism as binary oppositions in western political debates about cultural issues, more broadly" (see, e.g., Kramer 1989, 1990 [view 1] versus Rosaldo 1989 [view 2]). Paleolithic art has clearly been conscripted into view 1 ("aesthetic production") more so than as view 2 ("symbolic production"). This may well stem from the the earliest debate (1879–1902) over the Ice Age authenticity of cave art in which, it seems, the "art" could be taken as evidence of aesthetic sensibilities (and the art-for-art's-sake view still has active proponents, e.g., Halverson 1987), but not as evidence for "deep" cognitive and active symbolic production.

The artists' reconstructions of Paleolithic image-making almost never illustrate art being "used," only being "made." Burian's drawing (Augusta and Burian 1960: Plate 48) of the so-called bear ritual at Montespan stands out as an exception. In this reconstruction, a group of costumed dancers/hunters (all men) are shooting at the large clay "sculpted" lump interpreted as a bear. This was drawn during the late 1950s, while the sympathetic hunting magic account (cf. Breuil 1952) for the "why" of Paleolithic art held the interpretive sway. And, although there are one or two more recent illustrations that imply the con-text and practices of imagery, such as the so-called "shaman" holding forth, torch in hand, in the Lascaux Hall of Bulls (Pfeiffer 1986; see also the initiation scene in Prideaux *et al.* 1973: 32–33), the images of Paleolithic art are otherwise either of the art being made (in the aesthetic and art studio-like context) or of the art being passively worn or admired (see e.g. Figure 9.10b).

Lastly, although this is a related topic worthy of lengthy discussion and probing that I cannot take up here, we should not ignore the role that Paleolithic art – especially as documented *by* the French, and especially *in* France – has played in elevating and perpetuating not only a Franco-centric view of prehistory, but a Franco-centric (and more widely Euro-centric) history of art. To have "ART" is very much a part of constructing a certain version of "us" and "The Way We Were," as was once proclaimed on the cover of *Newsweek* (November 10, 1986). That the French Ministry of Culture had some of the imagery from the rather spectacular 1994 discovery of the new cave art site of the Grotte Chauvet up and around the world on the Internet within days of the discovery had the effect of reinforcing the longstanding association between "early art" and France. Given that the past few years have seen increasing acceptance of the existence of late Pleistocene imagery as a more global phenomenon (Conkey, Soffer, and Stratmann 1997), and that the appearance of modern humans in southwestern Europe was quite late in the spread of *Homo sapiens sapiens*, the re-assertion of the geo-focus of the emergence of human-ness as evidenced by art in France should not be passed over.

And yet, despite the techniques of re-presentation that promote an aestheticism, ambivalences about this imagery-as-art remain. The western art system – especially of the mid-nineteenth and twentieth centuries – emphasizes individual creativity, innovation, and formalized schooling, whereas (following Adam 1949: 32 and Murray 1991: 34–35), most "primitive" – and, by (not unproblematic) extension, prehistoric – art was considered to be "essentially religious," conservative, produced by untrained and anonymous (but naturally artistic) creators, "who were not expressing individuality but a direct and vital connection to natural forces" (Murray 1991: 35; see also Price 1989). Kubler (1986) has suggested that eidetic individuals – that is,

179

those with some specific mental envisioning processes that today are found rarely and mostly in children – may have played a primary role in the image-making of the Upper Paleolithic (see Kurten 1980 for the extension of this into Ice Age fiction). The assumption that, as Breuil called it in his sketch book [scene sixteen], (it was) "Big Game Hunting Which Brought Forth the Art" (1949: 63) lies behind the explicit premises of the sympathetic hunting magic hypothesis that held sway as the dominant account for "why Paleolithic art" well into the 1960s (which still lurks behind many current theories). On the one hand, the interpretations of the imagery since the Leroi-Gourhan interpretive revolution of the early 1960s have decidedly emphasized the "universal humanism" of Upper Paleolithic art-makers (deriving from the climate of opinion surrounding the founding of the Musée de l'Homme, see Clifford 1988; Conkey, in press), including the specific connection made by Leroi-Gourhan himself. Many of the titles ascribed to his *magnum opus* of 1965 include reference to this as a specifically *western* art (e.g., *The Art of Prehistoric Man in Western Europe*) (see Leroi-Gourhan 1965). But, on the other hand, much of the story for "why" the imagery has to do with its roots in "natural forces." For example, Leroi-Gourhan's entire schemata for the so-called "signs" found on many cave walls derive directly from depictions of male and especially female genitalia (Figure 9.3). Although the animals depicted on cave walls are no longer thought to be there because they were primarily "good to eat" (as the sympathetic hunting magic explanation held), but because they were "good to think" (after Leroi-Gourhan 1965), it is still the case that bison and horse, as the preferred species (comprising some 60 per cent of the wall imagery), are "natural forces" that inspired metaphoric and spiritual iconography. And despite many alternatives that have been put forth, and despite the fact that there are no substantive arguments to make the case, the female images are *consistently* interpreted as referring to fertility, reproduction (or even sexual gratification, cf. Collins and Onians 1978; Guthrie 1984); in other words, as deriving from and in "the service" of biological and natural forces.

That most French scholars today, among others, are reluctant to probe more deeply into the "whys" of the imagery than to say that it "must be something religious," perpetuates a vitalistic and abstracted account. Thus, while most treatments of the imagery convey some connections to the western art system – and indeed, it is usually the (all too briefly treated) subject-matter of the opening chapters in art history texts, and it is always in introductory archaeology texts as a visual hallmark of the achievement of fully modern symbolic behaviors – it is usually presented as a kind of visual appreciation. As with most formalist studies of primitive art, Paleolithic art is often treated in an "uncritical and breathless celebration ... that does little to illuminate the origins or meanings of these objects and much to reinforce stereotypes" (Murray 1991: 44).

Thus, it is not surprising to see that the same few images are repeatedly

	OVAL	RECTANGLE	KEY SHAPE		HOOK	BARB	DOT
NORMAL							
SIMPLIFIED							
DERIVED							

"WIDE" AND "NARROW" SIGNS are considered by the author to be symbolic of the sexes and to have evolved from earlier depic-

tions of female and male figures or sexual organs. Three groups of symbols are shown for each sex, in normal and more abstract forms.

9.3 As indicated by the caption on the graphic itself (from Leroi-Gourhan 1968), these geometric "signs" – that are widespread among the animal imagery in caves and on portable objects – are classified into shapes that are thought by Leroi-Gourhan to have derived from earlier depictions of male and female sexual organs. This is illustrated here to reinforce the point that many interpretations of Paleolithic art take it to have its roots in "natural forces."

shown – for wall art, it is inevitably (e.g., as in ten out of the twenty-six introductory texts I reviewed) either the "Chinese" horse or another image (or images) from Lascaux, *or* one of the bulls from the so-called "Sistine Chapel" (!) of Paleolithic art, Altamira. These very labels are indicative of the way aesthetic and culturally laden "connections" are made, linking the imagery inextricably to known features of art. For the portable art in textbooks, a "Venus" figurine has a 90 per cent chance of being *the* selected figure, either a specific one from those found at Dolni Vestonice (Czech Republic) or the "Venus of Willendorf" (which is, by the way, one of only three specific "Venuses" listed in the *Encyclopedia Britannica* [1984, X: 392] after the entry for "Venus" herself, the "original" Roman and Greek goddess). Often these Paleolithic figurines are displayed in a full-page format, whereas most of them are less than 10 centimeters high. In only one out of twenty-six texts surveyed are there other images of portable art without a "Venus"; in Gamble's (1986) text on *The Palaeolithic Settlement of Europe,* there is only one photograph in the entire book (all other illustrations are line drawings), and that is the cover bearing another widely celebrated "Venus" – head only – that of Brassempouy. Although as a head "she" lacks any primary or secondary sexual features, it is rarely (if ever) considered that "she" might not be a "she." The current excavator of the site refers to "her" as one of his Paleolithic wives, and his favorite one, at that. Occasionally, depending upon the genre of the text, other images are shown, but so-called "necklaces" and "jewelry" (or "decorated weapons") are prevalent in this supporting role. Given that there must be some 500,000 or more images of portable art, the "masterpieces" have, however, been codified into a very small subset of now recognizable and familiarized images.

Thus, there are several specific ways in which Paleolithic imagery, especially the female figurines, are portrayed and displayed that have facilitated the construction and mobilization of culturally-specific (to us, not to the Upper Paleolithic) ideologies, especially about gender. You don't even need to be a feminist to notice this (e.g., Bahn 1986). For example, there is the giganticization of images, so that the "Venuses" of only a few centimeters in size are displayed as almost life-sized, and almost never with a scale (the latter would diminish the aesthetic impact of the image). Oftentimes a wide range of Paleolithic imagery, including the female figurines, is lumped together in a single picture or chart, where images from a wide geographic range and from over tens of thousands of years are presented *en bloc* as a homogenized set of imagery that invites a homogeneous interpretation. In the repetitive selection of the same few images, the diversity of imagery is avoided and one or two images are, in effect, made to "stand for it all." In showing only the apparently "robust" female figurines (as on the distribution map of "Venuses" [Champion *et al.* 1986: 85]), the sense of a diversity is also inhibited and certain stereotypes are promoted. In the repetitive and routinized deployment of a limited – and thus, limiting – stock of images, one's imagination about meanings, about possible interpretations, and about "the past" are inhibited.

ON AMBIVALENCES: THE CASE OF THE "VENUS" FIGURINES

Despite the welcoming of art-in-Europe as a hallmark of modern humans and of "us," the ways in which Paleolithic images are selected and used in illustrations (and in reconstructions) attests to considerable ambivalence, as I will now suggest with specific reference to the so-called "Venus" female figurines. There is ambivalence about not just the status of these images as "art" (as we know it or, more properly, as we have constructed it), but also about our positionings relative to these "art-makers." There is a consistent tension at work, a simultaneous distancing and yet "pulling closer" to these makers and images. At some level we want these images – and, by extension, their makers – within "our" cultural prowess, yet not too close. We still use the label Cro-Magnons, although it has long been recognized that the people to whom the label refers are 100 per cent *Homo sapiens sapiens* and that the label is a "survival" from the 1860s' discoveries at the site of Cro-Magnon when the biocultural status of the remains was not assured. While some might argue that we use the term now to mark them, chronologically, as the earliest of the fully modern humans in southwest Europe, a certain distancing from us is, nonetheless, in effect, retained by the continued use of the term. Unlike what Hager (1992) has discussed with respect to the "swinging pendulum" of the relative "humanity" and relational status of Neandertals, our grand positioning *vis-à-vis* Upper Paleolithic "a.m. (anatomically modern) humans" has remained the same – we have always accepted them as modern humans – but there is a great deal of movement and ambivalence within this relational space. For example, as I have argued elsewhere (Conkey 1993, in press), the hunting-magic interpretation for cave art was based on a notion that the makers were not quite us, attributing their invocation of magic to their being pre-religious, pre-scientific humans. With the acceptance of Leroi-Gourhan's structuralist account (1958; 1965) for the imagery, which is founded on the premise that the makers engaged in the fundamental structuring processes of the fully human mind and that their works attest to a certain "universal humanism," the makers of Paleolithic imagery were more closely drawn into the circle of humanity (see also Leroi-Gourhan's 1964 volume, *Les Religions de la Préhistoire*.

One of the most popular set of images of Paleolithic art is the so-called "Venus" figurines. Although it is not exactly clear if *every* statuette, figurine, and certain bas-reliefs of females can legitimately be called a "Venus," since any precise definition of "Venus-ness" is never given, there is a recognized category that has been in place since the mid-nineteenth-century finds of female (and other) figurines. There are indeed a number of specific images for which the label "Venus of . . ." is regularly used – e.g., those from the sites of Willendorf, Brassempouy, Laussel, Lespugue; the first two are included as such in the *Encyclopedia Britannica*, for example, along with the Venus de Milo. What is infrequently discussed and almost never recognized is: (1) the marked diversity in the morphologies, shapes, and "appearances" of these images – no, they are not all "fat" and "reproductively charged" (but cf. Nelson 1990); (2) that there is a diversity in how humans are depicted in Paleolithic art that reveals that identifiably female statuettes are not the primary nor even the majority of human depictions (most are anthropo-morphic or un-sexable humans, cf. Delporte 1979; 1993); and (3) the historical circumstances of discovery, "naming," and interpretations that have led to the "Venus" nomenclature and all that that has implied (or fostered), in terms of interpretation and display.

Obviously, this is a much wider issue than can be taken on here, and one that involves more than just the visual displays and illustrative uses of the female figurines. On the one hand, are there powerful critiques to be made of the way these images – especially the ones that have been selected as "representative," although they, in fact, are not – have been used to promulgate deeply problematic gender ideologies (cf. Conkey and Williams 1991; Mack 1990, 1992; Nelson 1990). On the other hand, it is provocative to note that the uses of these images have continued to cultivate ambivalent notions of the "noble savage" that is in us – because it is in these figurines of "our" ancestors; they have been especially ambivalent with regard to certain racial implications.

One of the deeper observations about the use of these images to construct and reinforce contemporary (and now contested) gender ideologies has implications for considering racial ideologies as well. This is from the work of Rainer Mack (1990, 1992) who shows persuasively how the combination of the textual discourse about some of the Venuses – that is, what the (male) authors write about and how they describe these images – with the display of certain deliberately selected female images (that are, in turn, almost always "suspended" in an open and therefore "available" space) relies upon and effects a hierarchical and gendered subject–object relationship – that is, the appropriation of a female body by a masculine subject (see especially the discussion by Onians in Collins and Onians 1978). It is not irrelevant that just before the first discoveries of Upper Paleolithic female statuettes (the first in 1864, another in 1867), a shift in the art historical canon had taken place, with the female nude replacing (in the 1830s) the male nude not only as the idealized body of high art but as the embodiment of the erotic (Solomon-Godeau 1992; see also Adler and Pointon 1993; Pointon 1990). Furthermore, as the displays of human males and females in the first wax museums in France (late nineteenth century) attest, "the female" was both nude and pregnant (Solomon-Godeau 1992).

Although the first female figurines discovered – those from Laugerie-Basse

(Dordogne, France) (Figure 9.4) and another one that has never become much celebrated (from Trou-Magrite, Belgium) – are clearly (to us) not within what has become the stereotypic morphological ideal of the "fecund," "generous," "curvaceous," or "voluptuous" (e.g., Prideaux *et al.* 1973: 92, 98, but also "mis-shapened") Venus, the Laugerie-Basse one was named as "Venus" (by "her" discoverer, the Marquis of Vibraye). More specifically, she was named the "Venus Impudique," in that – with a vulvar mark and no clothing indicated – the slender, headless and nude female was considered "immodest" or "unchaste." The immediate predecessors in western culture to such a Venus label are the famous Venus de Milo (1820) and, perhaps more importantly in some ways, the so-called Hottentot Venus. The latter was a living woman, Saartjie Baartman by name, brought in 1810 from South Africa

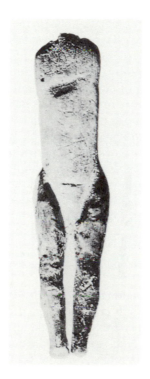

9.4 The so-called "Venus Impudique" from the site of Laugerie-Basse (Dordogne, France), which is reported to have been discovered around 1864. As such, it is likely to be the first discovery of a female statuette. While lacking what has become (to us) the stereotypic attributes of "Venus" figurines – namely, large breasts, wide hips and notable body fat – it nonetheless was named a "Venus" by the excavator, the Marquis de Vibraye (Delporte 1993: 67–68), but as "impudique" it is taken to be an immature and chaste female or a young girl ("une fillette"). The figurine is made from ivory, and is only 77 mm. in size. (Photo from Delporte 1993: 67.)

to London to be "displayed" (see Altick 1978; Schrire 1984 on this phenomenon of "displaying" living "primitives"); her sad fate soon thereafter was to
die in Paris where

> Cuvier examined her while she was alive and then dissected her after
> her death in 1815. Today her skeleton stands in the Musée de l'Homme,
> gazing up at her reknowned "tablier" or genitalia which float wistfully
> in a jar above Broca's similarly bottled, but now leaking, brain (Altick
> 1978: 268–272, Gould 1982).
>
> (Schrire 1984: 4)

Today, in a newly post-apartheid South Africa, there is considerable debate
and contest over these remains (which the Musée de l'Homme claims were
removed from display decades ago), their rightful resting-place (certain groups
are demanding they be returned for burial), and who should "own" them.
Saartjie Baartman has become a crucial symbol in the fiery crucible of the South
African politics of identity (e.g., Raghavan 1996; Schrire and Gordon 1996).

However, as this cartoon of the so-called Hottentot Venus unambiguously
conveys (Figure 9.5), her steatopygia – that is, the particular morphological
feature of her buttocks – was of considerable "interest", if not a fixation, to
the Victorian world in the years prior to the debut of evolutionary theories
and all that they came to imply (e.g., Gilman 1985). In fact, the label of
"Venus" for this Hottentot woman can easily be seen to have been as much
of a pun or joke as a label to evoke beauty (Schrire: personal communication).
In the 1830s and 1840s, the existence and documentation of South African
rock art was taken up, with its multitude of human images including the
regular depiction of females with greater or lesser degrees of steatopygia .
With the 1890s' discoveries of more female (and other!) figurines in Paleolithic deposits – especially at Brassempouy and the controversial ones from
Grimaldi – the implied link between at least some of the Paleolithic figures
with Khoi-San (Hottentot/Bushmen) or, more generally, African peoples was
very much in evidence.

Two particularly compelling images "tell" of this putative link and how it
persisted well into the twentieth century: first, there is the artists' drawing
that suggests not just a comparison, but a link, an affinity, between the so-
called "Venus" of Willendorf (excavated in 1908) and the steatopygous Khoi-
San peoples (Figure 9.6), although, as Nelson eloquently pointed out (1990:
12), the Willendorf figure does not, in fact, exhibit steatopygia (which refers
to protruding buttocks). Rather, if the Paleolithic figurine from Willendorf
is a realistic rendering (and that, of course, is another rarely asked question),
the figurine exhibits steatomeria, which is broad, not protruding, hips (that
the Khoi-San "mother" and "daughter" in the figure do not have). Another
striking implication of a link, and one that simultaneously also invokes the
problematic gender ideologies derived from "the gaze," is the image on one
of the columns of the Institute of Human Paleontology in Paris, built in 1926

9.5 One of many political cartoons that appeared in conjunction with the "showing" of the so-called "Hottentot Venus" (Saartje Baartman) in London in 1810, which attest to the fixation of the Londoners with her steatopygia. (Taken from Altick 1978.)

9.6 On the left of this illustration are two views of a cast of the "Venus of Willendorf" (which is only 110mm. in size, made from limestone, with traces of red coloring), which are juxtaposed (in Hadingham 1979: 222) with what Hadingham describes as "a reconstruction of a Paleolithic woman published in 1936 and based on an absurdly literal interpretation on the features displayed by the Willendorf and other stylized figurines." (Hadingham credits the American Museum of Natural History for both photographs.)

(Figure 9.7). Here the famous "Venus" from Laussel (or, "La Dame à la Corne," as it is sometimes labeled), also discovered in 1908, is shown being admired by a male of distinctly Khoi-San features. Whereas these visual renderings do not just allow or encourage, but also require, a link to be made, this is far more difficult to put into words, although the idea – and the ambivalences about its implications – is found in at least two not unimportant texts.

In Sollas's classic 1911 (second edition 1915) treatise, unambiguously titled *Ancient Hunters and their Modern Representatives*, he discusses the then recently discovered female and other figurines from Laussel and Willendorf in quite explicit reference to the presence of "negroid" attributes (such as "the hair is rendered in a way that suggests the 'pepper-corn' tufts of Negroid races" [Sollas 1915: 375]), and as presenting just those characteristics which we have enumerated as peculiar to the Bushmen, Hottentots, and Accas (Sollas 1915: 379). Sollas goes on to say that:

> Certainly the artists who carved the figurines have shown in the clearest manner that they were intimately acquainted with women who presented a close anatomical resemblance to the existing Bushwomen, and the presumption is that these women were of their own race. The supposed connexion between the Aurignacians and the Bushmen begins to acquire an appearance of probability
>
> (Sollas 1915: 381)

9.7 A provocative scene that has been carved onto one of the pillars of the Institut de Paleontologie Humaine (suggested date 1926), which depicts a nude man who is strikingly of Khoi-San/Bushman-like features and is here in the act of making the so-called "Venus of Laussel" (La "Dame à la Corne"), discovered in 1911 on a slab of limestone that was detached from the cave wall by the excavator Lalanne (the sculpture is 42 cm.; the site of Laussel is the Dordogne, France). (Photo by Marcia-Anne Dobres, with permission.)

Sollas then suggests that these Bushman-like peoples co-existed somehow with a more modern European sort (as evidenced then in certain skeletons), yet he even suggests that the Willendorf statuette is a very "Negroid-looking" one. Simplistically, the model he proposes is that the Negroid Aurignacians were of Mediterranean origin, who met some pressure from a European population, and so, in being "driven out of Europe," they retreated to suggestive locales such as pre-dynastic Egypt. In sum, their "nearer representatives, who retained most fully their culture, habits and disposition, were the Bushmen as we first knew them" (p. 389). "If we succeed in finding traces of the Aurignacian culture among the Bushmen, this is because these were a comparatively unprogressive race" (p. 388).

While we can forgive Sollas much of his version, this early discussion and correlation of the so-called Aurignacians (one of the earliest, c. 30,000 years ago, industrial cultures of the Upper Paleolithic) with Bushman/Negroid traits (all lumped together) was not only a way to account for the categorization of both Bushmen and prehistoric peoples into a single category of "unprogressive," but also a way to imply that the Bushmen were "survivals" of much earlier peoples (as was held by contemporary unilineal evolutionary theory). This also used the features of the female figurines to distance the figurine-makers and those they represented from the modern (civilized) humans of the early twentieth century.

As well, in the first systematic (and "most prestigious") collection and description of female figurines made by Edouard Piette between 1888 and 1902 (published in 1895, that is, prior to the Laussel and Willendorf finds), the author – perhaps the most important figure in the excavation and collection of portable art – is quite explicit about noting the diversity in the Paleolithic figurines and statuettes. Piette even sets up two distinct categories– the "svelte" ones and the "adipose" ones. Since he considered the figurines to be portraits of real individuals, he felt that we could "read" them directly as physical anthropological evidence on "racial types." In fact, Sollas cites Piette as his source that "as early as 1895, before the mural [cave] paintings had been recognized as genuine, Piette was able to assert that if we seek the nearest representatives of the people represented by the steatopygous statu-ettes, we shall find them among the Bushmen" (Sollas 1915: 379–380, quoting Piette 1895: 137). Thus, Piette had made links to the hair-dos of the pharaonic Egyptians and, by extension, suggested the presence of a Negroid population, at least at the Italian site of Grimaldi (Figure 9.8). Or, as Lalanne – the excavator of Laussel – said in 1912 (at an International Anthropology and Prehistoric Archaeology Conference), the apparent steatopygia of the statu-ettes was evidence for "an ethnic link between the races who peopled quaternary Europe and the Egyptian neolithic" (cited in Delporte 1993: 266).

This idea of geneaological links with (i.e., actually being of Negroid/African stock) or, at least, there having been some intermingling with a Negroid population had considerable hold on the prehistorians of the early twentieth century. And again, it is in illustrations that this possibility could be taken up more readily without having to engage in the specific implications if it were, in fact, the case. One of Breuil's explicitly "imaginative" drawings for children (Figure 9.9) – this time of a shell ornament trade fair – depicts, says Breuil, a "nomad Mediterranean population carrying their stock of shells from place to place across Western Europe" to exchange them. Thus, as Breuil describes this scene, "the six men and women on the left are of southern race, as is the old negroid slave in the center of the right-hand group who belong to the local population" (Breuil 1949: 75).

Although a great variety of interpretations for the female depictions has been bandied about over the century, our archaeological predecessors seem to have been willing to entertain a greater range of possibilities than current archaeologists – from the figures as representing real personages, to being priestesses, to being images of fertility, to numerous variants on the theme that they were representatives of an ideal aesthetic, often called "the barbarian ideal of beauty" ("l'idéal barbare de beauté," after Dechelette 1908, quoted in Delporte 1993: 266). Today, the diversity of the imagery is rarely discussed

9.8 The so-called "Negroid Head" made from green steatite (24mm. high), from the Grimaldi series of figurines, found in rock shelters along a cliff on the Mediterranean shore of Italy (see Bisson and White, in press; Delporte 1993: 97–107). It is particularly in the details of the hairstyle and in the similarities of hairstyle among figurines from Laussel, Brassempouy, and later Willendorf that authors, beginning with Piette (e.g., 1895), inferred a Negroid population at Grimaldi. They suggested perhaps this was a descendant Neandertal group who exhibit later manifestations, as seen in the hairstyles of the pharaonic Egyptians. (Photo from Delporte 1993: 106.)

(except in specialized treatises, e.g., Delporte 1979, 1993; Gvozdover 1989a, b; but cf. Nelson 1990 for an exception), and the "fertility cult" notion is almost always imputed, explicitly or implicitly: "Les femmes sont precieuse" reads the label on a set of female figurines in a French children's book on prehistory. That women are primarily to be thought of in terms of reproduction and in direct association with biological (more so than cultural) functions reinforces the deeply problematic hierarchical gender ideologies which dominate today's illustrative "use" of the female imagery, and which are aggravated by the blatant absence of women as active agents in the image-making, if not in Upper Paleolithic life then more generally. If the links between "us" and "them" are to be reinforced, it is interesting that just as in the case of Art more generally, the selected depictions, the artists'

191

9.9 This is one of the many wonderful – and informative – watercolors painted by
the Abbé Breuil, who is widely regarded as having been the key figure in the
documentation and interpretation of Paleolithic art well into the late 1950s. The
drawings were done for a children's book, and, as with most pictorial reconstructions,
reveal much about assumptions and imaginative possibilities for life in Ice Age Europe.
In this particular scene (Scene Twenty-Two in Breuil 1949: 73–75) Breuil depicts and
describes a scene of "trading with ornamental shells." In his description of what is
going on, he notes that the "six men and women on the left are of southern race, as
is the old negroid slave in the center of the right-hand group who belong to the local
population," with "local" here meaning a specific location in the Charente of France.
In the original, which is in color, the darker skins and hair of these negroids is quite
noticeable, and Breuil, as with other prehistorians, connects these negroid peoples
with the Mediterranean sites.

reconstructions, and the "use" and treatment of the figurines conform more
to the canons of the western art system – female as erotically charged, female
as a site of male desire, female as object, etc. – and thus "say" and illustrate
more about the attributes of a very gendered western art than about the
making of and involvement with the figurines in Paleolithic societies.

While Paleolithic art is "breathlessly celebrated" and drawn into the
Eurocentric sphere of cultural prowess (in which the west's tradition that
females, or parts of them – as in the so-called vulvas – are not only suitable but
desirous objects of depiction), there has been as well a simultaneous distancing from those features and aspects that evoke "savagery" or "the
primitive." Certain issues of racial ambivalence have more recently been

192

taken into some consideration, however, perhaps due to the increasing acceptance of the idea that there are earlier and earlier modern humans in Africa and the Middle East, before they "appear" in the Eurocentric heartland (France and Spain). New reconstructions of early modern humans are less Caucasian, such as that on the cover of the September 16, 1991 issue of *U.S. News and World Report* ("Early Man: The Radical New View of Where We Came From"). See also the provocative yet well-grounded notions on modern humans as "the Blacks," and Neandertals as "the Whites" (Kurten 1980, 1986), and note especially Gould's comments on this in the 1995 preface to Kurten 1980.

But there is still "gender trouble." In Figures 9.10a and 9.10b we can compare the white figurine-maker admiring his object (with, however, notably "dark-skinned" women in the background [in Howell *et al.* 1965]), with the newer version of a "darker" male – but still very much admiring his (female) object (drawn by Joubert, in Monnier 1992). Despite some changing racial notions, the issue of *U.S News and World Report* cited above has only one image of a female in the article, and this is in the form of a female figurine (the popular one from Dolni Vestonice), which is referred to as part of a probable "fertility cult." While the skin color implications of modern humans as being "out of Africa" are being taken seriously, the absence of depictions of females as active agents in Paleolithic life, coupled with their continued presence as objects of the cultural manipulation of natural forces, only perpetutates long-standing gendered stereotypes.

What I have tried to touch on so far is how pervasively the imagery of and about Paleolithic art has constructed, contributed to, and perpetuated a number of issues in our relationship with the past that have long troubled the interpretive integrity of archaeology. On the one hand, the way much of the imagery is displayed (what images are selected, how they are estheticized, etc.) and the artists' reconstructions (especially in the more popular journals and books) contribute to (if not actualize) the definition of these materials as "Art," and a very specific concept of "Art" at that. On the other hand, it is still an "art" that has links to that of the "primitive world," in its connections to "natural forces," in being essentially "religious" in motivation, and in being paraded about in our texts primarily for its qualities of "visual appreciation" that attest silently to its given position as either "a demonstrable pinnacle in the course of human symbolic evolution" – in direct association with *The Emergence of Man* (cover of Prideaux *et al.* 1973) – or "the beginnings of (western) art." We have yet to probe deeply into the imagery in its own local historical contexts, which has been denied by these more stereotypic positions that the imagery (and its display) have occupied.

Further, we can "see" similar ambiguities about a specific group of images, the female figurines: elevated to serving as icons of not just Upper Paleolithic material culture but of the position and attitude towards Upper Paleolithic (and, by extension, all) women. They are simultaneously "celebrated" for

9.10a

9.10b

9.10 These two illustrations are shown as a comparison to suggest that between 1965 (Figure 9.10a) and 1992 (Figure 9.10b), our ideas about the skin color of early anatomically modern humans have changed, primarily due to the "out of Africa" hypothesis and its implications. Figure 9.10a (Howell *et al.* 1965: 155) depicts "A New Kind of Man," referring to "the men who replaced the neanderthals in Europe" thought to be "intellectually and culturally superior" to their predecessors. The "new man" is noticeably white, yet the surrounding women are noticeably dark-skinned. While the "replacement" is dated to some 35,000 years ago, the actual appearance of female figurines is dated considerably later.

Figure 9.10b is a more recent pictorial reconstruction with a similar theme – the male artist making and gazing at "his" object and image, the female figurine. Here the intent man is darker in skin coloration although, as discussed in the text, the relationship of "man" to "female-object" is comparable to that in the 1965 drawing. This 1992 drawing is in a French children's book on prehistory (Monnier 1992: 22, illustration by Pierre Joubert).

certain attributes exhibited by only a few out of the many – large breasts, heavy thighs, wide hips (but only rarely protruding buttocks) – attributes which, through the discourses of the authors, have often been made into a list of "erotically-charged body parts" ("made passive and available for possession" [Mack 1990]); attributes that are marshaled in the service of fertility and reproductive success; attributes that have a historical link with Khoi-San (and, by extension, a problematically homogenized notion of Negroid/African) peoples that, at least in terms of the progressive evolutionary scenarios that informed initial anthropological inquiry (and have not fully gone away), were taken to be "closer" (in their relative primitivism) to these Upper Paleolithic peoples than are the modern (i.e., "civilized") Europeans. That it has become increasingly likely that modern humans – "us" – are, in fact, "out of Africa" renders it ironic that our late nineteenth- and early twentieth-century archaeological predecessors deployed certain African-like traits to distance us from full and unqualified acceptance of Upper Paleolithic peoples into the fully modern human circle.

While many of my colleagues in Paleolithic archaeology have tended to dismiss the study of "Paleolithic art" as too humanistic, as lacking a firm chronology, and as "noise" in the preferred concentration on the adaptive systems of Paleolithic technology and economy, their use and their sanctioning (if only implicitly) of illustrations indicates that there are entrenched, pervasive, and very specific ideas about the imagery as "art" and what it can "show" about "Life in the Upper Paleolithic". As Ernst Gombrich (1985: 79–80) once noted, it was by the 1920s (earlier, says Lears 1981) that "the visual arts provided us with the shortest route to the mentality of civilizations otherwise inaccessible to us." Since most Paleolithic archaeologists have yet to engage seriously with how we might make robust inferences about the mentality of Upper Paleolithic peoples, they have allowed and encouraged the use and deployment of visual strategies and visual images of the Paleolithic visual arts to "speak" for them. But, as I hope I have begun to elucidate, the pictures they have encouraged are ambivalent and say more about our relationship(s) with "the past" and about certain ideologies in the present than about how the visual images might have mobilized ideologies and relationships in Paleolithic times and contexts.

ARE THERE ALTERNATIVES? WHAT DO WE REALLY WANT IN OUR IMAGERY?

There has been an increasing interest in and concern for the uses of visual imagery in archaeology, what Moser (e.g., 1992a) has called "the visual language of archaeology," including recent symposia at national meetings (Conkey and Hager 1992; Conkey and Moser 1994), publications (e.g. Gifford-Gonzalez 1993; Moser 1992a, b; Gamble 1992; Moser and Gamble, in press), museum exhibits and corresponding catalogues (e.g., Musée Départemental de Préhistoire de Solutré 1990), and the incorporation of its role in prehistoric interpretation into more academic texts (e.g., in Stringer and Gamble 1993). Although certain interpretive positions in archaeology often seem to have solidified with acceptance and use, even these are constantly being reworked and refigured. Those images that are deployed in the service of archaeological interpretation are never fully conventionalized; their meanings are not static nor do they inhere in the imagery itself. While many images may seem to serve as tacit stocks of knowledge, implicating and mobilizing by their very appearance an entire range of further notions, assumptions, and even ideologies, even these images are not impermeable to multiple uses, meanings, and interpretive roles.

And yet, as I suggested above, there is little doubt that the repetitive and routinized deployment of a limited stock of images, such as of and for "Paleolithic art," have led to and then reinforced a limited, if not monolithic, understanding of the materials, the contexts, and the production of what are undeniably rich and diverse cultural and archaeological materials. While there is much more that could (and should) be said about how the visual cultures of the Euro-Russian Upper Paleolithic are presented both as objects/images and in artists' reconstructions, and about how an iconographic canon has been generated, deployed, and elaborated, the point of this last section is two-fold.

First, I briefly want to reaffirm – though I cannot here develop further – that the deconstruction of the visual language of archaeology is an important if not crucial part of historicizing archaeological interpretation and of making explicit the genealogies of archaeological interpretation. What we work with today are accumulated histories and accumulated conceptual frameworks that have been formed, enabled, and implemented by visuals. Precisely how these things have happened and are perpetuated and transformed is integral to interpretation today. Yet, although it is perhaps correct to say, as Moser has (1992b), "to analyze visual representations is to expose the conjurer's tricks," the analysis of visualization is more than mere deconstruction, even if it is deconstruction with an aim to understand more than to expose.

Second, and more substantively, I want to take up the question that was raised by the discussants – Whitney Davis and Lucien Taylor – at the American Anthropological Association symposium, "Envisioning the Past" (Conkey and Hager 1992): "Okay, if there are deeply embedded issues of race, class, gender, primitivization, etc. that are being defined and perpetuated in the visuals of archaeology, what's to be done?" That is, what do we want? Is it some form of "politically correct" archaeology? Or what? As Lucien Taylor (1992) noted: "In all the papers there was (inevitably perhaps) so much more about how *not* to envision the past than about the alternative strategies for its actual envisioning." Would everything be just fine if Neandertals were not so nasty, brutish and short, or if women and children were central and not just a "drudge-on-the-hide" (Gifford-Gonzalez 1993) or the servants to the making of Paleolithic art?

Thus, how then do we think about the use of visuals and enact the self-consciousness that we have gained from the deconstructions? Just how do we "defamiliarize the disinterested omniscience that so frequently characterizes the scientific gaze of archaeology" (Taylor 1992)? While this pursuit – of alternatives – could itself be a lengthy one, I will here just begin to suggest the paths along which it might proceed. And, to begin, I quote from the historian of science, Lorraine Daston, who has probed the question of "facts" and "evidence" through the literature on miracles and prodigies in early modern Europe (Daston 1991). In this, and in her other work, she astutely points out that "showing other alternatives are thinkable by no means debunks our current beliefs, it only exposes as fraudulent the absolute authority with which we think them" (as quoted in M.T. 1993: 35).

Of course, a starting alternative would be the rather obvious one of incorporating a fuller representation of actors, so that instead of only males running along the line of human evolution (e.g, as discussed in Conkey and Williams 1991: 116–117, figure 3) females would be included; or if, as is the case, we really have no direct or indirect information as to who the Paleolithic image-makers were, that the reconstructions might include a variety of possibilities – adult women, children, young adults, and so forth.

While the most simple, albeit problematic, reaction to biases has been simply to reverse the message, most of us realize this is not necessarily a solution in that it can itself become a limited and limiting bias. While no one would deny the powerful and important impact that Slocum's (1975) challenge to the "Man the Hunter" account for human evolution made, by taking up the insertion of "Woman the Gatherer" into the blatantly androcentric story, few would also agree that to simply replace "Man the Hunter" with "Woman the Gatherer" as the causal agent in the course of human evolutionary development allows for the exploration of the varieties of gender and social relationships, gender roles, and eventually gender ideologies that must have been at work over the millennia. There is no doubt that to raise such questions, as Slocum did, drew our heretofore numbed attention to the existence of bias and androcentrism (if not sexism), but there are examples of where one totalizing and homogenizing, usually male-centered, account is merely replaced by another such account (as has been suggested about the recent promotion of the "Goddess-centered" account of Old Europe: see Hackett 1989; Weaver 1989; Conkey and Tringham 1995).

Reversals, however, can have an important role in not just exposing bias but in understanding the sources and forms of bias; this is indeed what the Slocum article achieved. No discussion of reversals as one possible strategy can be had without reference to one of the most successful reversals I know, namely that of a pioneering feminist art historian, Linda Nochlin (1988). She begins with a nineteenth-century drawing of "A Woman with Apples," depicting a buxom, topless woman holding a tray of apples, so that the apples and breasts iconically co-mingle on the tray; few of us would look twice at such a drawing, and many might display it in a powder room context. It does nothing to challenge, much less affront, our (enculturated) sensibilities. However, Nochlin commissioned a reversal, which depicts a long-haired gangly man, nude except for his knee-high striped socks, holding a tray in the comparative locale, namely right below the groin, where his penis "co-mingles" with (yes!) a tray of bananas. This indeed takes the viewer aback, and when I show this slide in lectures or classes, the reaction ranges from outright laughter to puritan-like shock. By exposing (and with humor) the fundamentally different notions of what is "acceptable" and familiar imagery, Nochlin uses the reversal not to replace but to challenge the taken-for-granted representational ideologies – and all that lies behind them. Unfortunately, few, if any, such sophisticated reversals or modifications exist (yet?) for archaeology.

I have already discussed above the pressures of contemporary cultural censorship when a reversal is even suggested, as in the case of replacing the original drawing of an ambiguously female artist/shaman incising the lion on the wall at Les Trois Frères for *National Geographic.* But given that we just don't know who – in terms of gender, age, status, or experiential context (initiation rites? shamanistic re-creations of esoteric knowledge? doodling?) – the Paleolithic image-makers were (and it is likely to have been quite an array of possible peoples, over as much as a 30,000-year span of time), this is the very basis for encouraging diversification, varieties, and alternatives even more so than the repetitive, limited normativizing that can now be empirically demonstrated for archaeological reconstructions of Paleolithic art. As Tringham (1994) has argued, for example, ambiguities (such as that in the original artist's rendition of the artist at Les Trois Frères) are to be celebrated or at least made explicit. Alternatives are, in and of themselves, crucial to the development of critical thinking, pedagogy, and even hypothesis-testing (remember Chamberlain's [1897] "multiple working hypotheses"?!), to say nothing of enabling the imagination.

Perhaps my most adamant reply to "what do we really want?" would be to say that we must learn to develop and deploy alternatives and ambiguities, to harness them in our interpretive enterprise. Simply put, when viewers must choose between or among alternatives, the criteria for choice must be made explicit. Further, while competing and dual notions tend to be the preferred route to entertaining alternatives – as in the current duelistic (*sic*) debate over the origins of early anatomically modern humans ("out of Africa" or "regional continuity") – I suggest that, as with most reversals, we need to stretch for more than that, for more then "either/or" and choosing of sides (Moulton 1983, 1986). One particularly interesting case study springs to mind, although we now move out of the specific issues of the Upper Paleolithic and into a later period of archaeological interpretation. This is the case of the so-called "Ice Man."

In the wake of the recent discovery of a frozen man trapped in a glacier some 5,000 years ago at the present-day Austrian–Italian border, which gripped the imaginations and politics of many, the publicity and con-comitant visuals provide a wealth of interpretive fodder. In particular, it is striking to note the diversity of illustrations based on the very same archaeological evidence. Two immediate possibilities emerge. On the one hand, once could (as has Jacobi 1992) take several of the illustrations and compare them as illustrations of a singular scientific event and "find" in a kind of representational analysis. On the other hand, one could use a range of these reconstructions to probe into the relationship between the archae-ological evidence and the drawings, and into the relative validity and grounding for the assumptions behind each drawing.

What is fascinating about Jacobi's (1992) analysis for our purposes here is that he shows – similar to the point made by Mack (1990, 1992) concerning the "Venus" figurines – how there is a kind of Jakobsen-like "intersemiotics" at work. That is, there is a demonstrable relationship between the words and phrases of the text (about the Ice Man) and the drawing presented in each different article that he studied – all French ones: from *L'Express*, one in *Science et Vie* and one in *Paris-Match*. While the artists have each elicited from the text certain "visual stimulations" for their drawings, these very drawings themselves then re-interpret that which has been presented in the form of scientific information. Subsequent to Jacobi's study, which used only three reconstructions, at least a half dozen more – and all strikingly different reconstructions – have appeared in prominent articles. The three in Jacobi's study range from what he describes as (1) the "faceless mannequin," along with a very wordy text, making for a style of depiction that derives from the principles for an ethnographic museum of the early to mid-twentieth century (e.g., Rivière's Musée de l'Homme). With all the detailed equipment labels, an American might be more likely to label this after an outdoor camping display, as an L.L. Bean or REI-style depiction.

(2) the "man who came in from the cold," an ethnographic or travellers'

accounts visual reporting style with almost no text; a kind of "prehistoric Davy Crockett" with a remarkably detailed face.

(3) the Wagnerian Hero or a Bronze Age Tarzan, which is in full color and takes up a full page, which to Jacobi suggests that the artist is just as celebrated as the Ice Man. With, among other traits, the dramatic use of light to illuminate the arrival of the man at the top of a crest, and with cloak thrown open to expose quite a musculature, the journal (*Paris-Match*), suggests Jacobi, clearly allowed or encouraged the artist to imagine this hunter in ways that only tenuously link to the mummy itself.

How can these three (and others, even) be derived from the same archaeological data? Given that archaeological interpretations, and perhaps especially in the visual languages used by archaeology, always "go beyond" the empirical parameters of our archaeological data, what assumptions and agendas are allowed to fill in the space between "fact" and interpretation, between data and representation?

Further, what is interesting about these varied portrayals of the Ice Man is not only the potential for critical comparative analysis but also that they appeared in popular journals. Indeed, while we may think that we, as professionals and scientists, are not influenced or affected scientifically by popular discourse, I have come to see otherwise. In a compelling essay, Moore (1994) takes up the relationship between "the academy" of anthropology and popular writings, showing (using a particular novel, Angela Carter's *The Passion of New Eve*, in relationship to feminist anthropology) how the academic is often the popular "in disguise." It is not only that anthropological and archaeological knowledge goes into popular discourse – in the Ice Man journal articles, into *National Geographic*, into *Time*, or even into fictionalized accounts of the past and the movies based on these (e.g., Auel 1980; Kurten 1980; Thomas 1987) – but it is also the case that anthropological and archaeological knowledge is itself selectively re-confirmed and even reconstructed by that popular discourse.

Thus, it is not merely a matter of getting the editors at *National Geographic* (or *Time*, for that matter, with its March 14, 1994 cover still proclaiming "How Man (*sic*) Began") to reconsider, even to change, to question, and to engage with the labels and the imagery. More, it is to recognize first that there are certain aspects of archaeology – such as human origins, gender relations and gender roles – that have a great deal to do with the present that have become desirable or valuable to the public domain – of which we are a part. Second, therefore, it should not be surprising that many seemingly academic models, which are often only admissible or expressible in visual form, are little more than popular versions in disguise. If we want to acknowledge this and, more importantly, to show precisely and specifically how this is the case, then one way is to use alternative ways of thinking about our categories and concepts and processes of interpretation in order "to destabilize them, and force us to expand our horizons" (Moore 1994: 149). Moore endorses doing this by engaging with fictions, as she does in her essay.[2]

In fictional accounts, but also in the visual displays of everything from (selected) artifacts to pictorial reconstructions of "camp life" or cave painting, there can be imaginative possibilities that our academic and intellectual models must have but that they themselves cannot provide (Moore 1994: 149). A critical evaluation of the specific imaginative impetus that is given to our intellectual models by such things as artists' reconstructions and our visual props can reveal the "conditioned imagination" (Stoczkowski 1994) – "conditioned" that is, by tacit contemporary cultural assumptions and presumptions – that, in turn, almost inevitably "masquerades" (to use Moore's term) as an academic model.

SOME CONCLUDING THOUGHTS

In this chapter, I have tried to introduce an array of issues that have been entangled in the representation of the past, especially the Upper Paleolithic of Europe, and how these have been as much about our relationship to the past as about "the past" *per se*. I have suggested that the kind of ideologies that have been mobilized by artists' reconstructions, or even by the choices of archaeological materials to depict in our texts or lectures, have been more of a certain set of contemporary ideologies than those that might have been "at work" in prehistoric times. While this is no longer a very new kind of observation, I hope that by exposing some of the ways in which this happens we can establish a new archaeological integrity. While this is unlikely to lead us towards what the public or our students may want, namely a more definitive statement as to "this is the way it was" (in the past), there are more gains to be had than from those delimiting statements of closure that pervade the media and the academic reward system of archaeology. I have tried to promote the idea that by healthy critique, by generating alternatives and judicious reversals, by recognizing and exploiting ambiguity, and by using multiple or comparative imagery, displays, and varied reconstructions, perhaps there is hope for emancipation of the archaeological imagination that in turn not merely allows us to gain a better understanding of the human past but also encourages critical thinking.

With the increasing visualization of information in the computer and cyberspace era that is now upon us, with the deployment of computer-generated imagery, media, and visual-based learning systems, often being developed from outside our once less permeable academic circles (but cf. Michaels and Fagan 1993; Tringham 1996 for important exceptions), we must come to grips with what will be only an increasingly visual language for and of the discipline. We need to invest more in alternatives, ambiguities, and imaginations or we'll soon find that the popular media will be telling the stories for us, and, as feminists and scholars concerned with understanding patterned discriminations and difference, with promoting the understanding rather than the control of knowledge, and with encouraging and sustaining critical thinking in the making of responsible global citizens, we are not going to like what is done for us.

NOTES

1 I want to thank those who made possible my 1992 trip to South Africa, especially John Parkington, the University of Capetown, and the South African Social Sciences and Humanities Research Council. As well, many thanks are extended to others who made my stay there both stimulating and truly enjoyable: Jeanette and Hilary Deacon, Martin Hall, Tom Hufman, Chopi Jeradino, David Lewis-Williams, Aron Mazel, Ann Solomon, Lyn Wadley, Royden Yates, and others. In the preparation of this chapter, which is a revised and combined version of two different papers read in co-organized symposia on visual archaeology (Conkey and Hager 1992; Conkey and Moser 1994), I am especially grateful to editor Lori Hager for her infinite patience and encouragement. I owe special debts of intellectual stimulation to Whitney Davis, Diane Gifford-Gonzalez, Stephanie Moser, Carmel Schrire, Lucien Taylor, Ruth Tringham, and Alison Wylie. And despite the best efforts of the University of California, Berkeley, to swamp me out with administrative and student obligations, I deeply appreciate the rich community of scholars in archaeology at Berkeley.

2 As some of the references in the text have suggested, it is possible to take up this question through the fictions of Ice Age Europe, as I have done in an undergraduate course at UC-Berkeley: "Life in Ice Age Europe Through Fiction." By beginning with William Golding's *The Inheritors* (1955), we moved through Auel's (1980) *Clan of the Cave Bear*, then the two Kurten novels, *Dance of the Tiger* (1980, re-issued in 1995 in paperback) and *Singletusk* (1986, but now out of print), and then the two Thomas novels, *Reindeer Moon* (1987) and *Animal Wife* (1990). These last two can be provocatively juxtaposed with early ethnographic accounts by the same author (e.g., Thomas 1987) on life with the Bushmen. And the circle of implicating arguments, begun by our late nineteenth-century archaeological predecessors, can be taken up once again, now re-framed by Moore's suggestions about the source(s) of our academic models.

BIBLIOGRAPHY

Adam, Leonhard (1949) *Primitive Art*. London: Cassell (Penguin).

Adler, Kathleen and Marcia Pointon (1993) *The Body Imaged*. Cambridge: Cambridge University Press.

Ageorges, Véronique and Henri de Saint-Blaquant (1989) *Lascaux et son temps*. Paris: Casterman.

Alpers, Svetlana (1983) *The Art of Describing: Dutch Art in the Seventeenth Century*. Chicago: University of Chicago Press.

Altick, Richard D. (1978) *The Shows of London*. Cambridge, MA and London: Harvard University Press and the Belknap Press.

Auel, Jean (1980) *The Clan of the Cave Bear*. New York: Crown Publishers.

Augusta, J. and Z. Burian (1960) *Prehistoric Man*. London: P. Hamlyn.

Bahn, Paul (1986) "No Sex Please, We're Aurignacians," *Rock Art Research* 3(2): 99–120.

—— and Jean Vertut (1988) *Images of the Ice Age*. London: Bellew Publishing Co., Ltd.

Baxandall, Michael (1972) *Painting and Experience in Fifteenth Century Italy. A Primer in the Social History of Pictorial Style*. Oxford and New York: Oxford University Press.

—— (1985) *Patterns of Intention: On the Historical Explanation of Pictures*. Cambridge: Cambridge University Press.

Becker, Howard (1982) *Art Worlds*. Berkeley and Los Angeles: University of California Press.

Bisson, Michael and Randall White (in press) "Female Imagery from the Paleolithic: The Case of Grimaldi," forthcoming in *Culture: The Journal of the Canadian Anthropolgy Society*.

Bourdieu, Pierre (1984) *Distinction: A Social Critique of the Judgement of Taste*. Cambridge, MA: Harvard University Press.

Breuil, Henri (1949) *Beyond the Bounds of History*. London: P.R. Gawthorn.

—— (1952) *Four Hundred Centuries of Cave Art*. Montignac: Centre d'Etudes et de Documentation Préhistoriques.

Chamberlain, T.C. (1897) "The Method of Multiple Working Hypotheses," *Journal of Geology* 39 (2): 155–165.

Champion, T., C. Gamble, S. Shennan, and A. Whittle (1986) *Prehistoric Europe*. New York: Academic Press.

Clifford, James (1988) *The Predicament of Culture*. Cambridge, MA: Harvard University Press.

Collins, Desmond and John Onians (1978) "The Origins of Art," *Art History* 1(1): 1–25.

Conkey, Margaret W. (1988) "Images from the Ice Age," in *1988, Science Year. The World Book Annual Science Supplement*, pp. 40–55. Chicago: World Book, Inc.

—— (1993) "Humans as Materialists and Symbolists: Image-Making in the Upper Paleolithic of Europe," in *Origins of Humans and Humanness*. D. T. Rasmussen (ed.), pp. 95–118. Boston and London: Jones and Bartlett.

—— (in press) *Paleovisions: Interpreting the Imagery of Ice Age Europe*. New York: W. H. Freeman and Co.

—— and Lori D. Hager (1992) "Envisioning the Past: Visual Forms and the Structuring of Archaeological Interpretation." Symposium for the Annual Meeting of the American Anthropological Association, San Francisco, CA.

—— and Stephanie Moser (1994) "Visualizing the Past." Symposium for the Annual Meeting, Society for American Archaeology, Anaheim, CA.

——, Olga Soffer, and Deborah Stratmann (eds) (1997) *Beyond Art: Pleistocene Image and Symbol*. San Francisco: California Academy of Sciences and University of California Press.

—— and Ruth E. Tringham (1995) "Archaeology and the Goddess: Exploring the Contours of Feminist Archaeology," in *Feminisms in the Academy*. Domna Stanton and Abigail Stewart (eds), pp. 199–247. Ann Arbor, MI: University of Michigan Press.

—— and Sarah Williams (1991) "Original Narratives: The Political Economy of Gender in Archaeology," in *Gender at the Crossroads of Knowledge: Feminist Anthropology in the Postmodern Era*. M. di Leonardo (ed.), pp. 102–139. Berkeley: University of California Press.

Daniel, Glynn (1967) *One Hundred Years of Archaeology*. London: Duckworth.

Daston, Lorraine (1991) "Marvelous Facts and Miraculous Evidence in Early Modern Europe," *Critical Inquiry* 18 (1): 93–124.

Delporte, Henri (1979) *L'Image de la Femme dans l'Art Préhistorique*. Paris: Picard.

—— (1990) *L'Image des Animaux dans l'Art Préhistorique*. Paris: Picard.

—— (1993) *L'Image de la Femme dans l'Art Préhistorique*. (Second edition), Paris: Picard.

Dobres, Marcia-Anne (1992) "Re-considering Venus Figurines: A Feminist Inspired Re-analysis," in *Ancient Images, Ancient Thought: The Archaeology of Ideology*. A. S. Goldsmith, S. Garvie, D. Selin, and J. Smith (eds), pp. 245–262. Calgary Alberta: The Archaeological Association, University of Calgary.

Encyclopedia Britannica (1984) *Encyclopedia Britannica, Micropaedia*: Volume X (fifteenth edition). Chicago: Encyclopedia Britannica, Inc.

Figuier, Louis (1870) *L'Homme Primitif*. Paris: Hachette.

Gamble, Clive (1986) *The Palaeolithic Settlement of Europe*. Cambridge: Cambridge University Press.

—— (1992) Reflections from a Darkened Room. *Antiquity* 66(251): 426–431.

Gifford-Gonzalez, Diane (1993) "You Can Hide, But You Can't Run: Representations of Women's Work in Illustrations of Paleolithic Life," *Visual Anthropology Review* 9(1): 3–21.

Gilman, Sander (1985) *Differences and Pathologies. Stereotypes of Sexuality, Race and Madness*. Ithaca, NY: Cornell University Press.

Gombrich, Ernst (1985) *Meditations on a Hobby Horse and Other Essays on the Theory of Art* (1963; second edn 1985). London: Phaidon Publishers.

Gorilla Girls (1995) *Confessions of the Gorilla Girls*. New York: Harper Perennial/ HarperCollins.

Gould, Stephen Jay (1982) "The Hottentot Venus," *Natural History* 10: 22–27.

Guthrie, R. Dale (1984) "Ethological Observations from Palaeolithic Art," in *La Contribution de la Zoologie et de l'Ethologie à l'Interprétation de l'Art des Peuples Chasseurs Préhistoriques*. H.-G. Bandi, W. Huber, M.-R. Sauter, and B. Sitter (eds), pp. 35–74. Saint-Paul Fribourg, Switzerland: Editions Universitaires Fribourg Suisse.

Gvozdover, Maria (1989a) "The Typology of Female Figurines of the Kostenki Paleolithic Culture," *Soviet Anthropology and Archaeology,* special issue: *Female Imagery in the Paleolithic: An Introduction to the Work of M.D. Gvozdover* 27(4): 32–94.

—— (1989b) "Ornamental Decoration on Artifacts of the Kostenki Culture," *Soviet Anthropology and Archaeology,* special issue: *Female Imagery in the Paleolithic: An Introduction to the Work of M.D. Gvozdover* 27(4): 8–31.

Hackett, Joanne (1989) "Can A Sexist Model Liberate Us?" *Journal of Feminist Studies in Religion* 5: 65–76.

Hadingham, Evan (1979) *Secrets of the Ice Age: A Reappraisal of Prehistoric Man*. New York: Walker and Co.

Hager, Lori D. (1992) "Transformations in the 'Primitive': An Analysis of Pictorial Representations of the Neanderthals," paper presented at the Annual Meeting of the American Anthropological Association, San Francisco, CA.

Halverson, John (1987) "Art for Art's Sake in the Paleolithic," *Current Anthropology* 28(1): 63–89.

Howell, F. Clark and the Editors of Time-Life Books (1965) *Early Man*. New York: Time-Life Books.

Jacobi, Daniel (1992) "L'Homme des Glaciers: Sur une Découverte et Trois Dessins," *Alliage: Culture, Science, Technique* 14: 67–75.

Kramer, Hilton (1989) "Reflections on 'Bad Art'," *TNC* 8 (3): 5–8.

—— (1990) "Photography Until Now," *TNC* 8 (9): 5–8.

Kristeller, Paul Oskar (1980) [1964] "The Modern System of the Arts," in *Renaissance Thought and the Arts: Collected Essays*, P. O. Kristeller (ed.), pp. 163–227. Princeton: Princeton University Press.

Kubler, George (1986) "Eidetic Imagery and Paleolithic Art," *Journal of Psychology* 119 (6): 557–565.

Kurten, Bjorn (1980) *Dance of the Tiger*. New York: Random House/Pantheon. 1995 printing, University of California Press.

—— (1986) *Singletusk*. New York: Random House/Pantheon.

Lears, Jackson (1981) *No Place of Grace: Anti-Modernism and the Transformation of American Culture, 1800–1920*. New York: Pantheon Books.

Leroi-Gourhan, André (1958) "Repartition et groupement des animaux dans l'art pariétal paléolithique," *Bulletin de la Societé Préhistorique Française* 55: 515–552.

—— (1964) *Les Religions de la Préhistoire*. Paris: Presses Universitaires de France.

—— (1965) *Treasures of Prehistoric Art*. New York: Harry Abrams.

—— (1968) *The Evolution of Palaeolithic Art*. *Scientific American* (February): 58–74.

—— (1982) *The Dawn of European Art: An Introduction to Paleolithic Cave Painting*. Cambridge: Cambridge University Press.

Lorblanchet, M. (1992) "Le Triomphe du Naturalisme dans l'Art Paléolithique," in *The Limitations of Archaeological Knowledge*. J. Clottes and T. Shay (eds), pp. 115–140. Liège: ERAUL, No. 49. Université de Liège, Service de Préhistoire. Etudes et Recherches Archéologiques à l'Université de Liège.

Mack, Rainer T. (1990) "Reading the Archaeology of the Female Body," *Qui Parle* 4(1): 79–97.

—— (1992) "Gendered Site: Archaeology, Representation, and the Female Body," in *Ancient Images, Ancient Thought: The Archaeology of Ideology*. A. S. Goldsmith, S. Garvie, D. Selin and J. Smith, eds, pp. 235–244. Calgary, Alberta: Archaeological Association, University of Calgary.

Michaels, George and Brian Fagan (1993) "Introduction to Archaeology: A Computer and Internet Course," Santa Barbara, CA: University of California, Santa Barbara.

Michel, André (1886) "Art: General Considerations," in *La Grande Encyclopedie: Inventaire Raisonée de Sciences, des Lettres et des Arts*. 3, Part I. Paris: H. Laminrault et Cie.

Monnier, Jean-Laurent (1992) "Les Hommes de la Préhistoire." (Illustrations de Pierre Joubert). Rennes, France: Editions Ouest-France.

Moore, Henrietta (1994) "The Feminist Anthropologist and the Passion(s) of New Eve," in *A Passion for Difference*. Henrietta Moore (ed.), pp. 129–150. Cambridge: Polity Press.

Moser, Stephanie (1992a) "The Visual Language of Archaeology: A Case Study of the Neanderthals," *Antiquity* 66: 831–44.

—— (1992b) "Visual Thinking in Archaeology," paper presented at the Annual Meetings, American Anthropological Association, San Francisco, CA.

—— (1993) "Gender Stereotyping in Pictoral Reconstructions of Human Origins," in *Women in Archaeology: A Feminist Critique*. Hilary duCros and Laurajane Smith (eds), pp. 75–92. Occasional Papers in Prehistory, No. 23. Canberra: The Australian National University, Research School of Prehistoric Studies.

—— and Clive Gamble (in press) *Frozen in Time: Archaeological Images of Earliest Prehistory*. Gloucestershire, UK: Alan Sutton Publishing, Ltd.

Moulton, Janice (1983) "A Paradigm of Philosophy: The Adversary Method," in *Discovering Reality: Feminist Perspectives on Epistemology, Metaphysics, Methodology, and Philosophy of Science*. S. Harding and M. B. Hintikka (eds), pp. 149–164. Dordrecht: D. Reidel.

—— (1986) "Duelism in Philosophy," *Teaching Philosophy* 3 (4): 419–433.

M.T. (1993) "Challenging Assumptions," *University of Chicago Magazine*. April: 34–35.

Murray, Sarah (1991) "The Anthropology of Art," PhD Field Statement on file: Department of Anthropology, University of California at Berkeley.

Musée Départemental de Préhistoire de Solutré (1990) *Peintres d'un Monde Disparu. La Préhistoire Vue par des Artistes de la Fin du XXIX Siècle à Nos Jours*. Solutré, Saône et Loire, France: Maçon-Imprimerie.

Nelson, Sarah (1990) "Diversity of the Upper Palaeolithic 'Venus' Figurines and Archaeological Mythology," in *Powers of Observation: Alternative Views in Archaeology*. S. Nelson and A. Kehoe (eds), pp. 11–22. Washington, DC: Archaeological Papers of the American Anthropological Association, no. 2.

Nochlin, Linda (1988) *Women, Art, and Power, and Other Essays*. New York: Harper and Row.

Pfeiffer, J. (1982) *The Creative Explosion: An Inquiry Into the Origins of Art and Religion*. Ithaca: Cornell University Press.

——(1986) "Cro-Magnon Hunters Were Really Us: Working Out Strategies for Survival," *Smithsonian* 17(7): 74–85.

Piette, Edouard (1895) "La station de Brassempouy et les statuettes humaines de la période glyptique," *L'Anthropologie* VI (2): 130–153.

Pointon, Marcia (1990) *Naked Authority: The Body in Western Painting 1830–1908*. Cambridge: Cambridge University Press.

Price, Sally (1989) *Primitive Art in Civilized Places*. Chicago: University of Chicago Press.

Prideaux, Tom and the Editors of Time-Life Books (1973) *Cro-Magnon Man*. New York: Time-Life Books.

Raghavan, Sudarsan (1996) "Quest for Remains of African 'Venus'," (February 24, 1996): *San Francisco Chronicle*: A1, A7.

Rosaldo, Renato (1989) *Culture and Truth: The Remaking of Social Analysis*. Boston: Beacon Press.

Schrire, Carmel (1984) "Wild Surmises on Savage Thoughts," in *Past and Present in Hunter–Gatherer Studies*. C. Schrire (ed.), pp. 1–25. New York and Orlando: Academic Press.

—— and Robert Gordon (1996) "Re-searching the Hottentot Venus." A Symposium for the Annual Meeting of the Association for African Studies, San Francisco, CA.

Sieveking, Anne (1979) *The Cave Artists*. London: Thames and Hudson.

Slocum, Sally (1975) "Woman the Gatherer: Male Bias in Anthropology," in *Toward an Anthropology of Women*. Rayna Rapp (ed.), pp. 36–50. New York: Monthly Review Press.

Sollas, W.J. (1915) *Ancient Hunters and Their Modern Representatives*. London: Macmillan and Co, Ltd. (second edition).

Solomon-Godeau, Abigail (1992) "Male-Trouble: A Crisis in Representation," paper presented at the Annual Meeting of the College Art Association, Chicago, IL.

Stoczkowski, Wiktor (1994) *Anthropologie Naïve, Anthropologie Savante. De l'Origine de l'Homme, de l'Imagination et des Idées Reçues*. Paris: CNRS Editions.

Stringer, Christopher and Clive Gamble (1993) *In Search of the Neanderthals*. London: Thames and Hudson.

Taylor, Lucien (1992) Discussant: "Envisioning the 'Past': Visual Forms and the Structuring of Archaeological Interpretation." Annual Meetings, American Anthropological Association, San Francisco, CA.

Thomas, Elizabeth Marshall (1958) *The Harmless People*. New York: Alfred Knopf.

—— (1987) *Reindeer Moon*. Boston: Houghton-Mifflin.

—— (1990) *Animal Wife*. New York: Simon and Schuster Pocket Books.

Tringham, Ruth (1994) "Engendered Places in Prehistory," *Gender, Place and Culture* 1(2): 169–203.

—— (1996) "The Chimera Web: A Multi-Media Inquiry into Opovo, A Neolithic Village in Southeast Europe." Berkeley, CA.: unpublished CD-Rom.

Ucko, P. and A. Rosenfeld (1967) *Palaeolithic Cave Art*. New York: McGraw-Hill.

Weaver, Mary Jo (1989) "Who Is the Goddess and Where Does She Get Us?" *Journal of Feminist Studies in Religion* 5: 49–64.

Williams, Raymond (1977) *Marxism and Literature*. Oxford and New York: Oxford University Press.

—— (1983) *Keywords: A Vocabulary of Society and Culture*. New York: Oxford University Press.

Wolff, Janet (1981) *The Social Production of Art*. London: Macmillan and Co.

INDEX

122; emotions 121, 122; fine motor
tasks 123; language 121–4, 127,
129–33; left hemisphere 121–3, 126,
127, 130, 131; manipulation skills
121; mathematics 121; mental
rotation 121, 124, 126, 127, 131;
musical ability 122; in perception
121; reading comprehension 122;
reading maps 9, 123; right
hemisphere 121, 122, 126, 127, 130,
131; time sequencing 122; verbal
abilities 122, 126, 131; visuospatial
processing 117, 121, 122–7, 130–3;
writing 122, 123, 131, 133; see also
brain, encephalization, sexual
dimorphism
brain lateralization: in rodents 125–7;
circling behavior 125, 127;
dopamine 125; in the house mouse
126; maternal caring behavior 126;
in meadow voles 125; in voles 125,
126
Breuil, H. 176, 179, 180, 190, 192
Buckley, W. F. 30, 31
Burian, Z. 174
Bushmen 188, 189; see also Khoisan,
!Kung

Cann, R. 2, 8, 76, 77, 79, 81, 86; see also
Eve, models in human evolution
carnivores 98, 101
Caton-Thompson, G. 17, 20
Cavendish, M. 37
central–foraging concept: see models in
human evolution
chimpanzees: see nonhuman primates
China 77
coevolution 84, 153
Collins, P. 35
competition: and body size 14; female–
female 65, 66, 143; male–male 14, 81,
92, 93, 103, 131, 154–9, 164, 165; see
also nonhuman primates,
reproductive strategies
Conkey, M. W. 15, 177, 179, 180, 183,
184, 196–8
Curie, M. 36, 38
cut marks on bones 101, 102, 105; see
also subsistence
Cuvier, G. 186

Dart, R. 93, 101
Darwin, C. 3, 8, 129, 137

Darwinian models 153, 154
Daston, L. 197
de Scudery, M. 37
Delporte, H. 174, 184, 190, 191
demography 81, 82, 94
DeVore, I. 5, 45, 46, 94, 98, 103, 153
diet 6, 93, 95, 98, 102, 153, 163
digestion: guts 163
dioramas: see visual images
DNA 11, 77, 83–7; see also genetics
Draper, P. 96–8, 102
du Châtelet, E. 37, 43
Dunbar, R. 56, 57, 130, 131, 156, 165

Efe 140, 144, 159
encephalization 1, 4, 12, 76, 114, 116,
154, 155, 158, 163, 166, 168; brain
evolution 116, 128–33; brain
expansion 114, 116, 165, 166; brain
size 12, 116–18, 120, 128, 129, 162–8;
cranial capacity 162, 163; EQ 118; large-
brained infants 12, 155, 163; small-
brained infants 12; see also brain,
brain lateralization
ethnocentrism 47, 67; eurocentric 192,
193; francocentric 179
ethnographic studies 3, 6, 9, 46, 94, 96,
100, 101, 153, 159, 160, 165, 167, 176,
178, 199
ethology 114
Eve 2, 79, 80, 99, 200; African Eve 76,
79; as the Lucky Mother 83; mtDNA
2, 82–7; as the Straw Eve 83; see also
Cann, genetics, models of human
evolution
evolutionary biology 84, 137, 140
evolutionary theory 190; reductionist
approaches 137

Falk, D. 3, 8, 10, 13, 103, 107, 117, 121,
123, 125, 128–31, 133; brain
temperature 129; radiator theory 129
Fausto-Sterling, A. 56, 58
Fedigan, L. 3, 7, 8, 45, 47, 48, 57, 64–7,
100, 102, 109, 132, 141, 142, 153
Fee, E. 58–63, 70
female figurines: see Venus figurines
feminist movement 6; see also feminism,
feminist science
feminism 20, 29–32, 35, 51, 58, 63, 65,
70; see also feminist science, gender
feminist science 57, 58, 60–3, 65,
67–71; contextual values 61, 63, 67;